Child-Rearing in Ethnic Minorities

BILINGUAL EDUCATION AND BILINGUALISM

Series Editors
Professor Colin Baker, *University of Wales, Bangor, Wales*
Professor Nancy H. Hornberger, *University of Pennsylvania, Philadelphia, USA*

Other Books in the Series
Becoming Bilingual: Language Acquisition in a Bilingual Community
JEAN LYON
Building Bridges: Multilingual Resources for Children
MULTILINGUAL RESOURCES FOR CHILDREN PROJECT
Curriculum Related Assessment, Cummins and Bilingual Children
TONY CLINE and NORAH FREDERICKSON (eds)
Foundations of Bilingual Education and Bilingualism
COLIN BAKER
Language Minority Students in the Mainstream Classroom
ANGELA L. CARRASQUILLO and VIVIAN RODRIGUEZ
Languages in America: A Pluralist View
SUSAN J. DICKER
A Parents' and Teachers' Guide to Bilingualism
COLIN BAKER
Policy and Practice in Bilingual Education
O. GARCIA and C. BAKER (eds)
Multicultural Child Care
P. VEDDER, E. BOUWER and T. PELS
Teaching Science to Language Minority Students
JUDITH W. ROSENTHAL
Working with Bilingual Children
M.K. VERMA, K.P. CORRIGAN and S. FIRTH (eds)

Other Books of Interest
Encyclopaedia of Bilingualism and Bilingual Education
COLIN BAKER (ed.)
Asian Teachers in British Schools
PAUL A.S. GHUMAN
Coping with Two Cultures
PAUL A.S. GHUMAN
Making Multicultural Education Work
STEPHEN MAY

Please contact us for the latest book information:
Multilingual Matters Ltd, Frankfurt Lodge, Clevedon Hall,
Victoria Road, Clevedon BS21 7SJ, UK.

BILINGUAL EDUCATION AND BILINGUALISM 12
Series Editors: Colin Baker and Nancy Hornberger

Child-Rearing in Ethnic Minorities

J.S. Dosanjh and Paul A.S. Ghuman

MULTILINGUAL MATTERS LTD
Clevedon • Philadelphia • Toronto • Adelaide • Johannesburg

Dedicated to the memory of Derrick Sharp
and to Aneeka, Manisha and Kerry

Library of Congress Cataloging in Publication Data

British Library Cataloguing in Publication Data

Both Library of Congress and British Library catalogue records for this book are available.

ISBN 1-85359-366-4 (hbk)
ISBN 1-85359-365-6 (pbk)

Multilingual Matters Ltd

UK: Frankfurt Lodge, Clevedon Hall, Victoria Road, Clevedon BS21 7SJ.
USA: 1900 Frost Road, Suite 101, Bristol, PA 19007, USA.
Canada: OISE, 712 Gordon Baker Road, Toronto, Ontario, Canada M2H 3RT.
Australia: P.O. Box 6025, 95 Gilles Street, Adelaide, SA 5000, Australia.
South Africa: PO Box 1080, Northcliffe 2115, Johannesburg, South Africa.

Typeset by Solidus, Bristol.
Printed and bound in Great Britain by WBC Book Manufacturers Ltd.

Contents

Preface

This book represents the culmination of a research study initially undertaken by Jagjit Dosanjh under the auspices of the Child Development Research Unit at Nottingham University. That investigation, in turn, was part of a long series of studies of the way parents in fact bring up their children (as opposed to how they are advised to do so) in a whole variety of contemporary cultural situations, beginning with the publication of John and Elizabeth Newson's book *Infant Care in an Urban Community*.

Subsequently there have been Nottingham studies of child-rearing practices focusing upon children of different ages, on children with only one parent, on children suffering from a variety of different conditions such as cerebral palsy, hearing impairment, visual impairment, autism and Down's syndrome. Research has also been completed dealing with the children of Caribbean immigrants living in Britain, and with children living in the Kingdom of Lesotho. Moreover, the structured but open-ended interview pioneered by the Nottingham Child Development Research Unit has inspired a number of other studies of child-rearing practices in places as far apart as Japan, Greece and New Zealand. In their work on the children of Punjabi immigrant parents, Dosanjh and Ghuman were therefore in a position to benefit from the experiences of a number of different psychologists who had tried to grapple with the problems of comparative research in a wide variety of very different family and cultural contexts.

Researchers who are interested in making comparisons between groups with radically different cultural backgrounds inevitably face a series of complex problems. For instance, in making any kinds of statistical comparisons there is a difficulty in deciding what would be a comparable group within the indigenous population. The first generation of Punjabi immigrants were not simply moving to a strange new land, they were also leaving a predominantly rural background to adopt an urban lifestyle. The Punjab is a relatively affluent region of India. The land is fertile and well irrigated, and with improved farming practices has become prosperous and productive. Nevertheless, because families tend to be large there is not enough land for all the sons to inherit a viable amount of farmland and there has been a long tradition of young men being forced to emigrate to many different parts of the world in order to try and make a reasonable living.

Typically, the Punjabi population arriving in Britain initially consisted of single young men who were attempting to improve themselves financially by seeking their fortunes abroad. Many of these young men were reasonably well educated and had therefore expected to be able to pursue skilled and professional vocations in Britain; but they often found that in practice their qualifications were not recognised in this country, and they would then be forced to take rather menial jobs, and work very long hours, simply in order to survive economically. Women on the whole tended to join them later on, as it became clear that it would take a considerable time for the men to establish themselves and when they began to realise that it might take much longer than they had originally envisaged to be able to return to the Punjab with enough accumulated wealth to enjoy a secure future there.

The prejudices these young men encountered from members of the host community forced them to distrust the indigenous population. This was an additional reason to rely at first mainly on their relatives and compatriots for advice, help and moral support in coping with the problems of daily living in an alien environment. They had to learn the hard way how to negotiate with the authorities, how to secure decent accommodation and how to earn a livelihood. Their ignorance of local ways and their inadequate social status also left them open to various forms of exploitation. It is a tribute to their resilience, thrift and sheer hard work that many of them eventually succeeded in accumulating sufficient resources to contemplate getting married and raising a family here in the UK.

The immediate purpose of Dr Dosanjh's original study was to compare the child-rearing practices of these families with those of the UK population which had already been studied; but to do this it soon became clear that this would also involve investigating in some detail the wider values, beliefs, attitudes and aspirations which might have a bearing on how the parents were behaving towards their children. In other words, by focusing upon the practical details of child rearing one incidentally gains a valuable insight into the culture or distinctive way of life which typifies and unites members of a given community. This indeed was already evident in the work on indigenous groups.

The original survey study in the 1970s also provided a snapshot of the way in which Punjabi families were beginning to modify their traditional child-rearing practices, partly in response to the diminished role of the extended family and the decline of traditional multi-generation households. Thus the wives and mothers were coming increasingly under the influence of health professionals in the host community, rather than following the advice and example of older female relatives, who were now often not available to them. It is significant, too, that health professionals in the NHS increasingly included members of their own culture, so that the cross-cultural influence was not one-way.

Inevitably, then, the 1970s study revealed a sub-culture in a state of fairly rapid transition, though it is interesting to speculate why some cultural traditions proved robust against change while others were quite quickly being abandoned. It also began to be obvious that the next generation would not be content to maintain the traditional lifestyle of their parents, having come under the influence of the indigenous peer group within the British education system; clearly this had the potential to cause intergenerational tensions as traditional Punjabi values were gradually undermined.

The later chapters in this book attempt to address these wider issues by reporting further interview studies with second generation immigrant respondents from the Punjabi community. These studies were not on the same scale as the original investigation, and rely more on descriptive than statistical evidence. However, as respondents reflect on their own experience of cultural change, the reader is given a hotline to a community trying to come to terms with living permanently under the influence of modern Western values and a way of life which is itself in rapid transition.

Professor John Newson

Acknowledgements

The authors wish to acknowledge the great debt they owe to all the mothers who took part in the study. Without their help and co-operation the task would have been impossible.

Dr Ghuman wishes to acknowledge the general help of the following colleagues at the University of Aberystwyth, Wales: Daniel Chandler, Richard Daugherty, Bob Jones, Gareth Elwyn Jones and Gerran Thomas. He is extremely grateful to Colin Baker and Richard Lloyd for reading through the manuscript with great care and making many valuable suggestions.

Dr Dosanjh gratefully acknowledges the help and advice from Professor J. Newson, both in the initial and the present studies.

Dr Ghuman wishes to acknowledge the moral support, help and encouragement which he has received from his wife, Theresa, and from their young daughter, Michelle.

The division of labour for the compilation of this book was as follows: Dr Dosanjh carried out the first project between 1970–74 under the supervision of Professor Newson, formerly of Nottingham University, for his doctorate thesis. Dr Dosanjh carried out all except two of the interviews with the second-generation Punjabi mothers (1995 sample) in the English Midlands and, as he did in the original study (1976), translated into English those interviews which he conducted in Punjabi, Hindi or Urdu. Dr Ghuman went to the Punjab, India, to collect data from the native Punjabi mothers and grandmothers there and also interviewed white mothers in the UK. Dr Ghuman was wholly responsible for analysing the interview data and the researching and writing up of the final manuscript, including the compilation of the index.

Introduction

There is a fascination shared by most human beings about how people in other societies organise and run their lives. Other peoples' world views, motives, intentions, hopes, anxieties and ways of doing things are forever a great source of wonder and amusement rather than mere idle curiosities. Moreover, most societies in the world have become (or are in the process of doing so) multicultural, although some people find it hard to come to terms with this new-found cultural diversity. Therefore, in our view, it is imperative for all concerned to understand and, hopefully, appreciate the diversity of belief systems and ways of life of the ethnic communities in Britain, Australia, North America and throughout the world.

At an academic level, cross-cultural studies provide a valuable check against our ethnocentric world view and stimulate critical reflection and debate on concepts and theories developed within a specific cultural milieu. The field of comparative child-rearing practices provides an excellent opportunity for doing this. It embraces very many aspects of a community's culture, including family structure and its functioning, religion, basic beliefs, diet taboos, myths and superstitions, language and the way inter-personal relationships are built and sustained.

Most parents are keenly interested to know how best to care for their children. They see children as an investment in the future. The popularity of Spock's and other writers' books on child-rearing in Britain, the USA and elsewhere is eloquent testimony to the inherent parental interest in the subject. The desire to find out how children are reared and cared for has been with us since antiquity. Manu, an Indian social philosopher and lawgiver of the fourth century BC, had this to say on the treatment of children (Kakar, 1994: 192): 'The protective indulgence shown towards the child is manifested most clearly where it matters the most (at least to the child) – namely, in Manu's pronouncements on the chastisement of children. Children (and women) are only to be beaten with a rope or a bamboo stick split at the end.' Plato regarded the care of children as a grave responsibility. Rusk (1969: 6) quotes from *Laches* to show Plato's deep concern: 'For children are your riches; upon their turning out well or ill depends the whole order of their father's house.' One of the seminal influences on modern-day thinking about the nature of the child has been that of Rousseau who postulated that the child is naturally 'good' and 'equal' at birth. More recently, pioneering theories of Freud, Piaget, Erickson and Bruner have greatly changed the child-rearing practices of the western European and North American middle classes.

Early child-rearing practices have been linked to adult personality by psychoanalysts and to intellectual development by many child psychologists. Watson, the arch behaviourist, claimed the overriding influence of the environment on development. His extravagant claim was: 'Give me half a dozen healthy infants ... and my own specialised world to bring them up in, and I'll guarantee to take any one at random and train him to become any type of specialist I might select – doctor, lawyer ... and yes, even beggar man and thief, regardless of his talents ...' (Quoted in Hayes, 1993: 249).

For the anthropologists and sociologists, the child's early socialisation throws up insights into how a society/community culturally reproduces itself and how it sees its future. For society's capacity to survive depends on how effectively it can pass on its stock of knowledge and skills and its basic values and beliefs to posterity.

There is a paucity of literature in the field of the child-rearing practices of ethnic minority communities. We have not come across a single collated source of research about any of the Asian ethnic minorities in Britain or North America, though there have been a few research reports based on small-scale studies (Woollett *et al.*, 1995; Hackett & Hackett, 1994; Ghuman,1975). This present book aims to make a modest contribution in this important and somewhat neglected field. The book should be of special interest to social and health workers, nursery, infant and primary teachers, students in the field of child development and cross-cultural studies and others interested in the welfare of children.

The main aim of the book is to provide information on the changing patterns of child-care practices, bilingualism, and the nature of young children's identities among the Punjabis who have migrated in large numbers to Britain, Australia, Canada and the USA. The book is based on two research projects. The first was completed by Dosanjh under the supervision of Professor John Newson of the University of Nottingham. In this study, Dosanjh (1976) made detailed comparisons between the Punjabi parents' ways of bringing up children and those of the English sample studied by the Newsons (1976) in the early 1970s. The two ethnic groups were compared on: child-centredness, independence training, discipline and the role of physical punishment, patterns of play and friendship, adjustment at school and personality development. The second research has been conducted with a smaller number (40) of second-generation Punjabi families probing the same concerns as discussed above. Also included in the study are 12 white British families and 10 Punjabi families in the Punjab to broaden the data base. The main objective, however, was to find out to what extent the second-generation Punjabis have changed their child-rearing practices compared with the first generation. To give readers both the substance and tone of the mothers' experiences of, and attitudes towards, their children's upbringing, we have made liberal use of extracts from the interview transcriptions. The selection of quotes is essentially a subjective exercise, but an attempt was made to present as comprehensive a picture as possible and to eschew overt bias, at any rate. We feel that such an in-depth approach to the study of one ethnic minority group can be applicable in helping us to understand the tensions and apprehensions not only of other Asian groups, e.g. of Bengalis and Gujaratis, but also those other ethnic minorities in western Europe and the USA. The overriding dilemmas chiefly relate to the propagation of religion, the mother tongue, core values of the family and the support of kinship networks.

Chapter 1 describes the socio-cultural background of the Punjabis now living in Britain, Australia and North America within a wider context of post-Second World War migration. It reviews the history of migration of the Punjabis and deals with their patterns of settlement, family structure, religions, marriage systems, the position of women and *biraderi* (kinship) network. It also aims to give the reader an outline of the background of the second-generation Punjabis, the majority of whom were born in Britain, Canada and the USA.

The second chapter introduces discussion on the aims and objectives of the research, examines the samples and evaluates the methods of data collection and analysis.

Chapter 3 describes the child-care practices of the Punjabis, including: pregnancy, birth, toilet training, feeding, the role of religion and father's participation, and examines the changing family structure and its bearing on child care. The chapter is supported by in-depth interviews with the native Punjabi mothers and grandmothers in the

Punjab and the previously published researches, notably those by Kakar – a well-known Indian psychoanalyst. Finally, the views of some English scholars are presented to provide a broader perspective on the child-rearing issues. The discussion contained in this chapter should serve to put into context the findings reported in the subsequent chapters.

Chapter 4 relates the findings of our 1970s research on the myths and superstitions surrounding birth, and chronicles the mothers' comments on the role of religion and associated ceremonies. Conclusions are drawn concerning the 'changed pattern' of child care of the first generation of Punjabis.

Chapter 5 reports the empirical findings on the lifestyles of the second-generation Punjabis, which provide a context for the discussion of early child-care matters. The topics dealt with are: preference for baby boys, ante-natal and post-natal care and the learning of mother craft such as bottle-feeding, weaning and toilet training, the fathers' participation and cot deaths. The chapter discusses these findings within a wider perspective of published researches.

Chapter 6 recounts and then analyses mothers' views on a variety of topics: training for independence, discipline, rewards and punishments, play, the sharing of household chores and playmates. Further, it explores personal development – highlighting the main anxieties, fears and interests of the children. As before, the views of the two generations are compared and contrasted throughout and these in turn are compared with the small all-white British sample. All findings are placed in the wider context of previous researches.

Chapter 7 discusses bilingualism, religion, racism and identity and investigates family language, how it has changed since the early 1970s, and parents' attitudes and their role in promoting bilingualism. There is a description of the places of worship and their role in maintaining the community's language, and finally there is a full examination of the question of the identity of the third generation and their experiences of racism. The discussion on these issues include other ethnic minority groups.

Chapter 8 analyses home and school matters including: parental involvement in the 3Rs, adjustment at school, general activities of children after school and friendship patterns as revealed by the interviews; followed by a discussion of these matters in relation to the research extant in the field.

In the concluding Chapter 9, an attempt is made to draw together the various strands of the research projects into a coherent whole. The findings are placed within the wider context of previous researches carried out in various parts of the world. A summary of the findings and implications for bilingualism and the identity of Asian and other ethnic minority children is presented.

1 Setting the Scene

> Anthropology has ignored children in culture while developmental psychologists ... ignored culture in children. The result is ignorance of the process and content of the child's emerging competence as member of a culture. (Schwartz, 1981: 4)

Introduction

Since antiquity, homo sapiens has migrated from place to place, from one geographical area to another, in search of food, shelter or simply to better its economic circumstances. Other reasons for migration have included such imperatives as escaping persecution, staving off starvation and fleeing from mass-scale annihilation. Examples of this type of migration are to be found even in the modern-day world in parts of Africa, Europe and Asia. At the time of writing, a major migration of refugees from the former Yugoslavia is proceeding apace to Germany and to Scandinavian countries.

There was a massive migration of people after the Second World War. In addition to the migration of refugees from the various east European countries, there was a large-scale migration of people from the Third World countries to the developing countries in western Europe, North America and Australia. Cohen (1991: 15) has described this period of migration in some detail:

> ... the mix going to individual countries was different. Greeks, Turks and Yugoslavs went out Germany; Algerians, Portuguese, Spaniards, Italians and West Africans arrived in France; while the initial influx to Britain and the Netherlands tended to come from their former colonies.... Belgians 'foreigners' were largely drawn from Spain, Greece, Morocco and Turkey.... By the mid-1970s, when immigration restrictions were introduced in all the Western countries, some 13.5 million 'foreigners' were officially counted as residing in Belgium, Denmark ... the UK, Sweden and Switzerland.

Our concern in this chapter, however, is with the Punjabi migrants from the Indian sub-continent to Britain and North America – though the discussion should be of relevance in understanding the predicament of all minorities in Europe, North America, Australia and elsewhere.

Migrants tend to take with them their language, religion, dietetic habits, clothing styles and social mores, conventions and attitudes. In short, they migrate with their 'world views' and lifestyles. It is widely accepted now that it is important to understand the religious and cultural backgrounds of migrants to facilitate the processes of adjustment and integration. Moreover, the child-rearing practices of a migrant/ethnic community can only be fully understood within the context of its own religion and social mores. This chapter describes in some detail the social and historical background of the first and second generation of Punjabis living in Britain – though references are also made to North America and to other ethnic groups. The information and discussion should serve as a backdrop to the empirical researches described in the subsequent chapters.

First Generation

Indians have been associated with the British since the beginning of the colonial rule of India in the seventeenth century. Initially, a few personal servants and *Aýahs* (nannies) were brought home by returning officers of the East India Company. Queen Victoria, for example, had several Indian servants, the most notable one being Abdul Karim who came to England in 1887 after the Golden Jubilee. He was promoted later to be her *munshi* – a teacher of Hindustani. The Queen became proficient enough to greet visiting Indian Maharanis in Hindustani (Visram, 1986: 231).

Indian presence in Britain up to the end of the nineteenth century was confined to a few *Aýahs, lascars* (seamen), students from rich families and some medical practitioners. This number increased somewhat at the turn of the century when some Punjabi Sikhs and Muslims of 'British Indian' army background found their way here to become peddlers and hawkers. Rex (1985) argues that Sikh peddlers' pioneering spirit can be compared with that of the trail-blazing journeys of Livingstone in Africa. According to one estimate, however, there were only 7128 Indians in the UK by the year 1900 (Visram, 1986: 190). Visram describes their first settlements: 'The earliest settlers lived in the seaport cities of Glasgow, Newcastle, Liverpool, Southampton and London.' Desai (1963) argues that the total population of Indians at the turn of the century was around 5000, which included 1000 general medical practitioners and 1000 other professionals and students. The rest were mainly seamen in Cardiff, Bristol and Liverpool, or the Sikh peddlers who came to Britain after a period of service in the armed forces. Maan (1992: 119) gives this account of Indian immigrants, who were mostly from the Punjab, to Scotland:

> The number of such people in Scotland at that time (1920s) was very low compared with England or even Wales; and nearly all of them were in Glasgow. When Nathoo did well in travelling or peddling and realised the potential in that trade for hard-working young men, he sent for his two younger brothers from India, who arrived in 1924.

Punjabis also emigrated to the USA and Canada in the first two decades of the twentieth century. There were 2544 Punjabis, mostly in rural areas of California, by 1920 (Leonard, 1993: 4). Likewise, Punjabis were to be found in small numbers in Vancouver. According to one source (Buchignani *et al.*, 1985), there were 951 South Asians, mostly Sikhs from Punjab, in 1921 in Vancouver. A story of a Punjabi Sikh is illustrative of the immigration pattern (Buchignani *et al.*, 1985: 14)

> My brother Kapur Singh was one of the first Sikhs to go to Canada. He soon wrote back to our village saying that work was available at RS. 7 a day – a princely sum in those days. Sixteen of us assembled to go off and try our luck. I was just eighteen. Some were reserve army men, but most were farmers' sons. After a quick train trip to Calcutta and short voyage to Hong Kong we had to wait quite a while for the next ship to Canada. We were on the '113 boat' that arrived in Vancouver in October 1906. We were very worried about being rejected because of disease or some other reason – I think I aged two years – but none of us was. (Tara Sing Sidoo)

The Punjabis, both from India and Pakistan, are well known for their internal and external migration. The major reason behind this migration has always been the desire to improve their standard of living and thereby to enhance their social standing and influence in the community. A large number of farmers (240,000) left the overcrowded districts of the *Doab* (Jullundur, Hoshiarpur and Ludhiana) to cultivate the newly opened canal colonies in the west Punjab between 1921 and 1931. Subsequently, their external sojourn has taken them to the neighbouring countries of Malaysia, Singapore and farther afield to East Africa, Australia, Canada and America. For instance, from 1897 to 1901 around 32,000 Indian workers, mainly Punjabis, were recruited on a voluntary basis to work in East Africa on the building of railroads (Bhachu, 1985a: 21).

India was partitioned in 1947 to create a homeland (Pakistan) for the Muslims. The Punjab was at the heart of this divide. Nearly 15 million people were affected. As Aurora observes (1967: 140):

> The partition of the country and the Hindu-Muslim communal carnage which followed in Punjab, further aggravated the instability of this generation ... Munjeet came to England in 1954: his main plan was to get admission to a provincial university to read for B.Sc. in Mechanical Engineering ... but under the circumstances he got a factory job.

Another vivid description was given by a parent who was interviewed by Ghuman when he was researching for a project on the acculturation of young Asian people (Ghuman, 1994: 3):

> We had nothing left when we came to Julundur from Pakistan – just the clothes we were wearing We were in a refugee camp for six months. Then we were allotted 10 acres of land per household. A small grant was also given for buying some agricultural implements. It was a miserable existence. I then vowed to emigrate abroad, preferably to Canada or California because I could farm there or work on a farm.

The other salient factor in the migration of Punjabis is that of the scarcity of farming land amongst the peasants and the subsequent lack of employment for the young people. Shaw's (1988: 22) concluding inferences of the Punjabi emigration are succinct: 'Thus the tradition of army and navy service and of labour migration abroad and the experience of colonisation had the effect of instilling in Punjabis the desire and the confidence to seek their fortunes abroad....'

The tradition of migration is so well established that even the young people belonging to high castes and materially well-off families are trying to emigrate abroad. In our recent interview a retired engineer elucidated:

> It is not only the unemployed young who want to emigrate but the educated too. They want to live a peaceful life; they are fed-up with terrorism *(in the Punjab)* and the fact they are enchanted by foreign countries, especially America. Also most of them have their relatives living in England, America and Canada.

A village farmer explained yet other reasons for emigration:

Phinder has done well in England... now it takes 5 to 6 *lakhs* (£10,000) Rupees to migrate. Now some people are going to Arab countries. The thing is this: nobody wants to leave his home, but it has become imperative for some to emigrate because of recent police excesses – even terrorism. Also there is so much corruption and filth in this country; and then lifestyles are better over there.... The only person who came back to settle in the village is now planning to go to America, though he is highly successful here. *(Why?)* You know I have been to England; they are a very civilised race. I was given so much respect (*he has an amputated leg and walks with a crutch*)... they would stand aside and let my wheel chair pass. Here, I dare not go on a bus for fear of being crushed and general rudeness of bus conductors. So people abroad are really civilised; that is the main reason.

We feel it is important for the reader to appreciate that a large proportion of the migrants from the sub-continent were from the middle strata of their respective societies, though most of them – including university graduates – were only successful in finding manual jobs. Ballard (1994: 10) succinctly describes their situation: 'Overseas migrants are therefore usually drawn from families of middling status, whose members, are neither sufficiently prosperous to be wholly content with their lot, nor so poor as to be unable to afford the migrant's ticket, passport and visa.'

The Sikhs from Punjab have been emigrating to Vancouver, in Canada, and California since 1902. As in Britain, the first migrants were men from rural backgrounds who were employed in manual jobs (Ghosh: 1983: 91). In Canada, for instance, 225 persons were allowed to stay in 1940, but they were not allowed to bring their wives and children (Basran, 1993: 344). In the USA, the passage of the 1965 immigration laws put Third Word countries on a par with European countries and as a consequence the migration from India increased dramatically. Saran (1985) estimates the population of Indian-origin people to be around three-quarters of a million. Bouvier and Agresta (1985) estimate that their total number will be close to one million by the end of the millennium. Likewise, in Canada there has been a huge influx of people from India after the passing of the Immigration Act of 1967.

Chain Migration

This takes place within a tight-knit community through established links of blood relationship, *biraderi* (kinship) and sometimes through friends. Punjabi men, who settled in various parts of the UK during the 1950s and 1960s, started sending for their close relatives as there was an increasing demand for low-paid, unskilled workers in foundries, cotton mills and on the buses as conductors. Maan's (1992: 159) account of the Punjabi migrants illustrates this process:

> His elder brother Sardar Ali, came to join a cousin in Scotland, probably in 1949. Mr Yaqub Ali arrived in 1952 to join his brother. Then a number of new friends and contacts of the Ali brothers kept multiplying and the pool of sponsors in Scotland kept getting larger with every new arrival from the sub-continent.

A Birmingham respondent gave a personal account to show this process in action (Ghuman,1994: 5):

> I came to England in 1959. Got a job as a bus conductor. I worked overtime and made £30 per week on average – a lot of money at time. I spent £5 on food and rent and saved the rest. Some I sent home and the rest went on a house deposit: I could rent out rooms then. I contacted a *dalal* and paid £300 deposit for my brother's immigration.

Aurora (1967) gives very many examples of this migration process amongst the Punjabis who were residents of Southall in the mid-1950s. He gives an example of a Sikh worker who was the first to be employed in an all-white workforce and who created such a good impression with the firm that subsequently several more Sikhs were given jobs on his recommendation – a form of sponsorship which supported chain migration.

The migration from the Indian sub-continent became highly selective after the 1962 Immigration Act: entry permits were issued mainly to doctors, teachers, scientists and engineers. Primary immigration to Britain almost ceased when the second immigration bill was passed by parliament in 1970.

The vast majority of the migrants from the Indian sub-continent were men of rural background, belonging to middle socio-economic groups, who originally came for a limited period of time to make their fortune and then intended to return to the family-fold back in India and Pakistan. One estimate is that 95% of the migrants from Pakistan during the 1960s were of rural origin and over two-thirds of them were from the Punjab (Dhaya, 1972). Aurora (1967: 21) noted that in Southall – now the main enclave of the Punjabi community – there were only 11 Indian women on the electoral list in 1958. According to Maan (1992: 160): 'The first Punjabi Muslim family to come to Scotland was perhaps that of Mr M. Ismail in 1948. Mrs Sakina Ismail, who still lives in Glasgow, related that the all-male Muslim community of Glasgow did not approve of her coming over ... no other Muslim families came over until about 1952.' Shaw (1988) cites evidence from the electoral register to show that most of the Pakistani families were united in Oxford in the mid-1960s when there was an imminent anxiety over the increasingly tighter control of immigration from the sub-continent. According to the latest census data available, the number of South Asians in Britain is estimated to be nearly one-and-a-half-million – 2.7% of the population (see Owen, 1992); and nearly one-third of the Asians are of Punjabi ancestry. Almost half the Punjabis are from the Punjab in India (mostly Sikhs, but a quarter are Hindus) – the other half are Muslims from the Punjab in Pakistan (Ballard, 1994: 19–20)

Patterns of Settlement

The chain migration of Punjabis ensured the formation of enclaves within inner-city areas of Britain. The China-towns in San Francisco, Vancouver and elsewhere in North America are also well-known examples of the consequences of this process. Punjabi migrants found it difficult to get accommodation and were obliged to live in overcrowded houses. Aurora (1967: 37) cites an example of discrimination in housing:

> To let
>
> A decent single bed sitting room with facilities to cook in basement kitchen. Suit a working gentleman or a woman. Only respectable people need apply. No coloured please.

In England, Punjabis have settled in the Midlands, Yorkshire, and some London boroughs – notably in Southall, which is popularly known as 'little Punjab' amongst the ethnic communities and the local whites. Bath (1972) studied the geographical distribution of the Punjabi families in Smethwick, West Midlands. He found that the house-ownership pattern closely resembled the Punjabi village scene: adjacent houses were bought on *biraderi,* religious and caste bases. Likewise, Shaw

(1988: 41) found that Punjabi Muslims have settled in Oxford in line with their past village and kinship associations. Bhattra Sikhs in Cardiff have settled very close to Ninan Park, where they have also built a *Gurudwara* (Ghuman, 1980b). Punjabi settlements in the Sacramento Valley, California, and in Surrey and Victoria in British Columbia are also along the caste, religion and kinship bases. Anwar (1979: 11) summarises the situation succinctly: 'Extensive research shows that individuals with similar cultural origins tend to cluster together and thus become residentially segregated from the rest of society ... it allows it to preserve a sense of ethnic identity and to feel a familiar social networks.'

Formation of Gurudwaras, Mosques and Temples

Most Punjabis, especially Hindus and Sikhs, felt settled enough during the mid-1960s to unite their families in the UK. At that stage their lifestyles were very restricted and revolved around their jobs. Most men did excessive overtime: seven days a week and from '7 to 7' tended to be the norm. There was little time left for leisure, sports or social activities. One of our informants described his experience (Ghuman, 1994a: 11):

> When I arrived in Birmingham in 1958 I had to share a room with another person. Rates were ten shillings (50p) for a shared bed (i.e. on shift work basis), one pound to a share room with three to four people and £2 for a room. Then we have to pay for our communal *langar* (cooking) and take turns to make chapattis and cook vegetables and lentil curries. I could save fifteen pounds a week. It was a lot of money at that time. My other expense was a few pints of beer over weekends. Life was routine and dull. I did as much overtime as I could get. There was only 'lino' on the floor and very occasionally *Gymna* (landlord) would light a coal fire in the dining room. So it was always cold in the house. For our baths we had to go to the public baths near H.... park. It used to be freezing cold in winter. We listened to Punjabi folk music and Hindi pop a lot. There was a camaraderie in the house; we talked a lot about the Punjab and how we missed it.

Dhaya (1972: 26)) argues that, since the prime purpose of the migrant was to earn and to save as much as possible, there was a great reliance on thrift, hardwork and sober habits.

However, with the arrival of wives and children the situation changed drastically. As the Punjabi communities grew in size they recreated some of the cultural and social organisations of their home country, as migrants to a new country are wont to do. Places of worship for the Asian communities are pivotal in this respect. The institution of religion helps in maintaining their distinctive cultural traditions and social mores in addition to providing opportunities for collective worship and observance of religious customs and practices. Maan (1992: 174) writes: 'The Asian community at this stage had at last accepted the fact that they are here to stay.... New mosques, temples and religious schools were set up in every locality and every town with a viable Asian community, to ensure the spiritual welfare of the present and future generation.' Thus, run-down church buildings in the inner city areas have been bought and converted to Sikh *Gurudwaras* and Hindu temples and there are plenty of newly constructed Mosques in every major British city. A Hindu teacher informed us (Ghuman,1994: 14):

> We opened *Gita Bhavan* in the old church in L.... are in 1967. Statues of lord Rama, Sita, Sri Krishna and other deities had to be brought from India – Jodhpur. Also we arranged to get a Brahmin as a priest. Our temple is also a centre for social and cultural activities. We have a provision for free meals on Sundays. We have a lot of holy men and women from India and elsewhere for *Katha* (special sermons). We also teach Hindi to the youngsters twice a week.

Parekh (1994: 610) argues that Hindu religion has played an important part in the lives of Hindu migrants all over the world in providing them with a degree of stability and cultural continuity. This has happened in Singapore, Malaysia, East Africa, West Indies, Guyana, Britain, Canada and America.

Thus Hindu *Mandirs*, Sikh *Gurudwaras* and Muslim Mosques, though organised around sectarian, regional and caste bases, came to play an important part in the lives of first-generation Punjabis in Britain and elsewhere. This re-creation of religious and other social structures, such as Workers' Associations and economic/market niches, is a feature common to the Punjabis in British Columbia, Toronto and in California.

General Comments on Punjabis

The Punjabis have come from three distinct religious backgrounds, namely Muslim, Sikh and Hindu. The Muslims are mostly from Pakistan, which was created in 1947, and the other two communities hail from India. Despite their religious differences and dietary requirements, they share a common language (Punjabi), literature, music, dress, styles of cooking, ways of relating to one another, a spirit of entrepreneurship and a sense of humour. Before the partition of India, they lived cheek by jowl in relative harmony.

In Britain, relationships between the Punjabis of different religious persuasions have fluctuated from harmony through co-operation to downright hostility. Events in the sub-continent have, to a degree, influenced their social behaviour. India and Pakistan have fought three wars, for example, and within India the holiest shrine of the Sikhs at Amritsar was invaded and desecrated (in the eyes of most Sikhs, anyway) by the Hindu-led Central Government. Likewise, Muslims all over the world have been deeply shocked and offended by the incident at *Ayodhya,* in India, where a Mosque was demolished by an unruly Hindu mob under the glaring presence of the world's TV and press.

However, there was, and is, a solidarity and common purpose born out of the predicament of being together in a country, Britain, which has condoned racial discrimination in the past and treated them as second-rate citizens (see Brown, 1984; Jones, 1993). This has also been the case in North America, especially in the 1940s and 1950s. In Canada, for instance, the immigration laws prior to 1967 were extremely discriminatory against people from the Indian sub-continent. Basran writes (1993: 342): 'East Indians (*mostly Punjabis*) like other Asians, were also denied the right to vote ... remained alien residents, were vulnerable to deportation. East Indians also bore the brunt of racial stereotypes, facing considerable racism and open prejudice.' In America, at the turn of the century, the first Punjabi settlers were not given the right to bring their wives, so they married into Mexican families. The story of the Punjabi-Mexicans' struggle to build their distinctive identity is evocatively told by Leonard (1993).

Most Asians, we are sure, have heard the racial jibe 'Pakis go home' hurled at them sometime or another. The second generation, who are relatively free from the burden of traditional and religious loyalties, are prone to forge a common front to secure equality of opportunity and to fight racism. They are not too perturbed at being labelled with the generic term *Asians* by the indigenous whites.

Values and Belief Systems

Traditionally, Punjabi families are known to have been extended, where two or three generations of people lived in a single household in a patriarchal set-up. This meant sharing resources, pooling incomes and supporting the weaker and elderly members of the family. Most rural Punjabis came from such a background. But this tradition is being eroded both in India and Pakistan as a result of geographical mobility, though the bonds of *biraderi* (kinship) remain strong. The Muslim Punjabi communities perpetuate and reinforce the *biraderi* bonds through arranged marriages to first cousins. In contrast, Hindu and Sikh communities do not approve of marriages within their immediate kinsfolk. Their custom is to avoid the union of two families which have blood relations running up to three generations – some even avoid marrying into families which have the same *gotra* or *Jati* (sub-caste). Nevertheless, their affiliations with their kith-and-kin remain very strong and individuals often sacrifice their own advancement in the broader interest of the extended family.

Shaw (1988), who carried out an ethnographic study of the Pakistani community (mainly Punjabis), was surprised to discover her own misunderstanding of strong *biraderi* bonds. She writes: 'In fact my disappointments arose from my own prejudices.... From a western point of view, an individual who fulfils her or his role with the family, *biraderi* and community, does so at the cost of individual freedom. However, most Pakistani themselves, including the younger generation, do not see the matter in this way. They do not prize "individuality" as highly as westerners do, and for most of them the sacrifice of "individuality" that the culture requires is more than offset by the advantages of fulfilling one's role within the family, *biraderi* and community.' In our interviews with the second generation, we were struck by the sacrifices of the first generation. A Sikh mother told us this story:

> My father left us in the Punjab in 1960 – all five of us with our mother. We had our kinsfolk who helped my mum, but she took all the responsibility. My father, who was a graduate teacher in the Punjab, could only get a job in a foundry to start with, then he became a bus conductor and then a driver. He worked amazingly hard to save up for a house and for our upkeep and then paid our fares including our grandmother's. When we were here he worked on the buses day and night and even sent some money home to other relatives in the Punjab. I am sure his high blood pressure and

early death caused by a heart attack was all due to all the sweat he put into his job – and then he worried about us ... would we accept arranged marriages?

Cross-cultural psychologists (Kim & Gudykunst, 1988; Triandis, 1994) and anthropologists (Kluckholn & Strodbeck, 1961; Levy-Bruhl, 1985) have attempted to pinpoint the differences between the value systems of traditional *vis-à-vis* modern western European societies. One of the differences, which has surfaced from extensive empirical investigations, concerns the dimension of collective versus individual orientation. According to this conceptualisation, collectively orientated people seek achievement for the group's sake and stress the value of co-operation, order and self-control. In contrast, the individually orientated view achievement as for self-glory, and believe in competition and the pursuit of power. Triandis (1994) describes other differences between the two contrasting types of individuals in social norms, values, attitudes and behaviour. Stopes-Roe and Cochrane (1990), in a wide-ranging and in-depth study of two generations of Asian people report that, compared with the British, the Asian considered the interest of the family should come before that of the individual. Parekh (1986: 198) argues that 'For the Indians, it is the family rather than the individual which is the basis of social structure.' He has elaborated on this theme in a recent article (Parekh, 1994: 610): 'Children study for the family and believe that to fail to achieve what is expected of them is to let down the family.... Women go out to work for the family.' According to another researcher, who has worked extensively with Indo-Canadian communities (Buchignani *et al.*, 1985: 127), individuals in the traditional Indian family set-up were weak but families were strong because these hold the land resources.

The other attributes which are associated with collectivity are respect for and obedience to the elders and accepting the decisions of the head of the family, particularly in marriage arrangements and choice of work. These values no doubt had strong bearing on the child-rearing practices of the first-generation Punjabi migrants.

These values are antithetical to the cherished 'individuality' of people in Western countries. This chasm between the value systems of the migrants and that of the host society has posed very serious difficulties for the second generation Asians.

Arranged Marriages and the Position of Women

On the sub-continent, the practice of arranged marriages is the most important part of Asian social mores. This practice enhances the financial welfare and prestige of the family. Therefore it is the business of the family and not of the individual to arrange marriage. There is a popular belief amongst the Punjabis that 'love comes after marriage' and that pre-marital dating and courtship are only 'lustful' customs of the West. A comment of a parent amplifies this:

> I believe in this custom – otherwise what would our *bhaichara* say – they have become *Goras* (whites)! Our customs will pass on to the next generation – Punjabi language, our food, dress and music. Otherwise there won't be anything left of us and people at home will be shocked and terribly disappointed. Also our marriages last longer than *Gora's* ... all we hear is a lot of them get divorced in so-called 'love marriages'. (Ghuman, 1974: 17)

As much has been written on this subject, some scholarly (Vaidyanathan & Naidoo, 1989; Ballard & Ballard 1979; Wilson,1978), others in newspaper features and pamphlets (*The Observer*, 12 March 1994; *The Guardian*, 25 June 1994), the researchers do not think there is need for detailed discussion of this topic. But this issue, and that of dating, are the main antagonisms over which inter-generational tension does arise (Drury, 1991; Wade & Souter, 1991). The second generation are increasingly prone to question the traditional values and to exercise their right to individual choice. This threatens the very survival of ethnic groups which want to cling on to this custom of arranged marriage. From a survey of literature, it becomes apparent that it is the Asian/Punjabi girls who are more likely to complain and moan about the arranged marriages and their position within the family (Drury, 1991; Wilson, 1978; Anwar, 1979). There is a custom of lavish dowry-giving amongst the Punjabis when their daughters get married. An average family can spend up to £10,000 on jewellery, household goods, bride's clothes and lavish parties. This custom, to our knowledge, is not being modified or changed. It is widely practised in Canada, America and other places where the Punjabis have settled. This has a knock-on effect of lowering the position of girls in the family. In India, there is a flourishing illegal medical practice for aborting female foetuses for this reason. Indeed, girl infanticide was practised until very recently by some *high-Jati* Hindu *Rajput* to escape from the grip of this financially crippling social custom. The local newspaper in Chandigarh, *The Tribune* (20 April 1995), has highlighted the dismal plight of Indian girls by publishing reports which include incidents of 'bride-burning' among all strata of Hindu and Sikh communities.

The predicament of Punjabi women in the USA and Canada depends on the social class of the family. The long-established Punjabi Sikh families, which tend to be concentrated on the lower rung of the economic market, are still patriarchal in structure; whereas, the structure of the professional families is more akin to the Canadian pattern where women enjoy equality with men – which is similar to the situation in Britain (see Basran, 1993).

The first generation internalised the patriarchal norms of the Punjabi communities and believed in clearly defined roles for men and women and boys and girls. This observation must be qualified, however. There is a wide variation of attitudes on gender-related issues (e.g. equal opportunity of education and employment) within the Punjabi communities depending on the religion, caste and social position and status of the families. In Hindu polity, there is a strong matriarchal cult (Kakar, 1994: 84); the most widely worshipped goddess is *Mata Kali* or *Durga* in the Punjab. Then there are other goddesses: *Lakshmi* of good luck and fortune; *Sarsawati* of knowledge; and *Parvati* of security. Grandmothers are revered both by men and women in Hindu and Sikh households and similarly they can achieve a formidable status in Muslim families. Shaw (1988: 74) summarises their position in Muslim households: 'A woman who begins her married life under the mother-in-law's authority can gradually acquire a major role in managing the households, influencing the men and making decisions about her own children's marriages.' However, a visiting woman scholar (Akhtar, 1991: 288) from Pakistan made some very interesting comments about the attitude of Muslim men towards women in the UK: 'Villages are more advanced now in Pakistan but people here are still as they have left 40 years back.'

In India the position of middle-class women is changing owing to their newly found freedom to work. Sinha (1984: 12) sums up the changing position of women in India: 'From a purely subservient and dependent role in the traditional family system, she has begun to contribute to family earning. Because of their changed economic status, women have inevitably begun to have a say in decision-making and enjoy, at least partially, the income earned by them.'

A comment of a Sikh woman is very poignant of most first generation Punjabi women's plight (Ghuman,1994: 18):

> Firstly I was a *Guluam* (slave) to my father's wishes, followed by my brothers', then my husband's and after his death my sons'. When will I be free? We are human beings, too. Men have tea, beer, gossip, laugh and joke in their spare times, but us ... too busy cooking, cleaning, washing, looking after children and entertaining guests ... in some cases we are also beaten up by the *Jungalis* (savages).

This description echoes a dictum of Manu on the treatment of females. Manu, a social philosopher of the fourth century BC, was the architect of the Indian political, social, and *jati* (caste) system. According to his laws (Bhular, 1886: 145, quoted in Kakar, 1994): 'In childhood a female must be subjected to her father, in youth to her husband; when her lord is dead, to her sons; a woman must never be independent.'

Wilson (1978) has evocatively depicted the predicament of Asian women through her ethnographic researches. She highlights, particularly, some of the anxieties of second generation Asian woman who have to reconcile the conflicting demands of two 'cultural worlds'. We will return to this issue presently.

Knowledge of English

The vast majority of the Punjabi migrants were from a rural background and had completed their primary education, though the ones who migrated after the 1962 Immigration Act were mainly professionals (Ballard, 1994). Most of the Punjabis did not speak English at all, some had the basic minimum and only a minority of college graduates were able to speak with any fluency, but even they were handicapped by their different idioms and accents. Desai (1963: 9) describes it graphically: 'All university educated have had experience of writing and reading English, but very little of speaking it. Hence almost all immigrants need a severe adjustment in their knowledge of English before they are able to communicate with the English. Those who are not well educated have a meagre vocabulary, few phrases, little grammar and a sing-song accent. At best they achieve bare mutual intelligibility in everyday situations.'

A Punjabi Hindu woman described her predicament (Ghuman, 1994: 19):

> I joined my husband in 1967 along with kids. We came in January. It was very cold, but *Pitta Ji* lit coal fire so it was alright.... The real *Khusum nu khani* (damn) problem was English. I was like deaf-mute, couldn't do shopping, talk to the milkman or go to the doctor. My

> husband had to take me everywhere – who spoke English. A short while after a lady from the university came to my house once a week to teach me English. *Jhindi Rahe* (may she live long) she taught me a lot in two years. Then I went to her house once a week for six months.... Still now I find it difficult to explain my ailments to the specialist. My angina was not diagnosed – he said it was arthritis – that wretched language has caused me so much distress, I don't fully understand TV programmes and still can't read English newspaper.

This lack of full command in English has also affected the job opportunities of teachers and doctors who gained their qualifications from the Indian sub-continent (Anwar & Ali, 1987; Ghuman, 1995).

Racial Prejudice and Discrimination

The pioneering Punjabis in the first two decades of this century met with open racial discrimination whichever country they migrated to. Their situation began to change, somewhat, soon after the Second World War when India gained independence from the British in 1947. For instance, the American laws of nationality and immigration denied them the right of citizenship and property owning and leasing until 1945. Full rights of immigration and citizenship on a par with Caucasian whites were only achieved in 1965, after which the population of South Asians in the USA increased dramatically. This is illustrated by the fact that the Punjabi population of Sacramanto Valley in 1965 was only 700 but it shot to 60,000 by 1980 (Gibson, 1988: 219). In Canada, the early Sikh settlers faced discrimination in housing, employment and the right of domicile. There was a steady improvement of their situation after the 1952 Immigration Act – but full rights were not accorded until 1967 (Buchignani *et al.*, 1985; Basran, 1993).

In Britain, there was no formal or legal discrimination against people from the Colonies and Commonwealth. They had the right to vote and indeed the first MP of Indian origin was elected in 1892 for the Finsbury Central working-class constituency. However, discrimination was rife at an informal level in all walks of life and the Asians and Blacks were the two main groups against whom it was directed. The first Race Relations Act came into force in 1971, thus officially acknowledging the prevalence of widespread racism in British society both at institutional and individual levels. As Ballard writes (1994: 2): 'Right from the outset, non-European settlers found themselves subjected to racial exclusionism, and to this day skin-colour remains an inescapable social marker.' A Hindu bus conductor explained (Ghuman,1994: 19):

> Though I had an MA in History the only job I could get was a bus conductor. There were a lot of Asians in this work at that time (1960s). After a few years service I applied for a vacant post of wage clerk in the transport department. I had a flat refusal. At job our white mates always used to talk negatively about us. We got overtime only if whites refused to do it. I used to get very upset – but what could you do? You are in their country uninvited. We have also to put up with racial taunts and insults from passengers at night. Several of us got assaulted.

There is a growing body of objective evidence from research investigations (Brown, 1984; CRE, 1987; Jones, 1993) which supports the personal impressions of the first generation Punjabis that racism is endemic in the institutional structures of the Law, the Police, the Civil Service, the National Health Service, Education, the Army and indeed in all areas of social and economic life.

In our view, Rex and Tomlinson (1979: 207) have summarised the situation of first-generation Asian immigrants in Birmingham quite accurately, which also applies to the Punjabis:

> The range of jobs occupied by West Indians and Asians, ... in fact concentrated more in the lower reaches of the occupational system ... they work longer hours for the money they earn and do more shift work ... Their houses, apart from the council houses which some of them live in, are worst houses in the city which have not been demolished ... their children go to primary and comprehensive schools which are largely segregated or are, at least, immigrant majority schools.

The situation of the ethnic minorities in the UK has further deteriorated since the above research was carried out in the mid-1970s (see Brown, 1984; Jones, 1993).

Second Generation

The second generation of Punjabi origin, who were either born in Britain or joined their families at a young age, have different expectations, values and social attitudes compared with their parents. They have experienced two distinct cultural norms and value systems, one of the home and the other of the school and wider British society. They have been described by researchers as a 'Half-Way Generation' (Taylor, 1976), 'Between Two Cultures' (Taylor & Hegarty, 1985), a generation who have the 'Best of Two Worlds' (Ghuman,1994) and a generation who are caught up in a 'Culture Clash' (Wilson, 1978).

In Britain, the second-generation ethnic minority young people have been hard hit by the long economic recession. Their unemployment rate is nearly double that of whites (Jones, 1993). They have to apply many more times to get interviews, even when they are better qualified than the indigenous whites (*The Guardian*, 13 September 1994). Many Asian young people have Anglicised their names to conceal their Asian origins (*The Independent*, 1 September 1992 and *Nottingham Post*, 2 September 1992). Despite their British citizenship they face racial discrimination and sometimes harassment even from the Police.

To cope with the ensuing tensions and anxieties, most young people have developed bicultural identities; i.e. they think of themselves as British Sikhs/British Punjabis. Some have rediscovered their religious values and have anchored their identities in their ethnic culture. Shaw's (1994) observations on the religious identity of the second generation Muslim young people are very telling indeed. The bicultural identities, however, are constructed as a functional response to their predicament – to be a Sikh at home and English at school or place of work is an effective way of dealing with the world. Ghuman (1994: 56) was informed by a successful head of department in a secondary school:

> ... but I am very traditionalist at heart. I can fit into both cultures. In Indian society, I behave like an Indian, here in school I behave like an English. I am bicultural.

Some young people can become alienated from both cultures as they face racial discrimination and rejection from the host society and disenchantment with their family's rigid insistence on maintaining traditional values. Witness the recent riots of young Muslim people in Bradford. It shook the community leaders, who generally kept a low profile and coped with racial discrimination and unemployment in a passive way. Parekh (*The Independent*, 12 June 1995: 15) argues that this has come about because of the complex interplay of inter-generational tensions and inner-city degeneration resulting in massive unemployment of Asian youths with many drifting into drug and crime culture. His analysis of the situation is: '... they define their cultural identity differently from their parents and stress such Western values as the equality of the sexes, greater freedom of choice in matters relating to marriage and occupation, and freedom of social dissent. The political struggle in the hands of young Asians therefore acquires a complex form, primarily against the wider society, but secondarily against their own elders.'

The second generation, therefore, has different expectations, personal identities and values from their elders. Furthermore, there have been radical changes in the way the second generation is organising its family life. It is more than likely that women are in full-time or part-time employment and family structure is more akin to the British norm, i.e. nuclear rather than collateral. Grandparents are not at hand to look after the next generation and to pass on the cultural and religious values of the community. Also, the second generation has tended to move away from ethnic enclaves to white suburbs (Ballard, 1994). Ghuman was given an interesting account by a village grandfather from a Punjabi village whose one son lives in England (farmer, aged 62):

> We went to see our grandchildren last year – they live in Coventry. I observed that they will become like *Goras* (whites) slowly.... They speak English and behave like white children. My son and his wife run a store and haven't got time to teach them Punjabi language or our culture. Our *Gurudwars* should do it but these are badly managed. Kids will choose their partners like them and most probably their children would lose all our traditions and way of life.... They will never come back to live here. My granddaughter wrote back to me after she came to the village: 'I thought India was nice in most places but it is very dirty. They don't here have rules for driving. Nobody takes any notice. Driving is very dangerous, and the police is no good.'

Another grandfather observed (farmer, aged 75):

> My grandchildren in England can speak a little Punjabi – the girl more so than the boy. When I was there, my daughter-in-law insisted that he (the son) should greet me in Punjabi – he very reluctantly did... I can't go (*meaning legally*) and live there to tell kids a bit about our religion and history. Anyway their way of life is so different that I will feel very uncomfortable – a deaf and dumb in a sweet prison really ... I do miss them but this is our compulsion, I am not happy about it.

Changing Family Structure

Objective evidence on the changing pattern of Punjabi family life is very sparse. However, Stopes-Roe and Cochrane (1989, 1990) have conducted a very comprehensive inquiry into the changing values and attitudes of the second generation Asians. They found rather a mixed response to the question of living with parents: two-thirds of the young men preferred to live in a joint household, whereas only one-third of the young women wanted to do so. Young women's reluctance to live in an extended family is owing to the Asian tradition where a new bride moves into her father-in-laws' household. They conclude (1989: 157): 'But they differed more in their views on family structure; the Asian young people, while wanting elbow room, as it were, still preferred to be closely and continuously involved in the parental family unit. While British family members were often willing to help if they have to, they did not see close family living as desirable.... They (the young) made it clear that they preferred, and would maintain if they could, the old spirit and structure of the family.' Some of the respondents in the study suggested a 'non-residential extended family' situation where newly married sons/daughters live in close proximity to their parents – sometimes as neighbours. Shaw (1994: 56) found this pattern of living arrangements to be common amongst the second generation Muslims in Oxford. She concludes her comments on the second generation: 'Most maintain close links with relatives, friends and peers, and still routinely participate in family and community events. They also take for granted the obligation to support and take care of their parents.' Likewise, two generations of Bhattra Sikhs in Cardiff have bought houses in the immediate home neighbourhood to retain 'extended joint households' (Ghuman, 1980).

Bhachu (1985a: 67) researched the lifestyles of the Sikhs of Punjabi origin, who migrated from East African countries from the mid-1960s onwards (hence the title of the book *Twice Migrants*), and came to the conclusion that, though most of the households are nuclear, they are involved in a complex kinship network within extended families. This is an interesting example of accommodation to the mores of their chosen host country.

Conclusions

It appears from these studies that there is a continuity of the Punjabi/Asian family traditions, but with some modifications to take into account the imperatives of available accommodation and the growing awareness amongst the young people – especially young women – of a strong personal identity.

All the research reports on the second generation (Stopes-Roe & Cochrane, 1990; Ballard, 1994; Shaw, 1988; Nesbitt, 1993; Parekh, 1994) reveal that the vast number of marriages are still arranged and endogamous, i.e. within religion and caste, despite the wide media publicity afforded to a few cases where young men and women had defied their parents. This custom, in our view, is going to ensure the perpetuation of at least some traditions of the family, important *jati* (caste) rituals and, more significantly, the religion of the community.

In the next chapter, the reader is given information on the research methodology including sample selection and the use of questionnaires and semi-structured interviews. Readers who wish to follow the main discussion on child rearing can move to Chapter 3.

2 Investigating Ethnic Minorities

Introduction

The second generation's changing lifestyles, values, personal identities, expectations and their perceptions of their economic and social positions in the wider society are bound to affect the way they are rearing their children. In some ways their techniques are going to be close to their parents' methods, but in many other respects they are going to be quite different. This situation may be summarised in a phrase: continuity and change. The researchers thought it would be of great interest to find out, empirically, how far an ethnic community has changed one of the most important customs in its way of life, namely child-rearing practices, which will reflect in an important way both how a community reproduces itself culturally and how it projects its hopes and fears for the future. The personal concerns, anxieties and other issues arising from such an inquiry should be of value in understanding the predicament of other ethnic minorities in western European countries, North America and elsewhere.

A major aim of this book, as discussed in the introduction, is to report the findings of two studies which compare and contrast the child-rearing practices of two generations of Punjabi parents living in England. The first research was carried out in Nottingham and Derby with a sample of 200 families during 1970 to 1972 (Dosanjh, 1976). The objectives of this inquiry were to give a detailed account of the Punjabi way of life and to compare Punjabi parents' child-rearing practices with those of the English.

The second research was carried out between February and October 1995 with a smaller group (40) of second-generation Punjabi parents who are no longer immigrants but permanent settlers, the majority being British citizens. They regard Britain as their home country.

Research Methodology

Instrument

Dr Dosanjh translated into Punjabi the questionnaire (relating to seven-year-olds) developed by the Newsons (1968). In view of his special knowledge of the Punjabi culture, Dr Dosanjh added a number of questions on the social customs and religious ceremonies. For example, items relating to superstitions and myths surrounding pregnancy and the childbirth were deemed to be important for the inquiry. The questionnaire formed the basis for a semi-structured interview with the parents (see Appendix).

There were considered to be a number of advantages in employing the interview technique over a structured questionnaire and attitude scale. In the first place, the main objective of the inquiry was not only to collect factual data but to find out, as far as possible, associated attitudes and sentiments which go with facts. Therefore, the questions were designed to trigger off the mother's own train of thought and subsequently – it was hoped – she could introduce topics which interested her. Secondly, in-depth interviews have produced rich illuminating information which is not normally possible in a conventional questionnaire, and it was hoped that with Punjabi mothers this would prove to be an appropriate technique (see Newson & Newson, 1968). Thirdly, most first-generation Punjabis have had a bitter experience of endless form filling back at home and they tend to be sceptical of this exercise. It was thought that the information gained through such a technique may not be as reliable and valid as that gained through personal interviews.

With the first generation, all the interviews, except seven, were conducted with mothers in the presence of the fathers by Dr Dosanjh in the parents' home. Mrs Dosanjh was also present at most of the interviews to help create an atmosphere of cordiality and family-gathering which the Punjabis tend to appreciate. However, with the second generation, the majority (32 out of 40) of the interviews were again conducted at the interviewees' homes, but this time mostly without the presence of husbands. Only in a few cases were husbands present. Again Dr Dosanjh did the bulk of the interviews, except six which were to be conducted with Muslim mothers for it was proving extremely difficult to persuade Muslim women to be interviewed by a male researcher. In the event, we were fortunate enough to get the help of a young Muslim girl who has achieved advanced level qualifications at school ('A' levels) and is going to study law at a university. Dr

Dosanjh explained to her the objectives of the inquiry and briefed her about conducting semi-structured interviews. She carried out a couple of interviews in the presence of Dr Dosanjh, who was able to help her improve her interviewing skills for the subsequent interviews. She turned out to be an extremely competent and reliable interviewer.

Reliability and Validity of Interviewing

There are two main problems associated with the interview method of data collection. The first one is termed 'social desirability response set' – the desire to please the interviewer by the respondent. The second, interrelated problem, is that of the validity of the information collected, especially in our case where mothers were asked some questions which required them to reflect on their experiences of early child-rearing. As regards the first concern, the purpose of the interview was explained clearly to mothers. They were told that the main motive is to find out how Punjabi parents bring up children so that teachers and others concerned understand children's needs and abilities and thereby help to fully develop their educational potential. Also, in general, questions were open-ended and mothers were encouraged to talk freely without any implicit or explicit approval or disapproval of their comments. We feel these measures helped to overcome 'the desire to please' response set.

As regards the validity of the data, it has to be conceded that there is a risk involved in 'recollections' tending to follow certain directions of distortion. A mother is likely to present a 'rosy picture' of her child (see Yarrow *et al.*, 1968). Furthermore, inaccuracies tend to be in the direction of recommendations of 'authoritative experts' in the field of child rearing (see Robins, 1963) – but this particular objection is not applicable to our sample as Punjabi mothers were not likely to follow the trendy theories of Dr Spock and others!

As far as the reliability and validity of the mothers' recollections of events is concerned, the reader's attention is drawn to the fact that, firstly, the questions which relate to retrospective information are only a small part of the interview schedule and the data was obtained contemporaneously, but in both cases we are asking mothers to recall information, and are not observing mothers' behaviour in real settings – which, incidentally, would be extremely time-consuming. Secondly, Rutter, Tizard and Whitemore (1970: 61) argue: 'In a quantitative analysis only large differences can be considered as due to anything other than faulty recall.' Thirdly, we feel that in 'recollections', although exact details are likely to be forgotten, the essence tends to be remembered. In this study, our concern was more with the qualitative aspect of the data, viz, how Punjabi mothers viewed their child-care practices in retrospect and prospect. Finally, the presence of fathers in nearly all interviews also helped mothers in their recollections of past events; since fathers interrupted to pin-point certain incidents relating to bottle-feeding, toilet training and other matters relating to child rearing. Furthermore, the use of attitude scales to assess parental child-rearing attitudes has been seriously questioned by Holden and Edwards (1989: 52). They looked critically at 83 attitude scales and came to the conclusion that the reliability, validity and conceptual under-pinnings of such instruments is far from satisfactory. Therefore, they recommend: 'It is advocated that PCRAs, in their current manifesta-tion, be abandoned.'

The major drawback of the interviewing technique is that it is very time-consuming and laborious and it is often not feasible to undertake research with a large sample. The sample in the second study is comparatively small for this very reason. For the second inquiry, we have retained the core of the interview questionnaire to facilitate the comparison between the two generations. Some pruning of the items, however, was necessary to simplify the very lengthy questionnaire used in the original study and to add some items deemed relevant (bilingualism, religion and identity) to the present-day predicament of the Punjabis and other Asian groups living in Britain. The mothers were assured the complete confidentiality of the data collected, and the fact that Dosanjh lives and worked in the area and knew the *biraderi* well and was fully trusted, helped matters considerably.

Samples

For the first study, Punjabi parents, who had children between the ages of five to nine, were contacted through schools in the Nottingham and Derby area. From the list thus compiled, a selection was made by taking every fourth child in Derby and every third and fourth child alternatively in Nottingham to reduce the final sample to 240, with the eventual aim of interviewing 200 parents as a 20% refusal rate was anticipated. The mothers included in the sample are those who had children or a child within the age range seven to nine years. With the consent of parents, a tape recorder was used in all the interview sessions. Whilst the majority of mothers conversed in Punjabi, some preferred to use Hindi or Urdu. The tapes were transcribed and subsequently translated into English by Dr Dosanjh.

Because of the constraints imposed by time and finance, it was decided to limit our present study with the second generation to a smaller sample of approximately 50. We approached the local schools, as in the 1970s sample, to help us make initial contacts with the neighbouring Punjabi families. But the response was not encouraging so we had to abandon this strategy and rely on our personal contacts within this Midlands (England) community to complete the project. In the event, we were able to interview only 45 families and the data from five of these is excluded from the analysis because these mothers, by confining themselves to 'yes' or 'no' answers to all questions, were considered not articulate and co-operative. The final sample therefore consists of 40 families. All the mothers, except eight, were interviewed in English and with the consent of the mothers a tape recorder was used as in the 1970s research. All the tapes were subsequently transcribed (and translated by Dosanjh where appropriate into English) for textual analysis.

It was thought prudent to interview some white mothers (12) to provide some valuable data for comparison. In the event, 12 indigenous white mothers were interviewed to broaden the basis of the data (these interviews were conducted by P.A.S. Ghuman). The interviews were based on the same questionnaire, except that questions relating to ethnicity and bilingualism were omitted.

Religious Composition

As religion plays an important part in the lives of Punjabi people, it was deemed important to include in our samples mothers from the three main religions of the Indian sub-continent, namely, Sikhs, Hindus and Muslims. The details appear in Table 2.1.

There is a high proportion of Sikhs in the sample and, therefore, the

Table 2.1 Religious composition of the Punjabi samples

	Sikhs	*Hindus*	*Muslims*	*Total*
1995 study	20 (50%)	10 (25%)	10 (25%)	40
1970s study	138 (69%)	37 (18.5%)	25 (12.5%)	200

reader is cautioned that the sample cannot be fully regarded as representative of the Punjabi population in Britain or in Punjab. In British studies, the Registrar General Classification of occupation is normally used to split samples into working class/manual and middle class/non-manual categories. This is not considered entirely satisfactory for the Punjabi groups as there was, and is, often a mismatch between their education, aspirations and attitudes and the jobs which they managed to secure owing to the widespread racial discrimination in England. In the event, the mother's educational level was thought to be the best indicator of the Punjabi parents' lifestyles as it has a strong bearing on the quality of mother–child interaction and family culture. The educational level of mothers is given in Table 2.2, and in Tables 2.3 and 2.4 we tabulate the manual and non-manual data on Punjabi and British mothers and fathers respectively.

The occupational make-up of the Asian population in Britain has dramatically changed since the 1970s (see Jones, 1993; Smith, 1977) and the Punjabis are no exception to this generalisation as is clear from Table 2.4. However, Punjabis of Indian origin have done better than their counterparts from Pakistan. Thus, in our present sample nearly half of the Hindu and Sikh fathers were in 'professional, intermediate and skilled non-manual' jobs, whereas only one Pakistani-origin Punjabi was in this category, six were doing manual work and three were unemployed. Statistical data from the Social Trends (HMSO, 1995: 20) support our observations: 57% of Indian-origin people are in non-manual occupation compared with only 34% of Pakistanis.

House Ownership

All the second-generation families, except one, own their houses: nearly a third are in detached, over a half in semi-detached and the rest are in terraced houses. These figures match very closely with the national statistics and there has been little change since the 1970s (see Social Trends: HMSO, 1995; Jones, 1993). The corresponding figures for the white mothers studied are: half of them own their houses and half of them are in council houses. The figure for ownership in this sample is lower than the national figure, which is 65%.

Family Size

One of the important variables in understanding the effect of acculturation on child-rearing practices is to compare the family size of the 1970s sample with that of the 1990s, and to compare both with the indigenous white families. The data is presented in Table 2.5.

It is clear from Table 2.5 that, in the 1970s the size of the Punjabi

Table 2.2 Educational level of mothers

	Degree, 'A' Advanced levels and College Diplomas (normally achieved at the age of 21)	*'O' levels, GCSE and CSE (School-based qualifications normally achieved at the age of 16)*	*No qualifi-cations*	*Total*
1970s study	20 (10%)	35 (17.5%)	145* (72.5%)	200
1995 study	14 (35%)	16 (40%)	10 (25%)	40
1995 study: British sample	3 (25%)	5 (41%)	4 (33%)	12

*Included in this category are 67 mothers who did not go to school at all

Table 2.3 Social class based on mothers' occupation (shortened version of the Registrar General's Classification)

	Non-manual (1, 2 & 3a)	*Manual (3b, 4 & 5)*	*Housewife*	*Total*
1970s study	10 (5%)	60 (30%)	130 (65%)	200
1995 study	10 (25%)	19 (47.5%)	11 (27.5%)	40
1995 study: British sample	3 (25%)	6 (50%)	3 (25%)	12

Table 2.4 Social class based on fathers' occupation (shortened version of the Registrar General's Classification)

	Non-manual (1, 2 & 3a)	*Manual (3b, 4 & 5)*	*Unemployed*	*Total*
1970s study	22 (11%)	158 (79%)	20 (10%)	200
1995 study	17 (42.5%)	18 (45%)	5 (12.5%)	40
1995 whites	3 (25%)	8 (67%)	1 (8%)	12

Table 2.5 Punjabi and English family size – in percentages

Number of children	*1–2*	*3–4*	*5+*
Punjabi family (1995 study)	62.5	30	7.5
Punjabi family (1970s study)	18	45.5	26.5
White family (1995 study)	91	9	–
White family (1970s study)*	36.7	38.6	24.7

*See Newson & Newson (1970)

families was larger than those of the English. This situation has changed since then: the 1995 sample shows a decrease in family size, although it is still higher than that of the indigenous whites. Another interesting fact is that in the present Punjabi study only one-fifth are extended families, whereas in the 1970s sample nearly a quarter of the families lived in joint households – a slight decrease in the extended family set-up. In Table 2.6 we give details of mothers' residential status.

It is clear from Table 2.6 that the majority of the mothers in the present group were either born or had their schooling in Britain and are therefore more familiar with the British norms, social mores and customs and practices and have a greater knowledge of English than the 1970s sample, where the vast majority of mothers were of recent arrival. The age description of the samples is given in Table 2.7.

There are a number of significant features to note from Table 2.7. First, the mean age and range of the Punjabi mothers is higher than that of the whites. Second, that the present study is concerned relatively

Table 2.6 Mothers' domicile status – 1995 study

	Born in Britain	*Resident over 20 years in Britain*	*Resident over 10 years in Britain*	*Total*
Sikhs	9	6	5	20
Muslims	2	4	4	10
Hindus	–	6	4	10
Total	11 (27.5%)	16 (40%)	13 (32.5%)	40

Table 2.7 Mean age, range and standard deviation of the 1995 samples

1995 study	*Mean*	*Range*	*Standard deviation*
Punjabi mothers	34.8	20	4.9
Punjabi fathers	35.8	29	4.9
White mothers*	30.5	15	3.5
White fathers	36.0	18	6.8

*Two of the white mothers were single-parent families

with the younger age group of mothers who might still have more children. In the sample, as a whole, there are 21 boys and 19 girls. The age range of children is from seven to nine years.

Conclusions

In sum, there are a number of differences between our two Punjabi samples. A significantly higher proportion of the second-generation are in employment, have better types of jobs, were born and / or had their full schooling in Britain and speak English fluently. Furthermore, they have fewer children and fewer live in an extended family situation. The only commonality with the 1970s mothers is that the majority in both samples own their houses and that none of them are single-parent families. The white sample in the study is comparatively younger, fewer own their houses, they have fewer children and the sample includes two single-parent families. All the above parameters have significant effects on child rearing and we will explore these in subsequent chapters.

In the chapter that follows, the traditional child-rearing practices of the Punjabis are described in order to contextualise the discussion of our research data. The description of child rearing in the Punjab is based both on the existing literature and upon some empirical data which was collected by P.A.S. Ghuman in April 1995 during his four-week visit to the 'Indian' Punjab. Ten mothers (four from the manual class and six from the non-manual class) and six grandmothers were interviewed using a semi-structured interview method. The topics included in the interview related to ante- and post-natal care, children's upbringing, medical improvements, family planning, the role of the extended family in child care, and the changes which have taken

place in the craft of motherhood. The major thrust of the interviews was to explore issues and generate discussion rather than seek answers to predetermined questions. The interviews were held in two locations: in an urban setting – Chandigarh, and in a rural village – Mahalon. With the consent of the mothers, a tape recorder was used throughout. All mothers and grandmothers, save two, spoke in Punjabi. The translation of Punjabi transcriptions was by P.A.S. Ghuman.

Note

Separate analyses of the data by social class and religion were not carried out because the numbers involved are too small and the ensuing generalisations could have been misleading.

3 Child-Rearing Practices of Punjabis

> ... we should do well to remember that in terms of loving care and family support, their children may be receiving far more than our own children; our material conditions of living are so transformed that we might be living on another planet, but that does not mean that we do not have to learn much about child rearing from developing countries. (Brimblecombe, 1980: 6)

Learning of Mother Craft

Traditionally, in Indian society, the status of the expectant mother was in sharp contrast to the new young wife. She was accorded every respect and considered to be part of the husband's family, whereas the new bride was treated as an apprentice who had to earn her place in the new family. Kakar describes her position evocatively (1994: 79): 'For an Indian woman, imminent motherhood is not only the personal fulfilment of an old wish and the biological consummation of a lifelong promise, but an event in which the culture confirms her status as a renewer of the race, and extends to her a respect and consideration which were not accorded to her as a mere wife.' According to some feminist thinkers (see Phoenix *et al.*, 1991: 49), there is still a resonance of this notion in the Western world: 'For women a major reason for having children is the identity and status which motherhood provides ... it is seen as providing a means by which women achieve full adult status and demonstrate their feminine identity.'

On the Indian sub-continent, expectant mothers are, or were, very rarely taught about children and how to raise them. In most cases, the first delivery was in the young mother's parents' home where her own mother and other elderly women looked after the infant for the first six to 12 months (see Kakar, 1994: 77). The young mother picked up child-rearing skills by imitating and emulating the senior women of her father's household. Currently, this practice is fading due to the

occupational mobility and an increased awareness that advice on child care can be sought from nurses and doctors. This transition, however, is not without its problems as we were told by a young mother (Teacher; aged 27):

> We are not given any training at all – this is one big drawback in India. They get a little idea by watching their aunts and other relatives. There is no reading material available – I tell you there is nothing. There may be a little about pregnancies but no knowledge of motherhood. My mother did not tell me much. The first child is a sort of experiment only. For the second child, I was better prepared ... My mother learnt from her mother, but because I was away with my husband there was no help.

Gender of the Child

In Punjabi families, boys are generally preferred to girls to the extent that in some families women who have girls are made to feel inadequate, but the situation is changing somewhat. A grandmother (aged 60) from a farming background informed me:

> On having a baby boy or girl – I do not think there is any difference to me, personally. It depends on your thinking. I celebrated the birth of my grand- daughter by distribution of *Barfi* (*high quality Indian sweet*) whereas on the arrival of my grandson it was only *Ladoos* (*ordinary sweet*). But our society approves of boys, but to me it doesn't make any difference.

Another grandmother (retired professor; aged 63) was somewhat guarded in her response:

> This custom has not changed much. Even now the wish of most parents is that a boy should be born. (*Reasons?*) There is a widespread belief that a boy will look after us in old age. Our society is very macho and male dominated. Only a man is considered to be good for many jobs. But people now don't mind having mixed families.

The notion that a son would look after his parents is very much part of the Punjabi and Indian psyche. Kakar writes (1979: 450): '... given the infant mortality rate which used to range above 20 per cent, a surviving child (especially a son) was accorded the most deferential care by his mother and the family, for he would become the parents' source of economic support in later life and through his participation in the ritual of death and mourning, their guarantee of religious merit and righteous passage into the next life.'

There are some parents, however, who would also like to have a daughter in the family. A mother of two boys wistfully remarked (Clerk, aged 42):

> People undergo 'sex-test' to abort girls. They must have a boy. Very few can accept all girls in a family. We know of a couple who had six girls because they were trying for a boy.... Now, in our case I think, to my mind, I want a girl in my family. But I had very difficult pregnancies and faced many problems. Maybe we should have tried another time.

There is some statistical evidence (Booth & Verma, 1992: 1155) to show how Hindu and Sikh parents in the Punjab differentially treat the young children for medical care. They conclude: 'The magnitude of restricted access to hospital care for girls as shown by our data is impressive; the M/F ratio of 4.13 suggests that about three out four girls (75%) who are ill enough to require hospitalisation are denied this essential medical care simply because of their sex.' According to the authors, this accords with the social and cultural mores of Punjabi society in which it is the sons who inherit family land and are responsible for looking after the elderly parents whereas the daughters have to be married off with dowries.

Regrettably, in some parts of India, these traditions have such a stranglehold over people's minds that they go to great lengths – mainly for economic reasons – to avoid having girls (foetus abortion) and baby girls are killed by a variety of cruel methods, which include poisoning, starving to death and suffocating. Goledenberg writes in *The Observer* (22 October 1995: 21):

> For Amarvati, who thinks she is 38 although she looks much older, the arrival of a second unwanted daughter meant the end of her marriage. Her husband, a woodcutter, balked at the expense of raising a daughter and left her. 'My husband would not have left if it had been a boy,' she said. 'I had to kill it, there was no alternative. God made a plan for us to suffer, but we killed the baby and escaped.'

This quote crystallises some of the dilemmas which the poor in the Third World countries face and also shows their ontological outlook – which may be termed as a fatalistic attitude to life.

Family Planning

The middle-class mothers interviewed in Mahalon village and Chandigarh have only two children each, with the exception of two mothers who had three. However, two *Chumari* (untouchables) mothers had four and they were in their mid-30's. It seems to me that most middle-class Punjabis, in India at any rate, are extremely keen on family planning. We were informed by a grandmother from a farming background (Housewife, aged 58):

> All our people (middle-class *Jats*) now believe in having two kids – it was OK in the old times. But it can be difficult with, say, one boy and a girl. Suppose the only son decides to live away or go abroad, then there is no one left with you because the girl is going to her in-laws as is our custom. You really need two sons for this reason – also a tragedy might strike. I know now-a-days it is expensive to bring them up and educate them. Look at us, we are on our own – we feel quite sad and dejected at times – because our son is in service and lives in a city. In old age it will be a real problem for him and us.... As regards the *Ad-dharmis* (untouchables), still they have four or five. They think it is their investment for old age. The village nurse gives them advice on birth control, but they reject it and are cynical of small families. Their attitude is: 'Our children are not going to "divide" our land – they are born to work and earn money, and so be it.'

Ghuman interviewed a doctor (aged 32) on a variety of issues ranging from birth-control to the health-care of young children. The doctor gave a thoughtful reply:

> Family planning with the poor strata has failed – there is so much deception and corruption. Some officials are supposed to bring forward men who can be sterilised because they had two or three children. But it is all in papers – nothing gets done in reality ... Doctors don't go to the villages to attend to the patients. There is a lot of malnutrition and poor hygiene amongst the poor. Then there is scabies and water borne diseases. TB and malaria are widespread.... The future is bleak unless population is controlled – the public medical facilities are stretched to the limit.

Pre-natal Care and Child Birth

The facilities in India and Pakistan have improved since Independence in 1947, but are still paltry compared with Western countries. In the village where we did our interviewing, a nurse is working full-time and the services of a doctor are shared between several villages. As a consequence of improved care, the infant mortality rate has declined and people are more aware of hygiene matters relating to delivery and child care. A farmer's wife (aged 56) gave a potted history:

> We have a nurse in the village for deliveries – also *Dais* (traditional midwife) work along with them. *Dais* have to attend a course as well. In the old times we used to have Muslim *dais* – they were very knowledgeable. And then lower-*jati* women (untouchables) learnt the skills from the old-hands or did a short course, but they were not fully qualified. Sometimes they did not know whether a baby in the womb is all right or not. Whenever there was a problem people would have to go to a nearby town hospital. Now the situation has much changed. After birth babies are given a course of injections – some after few weeks, others after three months, and so on.

Medical facilities in cities, both public and private, are much superior to those found in villages. The upper-middle classes enjoy the more up-to-date provisions. The wife of an Army officer (aged 29) commented:

> I was having a very good care – actually I had some problems which they did not understand, so I suffered a lot. But for my first child I was in a private clinic and the second was in an Army hospital. I had regular check-ups and advice.

Likewise a grandmother (retired professor, aged 63) recounted:

> Before my time the deliveries were at home with little care for hygiene and other matters. The first delivery was usually at a girl's parents' home – because daughters could talk freely to their mothers. Even now some deliveries for the first child are in this way.... But now educated girls are not shy and can freely explain and discuss things, so it doesn't matter.... Both my kids were born in a hospital. I had medical check ups – first weekly and then monthly.... She was a very good doctor. I stayed in hospital for ten days after my delivery. Old-fashioned notions were discarded: I could sit and lie under the fan, have cold drinks and 'cold fruit' (*Some foods are considered to be 'cold' and others 'hot'; for instance, almond and ginger and certain lentils are hot, and fruit and rice are cold*).

Another grandmother (farmer's wife, aged 65) explained some of the old traditions:

> In our times babies were delivered at home – the first one being in girl's parents' home. *Dais* were midwives. Then nobody knew about hospitals – because girls had fresh food, plenty of milk, yoghurt and fresh vegetables. They were active, walked a lot and were healthy. So you don't need doctors. When girls were pregnant they were not allowed to go out during the last month of pregnancy – in case of a fall and subsequent abortion. After the delivery, the mother was not supposed to do any household chores for a month and quarter. Then we have to perform a simple ceremony: a *Jhir* (water-carrier) took boiled wheat, which was blessed by a priest, to the farm-well and there it was distributed.... The mother, in the meantime, was given a special food supplement called *Dh̊abra*, which was made of *ghee*, flour, dried-grapes, ginger, aniseed, raisins and almonds. The idea was to build up mothers' lost strength – you know woman is literally physically shaken by the birth. If it was a boy, there were great rejoicing and presents were given both to the mother and the baby boy – gold jewellery, dress and bed-clothes and kitchen-wares were the common gifts. Men threw extravagant drinking parties and these went on for a month or so.

Feeding

Traditionally, babies were breast-fed and mostly on demand. This was one of the reasons why young mothers were encouraged to drink a lot of milk and a special food supplement was also prepared. Solid foods were started around the age of six months – a piece of chappati, yoghurt, boiled rice and lentils were the common offerings. The whole thing was taken very lightly; grandmothers did feed babies and sometimes even suckled them. A grandmother (farmer's wife, aged 50) explained:

> In our times breast-feeding was the natural thing to do. We have heard of some cases where a mother could not feed her baby because milk won't come. In this case another mother from the kin-group suckled the infant until he could take cow's milk. In rare cases, well-off people gave powder milk – *Cow and Gate* – I think. Babies were fed whenever they cried for milk – day or night.

It is difficult to specify a precise date, but we think somewhere in the 1970s it became fashionable amongst the upper-middle classes to feed the baby by a bottle using powdered milk. Its advantages were perceived to lie in the convenience with which babies could be fed by

Ayahs or a mother substitute. A young mother explained (Army officer's wife, aged 28):

> I breast-fed my first child only for four months – I was never told the benefits of doing so – after that it was convenient to use a bottle. Also, I used to get very little milk. My boy suffers from asthma and generally remains unwell. Now I feel guilty – I should have persevered for a longer period. With the second baby, I fed her for two-and-a-half years. She is very intelligent and has hardly fallen ill. I learnt from my mistakes.

The fashion of using a bottle with cow's or buffalo's milk became popular with a lot of working mothers even in lower socio-economic groups, but doctors and nurses have been stressing the value of mother's milk because of a widespread occurrence of gastro-enteritis. A doctor (aged 32) explained:

> Mothers prepared milk often in unhygienic conditions – flies, water not fully boiled, bottles and nipples not cleaned properly, etc. – so we have a big education/awareness programme to tell mothers that breast milk is the best for babies. You know there was a bit of snobbery attached to bottle-feeding – it was thought to be modern and high class. I think mothers are going back to breast-feeding now.

Help with Child Care

The joint family system provided an excellent framework to support young mothers in child care. In a lot of cases, the grandmother became a surrogate mother to the first born. But this joint family system of the middle classes is breaking down because of wider occupational choices and geographical mobility (see Sharma, 1990). A farmer (aged 62) analysed the situation:

> Joint family is finished here as well. There are two reasons for this: all young people of our class are educated and they want independence – want to do their own thing; second there is this awareness that they want to be sole in charge of what they earn and how they spend. I don't see any joint household save one in our village. But they fight all the time – why haven't you done this? So and so had drunk more milk? The situation my be different in remote villages. We have been exposed to TV – as you know there is a cable system as well, and almost all houses have electricity and there are several households with telephones and cars. A lot of people are abroad.... This has brought in individualism and even

> selfishness – the old values are fast disappearing. Before children obeyed their parents. Now they make their own choices: what subjects they want to study at school and which line of occupation they want to pursue.

The changing pattern of family structure has been described by many scholars (Sinha, 1984; Gupta, 1978; Ramanujam, 1972). Sinha (1984: 9) argues that village people are increasingly moving away from their traditional family and caste occupations to seek jobs in the burgeoning industries in urban areas. As a consequence, families are rejecting some of the old-established values and attitudes. He concludes by suggesting that the traditional extended family is in a transitional phase and this, therefore, has serious implications for the care of young children.

Regrettably, there is virtually no research material on this topic in the two universities Ghuman visited (Guru Nank Dev at Amritsar and The Punjab at Chandigarh) in the Punjab. A single M.Phil. thesis (Singh, 1992: 3) at Chandigarh dealt with the topic of child rearing in a peripheral way. The writer found that working mothers are facing considerable difficulties in finding child-care facilities and he notes the changing position of working women: 'A woman exercises considerable power in the family matters and most of the important decisions in the family are made in consultation with her.' Another research on child rearing was published by Sharma (1981) – some 17 years after the fieldwork was carried out by another scholar. In our view, this study is out of date owing to the very many social and economic changes which have taken place.

As the extended family network is fragmenting, the strain of rearing children is becoming more acute. A woman clerical worker (aged 42) was very candid:

> I was alone in Chandigarh. It was difficult for my in-laws to come from *Roper* (a town 25 miles away) to help. Anyway, my mother-in-law was not happy because she wanted us to live with them. She was very angry with me – she thought I have led her son astray. So I had no co-operation from her. With my first child I was very tense. I had a full-time job and a new baby. I used to get very tired after work and then there was this problem of feeding. Because I was tense, my milk dried up. Then I have to leave my son in a crèche … Now, my boys are not close to me because I did not spend that much time with them. I wonder whether working full-time was worth it – but we needed the money.

The conflict between the new bride and her mother-in-law has been the subject of numerous folk-tales, ballads and popular jokes. Kakar (1994: 74), in his seminal work on Indian childhood and motherhood, describes the situation of the new wife succinctly: '... a bride comes into her husband's family with a tremendous burden of anxiety and nostalgia, with a sense of antagonism towards her mother-in-law who has, after all, usurped the place of her own sorely missed and needed mother.... For it must be noted once again that the new bride constitutes a very real threat to the unity of the extended family.... The nature of the danger she personifies can perhaps best be suggested by such questions as: Will the young wife cause her husband to neglect his duties as a son? As a brother? A nephew? An uncle?' There is still a resonance of such attitudes towards the new wife by the in-laws although, increasingly, middle-class couples tend to live away from their parents.

A grandmother (aged 54), who is living in an extended family, analysed it as follows:

> My kids were born at home – there was no problems then. Nowadays, ladies are weak and delicate so they want to go to hospital to have a caesarean birth. Also medical profession has been commercialised and sometimes they compel you.... Both my children were almost brought up by my mother. In the same way I help my daughter-in-law. Young wives – even when they are not working – don't know much about feeding, massaging and bathing babies. They also get tense and anxious when something goes wrong ... the thing is young people want freedom and independence and want to live on their own, but then they can't cope.

A mother belonging to the *Harijan* caste (untouchable) had the full support of her mother-in-law (housewife, aged 35):

> My husband is away in Dubai. I have four kids and I can only cope with the help of my husband's mother. She helped me with children when they were babies in every way. Even now one of them sleeps with her.... She is more than part of the family; she is the very *mudd* (foundation) of the family.

In lower *Jati* and in working classes, the traditional pattern of family organisation tends to persist. Therefore, the child-care practices of these groups have not been affected to the same extent as that of mobile middle-class and high-caste families.

Toilet Training

Traditionally, the toilet training of children was handled very lightly indeed (Luschinsky, 1962; Ghuman, 1975). A new baby was usually wrapped in a *Potra* (a square piece of home-spun cotton), which was changed as the occasion demanded. A mother would start holding her baby (at around the age of six months) over her feet, and this was the beginning of the toilet training (see Kurtz,1992). This would continue until the baby could ask to go, usually around the age of two-and-a-half years. Grandmothers usually helped the young mother and so did the *dai*. The latter also acted as a midwife and trained the young mother in massaging, bathing and toilet training the baby for anything up to nine months. Babies around the age of one year would go in a bigger nappy called *langot*, which lasted till the baby was dry. A grandmother (housewife, aged 55) informed:

> Nowadays you can buy nappies and potties from a *bazaar*. Before women used to make them at home – anyway these were not available then. Babies are usually dry by the age of one-and-a-half or two. They start telling you that they want to do *Shee*. But you have to train them, otherwise they mess up their *langot*. I say to my daughter-in-law: take it easy, babies will come along in their own time. I had no problems with mine.

A young mother (teacher, aged 28) gave the following account:

> Most of the Indian children don't take very long to be toilet trained. Here we have diapers and all – but people don't think it is a very good habit. So from six months on we try. My first child was not so soon as my second – she was more independent and intelligent My children were dry after one-and-a-half year. My mother-in-law helped me a lot.

Overall, Punjabi mothers are very caring of their young infants – even to the point of indulgence. Kakar, an acknowledged authority on Indian childhood, writes (1979: 449): '... which lead to the conclusion that certain tentative generalisations on childhood in traditional India, in the sense of describing a dominant mode in a variable range, are indeed possible.... An Indian mother is inclined towards a total indulgence of her infant's wishes and demands, whether these be related to feeding, cleaning, sleeping or being kept company. Moreover, she tends to extend this kind of mothering well beyond the time when the "infant" is ready for independent functioning in many areas.' It appears to us, albeit from a small sample and personal observations, that this way of 'mothering' children is changing in the middle-classes due to structural, demographic and occupational changes taking place in the family (see Sharma, 1990).

Religious Dimension

The influence of religion on child-care practices has been very strong in the traditional family set-up. The notion of a child's nature was derived from religious texts as is his/her name and rites of passage into childhood (*Bhaddan* ceremony). For instance, according to Kakar (1979: 448), the Hindu views on child nature have been shaped by the sacred texts of *Ramayana* and *Mahabharata* and *The Laws of Manu.* One of the interpretations is that the child is idealised in the holy texts as a creature without desires and aversions and thus nearer to God. And 'That begetting of a son is one of man's highest duties and the only way he can discharge the debit he owes to his ancestors.' A grandmother (housewife, aged 55) gave a vivid account to illustrate the influence of religion:

> Child's name is chosen from within the religious texts – *Gita* for the Hindus and *GranthSahib* for the Sikhs – we had it from the *GranthSahib.* Then at the age of about one month he is taken to a *Mandir* or *Gurudwara* for prayers. Our babies are given holy water from the Ganges. Incidentally I am from a Sikh family and my husband is a Brahmin – so we tend to follow rituals of both religions. We also had a *Havan* (*a ceremony in which wood is burnt and Mantras recited by a Brahmin after the birth of a son*) – this was done after the 13th day after the birth of my grandson ... Our boy had to go for *Mundan* ceremony (*clean shaving of first hair*) in Panchcool. *Bhai Sahib* (husband's elder brother) joined us from England. Also we had a religious thanksgiving ceremony organised at home when my son was born ... Then there is the ceremony of *Chaunka-Chadhana*; this is to do with *pavatar hona* (purification) of the new mother. After 40 days the new mother cooks for the family and prayer are said for her and the child's safety, and from then on she carries on with her domestic duties.

Most Hindu families have a little holy shrine in their homes. Here they worship their favourite *Murtis* (the most common ones being statues of Hanuman, the goddess Lakshami and Ganesh) and impart religious consciousness to their growing children in the privacy of their own homes. We were informed by a Hindu grandmother (aged 58):

> Children learn our religion by copying us praying daily to our deities. We have statues of *Lord Rama, Sita* and *Hanuman.* In *Arti* (evening prayer with candlelights) children join in as they do in the morning prayers. Special prayers are said before starting a new year at school. The blessings of our *Murtis* are sought before the examinations. Children are not excluded from any religious events. They come with us to the mandir. They listen to the *Bhajans.* Before *Dussehra* (an important Hindu festival) the story of *Ramanaya* is enacted and a procession is taken out. Then there are *Diwali* and *Navratari* celebrations. All the year round there are holy festivals and children are part of the whole thing ... our religion is not in books but in our lives and that is the way children learn it – by living it with us. They learn food rituals and its 'purity' – whether it is *Sucha* (pure and truthful) or *Jutha* (impure and defiled) by watching us prepare food and how we serve it. Fasting is another important part of our religion, especially for girls and women ... and many many other things.

Some Sikh families also have their holy book (*Guru Granth Sahib*) in their homes and this is used for invoking blessings for special occasions and for saying daily prayers. Normally there is a family service once a week; otherwise individuals read their daily prayers from this holy book. A Sikh mother explained (housewife, aged 35):

> We have *Guru Granth Sahib* in our house. I don't perform a daily service but read it on *Sangrands* (the first day of every new month) and on festive occasions. My children are with me when I am reading the holy book ... I also read *Guru Sakhis* (narrating the good deeds of the Sikh gurus) to them. Children go to *Gurudwara* with me – they are not excluded.

For the Punjabis and for other Asians their religions are part and parcel of their daily lives and are closely woven into the life-cycle rituals (rites of passage). They think it is important for growing children to be full participants in all aspects of their lives so that they can internalise both the rituals and quintessence of religious piety and spirituality.

Rewards and Punishment

Punjabi parents are often very indulgent towards their children until the age of about three. Very few would contemplate punishing a child in any way before this age, let alone by physical punishment. A crying infant will be instantly picked up by a mother or another female relative. However, the situation changes quite dramatically when the next baby arrives. Gentle smacking is used by some parents to discipline their toddlers. Generally, the tendency of Punjabi parents is to spoil the babies at the expense of the toddlers, especially when they happen to be boys. A young mother (teacher, aged 28) who mostly spoke English but switched to Hindi and Punjabi at intervals (which seems to be the fashion amongst the upper-middle-class Punjabis) explained:

> My son used to cry a lot when he was a baby – I thought he was naughty. But now I know he was asthmatic and wanted to be comforted. I did not use to hit him (meaning smack) but now he is older (8 years), I hit him sometimes – not my daughter (5-year-old), she is very sensible.... Well, first four years I would scold them: like told them I will lock you in the store or bathroom. That was the maximum. They did throw tantrum – I would ignore it. Sometimes when they annoy me now, I give them one *chupaer* (slap). (*Has there been a change in this?*) In my case, I can't remember my parents hitting me even once. They were patient – both mother and father. They let us do everything. We were good children except that my brother was more temperamental and they gave in to him. He is suffering on that account – very self-centred.

However, a grandmother gave a very different account (farmer's wife, aged 65):

> *Chaddoo ji* (leave it), I used to smack them a lot – you know that. A child of three years upwards must be chastised, otherwise they become very naughty.... My grandson (6 years) was not going to school this morning. He said: 'Leave me, I will go myself'. He played a trick on me – he sneaked off home. I gave him two. That brought him to his senses. If I had not given him those slaps, he would have tried it again. You know your uncle's grandson, he used to cry and yell before going to school: 'Oh, grandfather save me they are beating me'. Grandfather used to take pity on him, and would say: 'Leave him today, he will go tomorrow'. For the boy, tomorrow never came; and he is now illiterate. Times have changed, though. Children in my times were easier to deal with: sometimes we would give in, other times we *Pitai* (coax) them. But now parents give in a lot which I don't like. Our children were happy playing with *khudo* (ball made out of rags), now my grandchildren have broken six bicycles – what can you do? In my times, children have to wait until they were 15 to have a bike.

There is an old saying in Punjabi which recommends: A farmer's son and a scythe need regular chastisement – the more the better (*which may remind the reader of: Spare the rod and spoil the child*). The older generation tended to believe in this type of folk-wisdom and therefore a boy was treated quite severely in village families. Kakar describes it succinctly (1979: 451): 'Anywhere from the fourth or fifth year onwards, and for the male child especially, involves a virtual reversal of everything that is expected of him. The most striking feature of this change is the contrast between an earlier, more or less unchecked benevolent indulgence and the new inflexible standards of absolute obedience and conformity to familial and social standards.' Likewise, Segal (1991: 235) notes that infants are generally over-indulged but young children are reared in an authoritarian atmosphere.

Independence Training

It is a well-established custom in Punjab that young infants, and even toddlers, sleep with their mothers or a mother-substitute. Indeed, very few mothers would contemplate putting a new-born baby in a separate cot in her room, let alone in a different room. As discussed earlier, babies are indulged to the point of being spoilt. A grandmother mockingly remarked: 'We are not like the *Goras* (whites) who after feeding the baby leave her in the upstairs bedroom – cry or no cry ... In my family, if a baby is slightly ill the whole family is awake to comfort and support the young mother. A completely different *Tarika* (way of doing things).'

In our judgement, there is no conscious attempt made to train the children to be independent as is understood in Britain and America. If anything, children from the age of four or five years onwards are encouraged to be obedient (*Akhe Laggo*) and to honour the elders (*izzat karo*). The popular notion of a good child is, and was, firmly tied to the notion of being a *Kahne Kar* (do as you are told) child. In our view, Segal (1991: 232) describes the expectations of Indian parents quite accurately: 'Children are docile and obedient. Their role is to bring honour to their families by exhibiting good behaviour, high achievement, and contributing to the well-being of the family.... Children are dependent emotionally and often socially on their parents throughout the parents' lives.'

Fathers' Participation

This modern European practice is still a matter of mirth and hilarity amongst even the middle-class Punjabis. The working mothers don't expect to get much help from their husbands. They seem to get help from baby-sitters and/or have to make other *ad hoc* arrangements with their neighbours. Sometimes, a grandmother or a close relative might come to live with the couple during the first few months of a baby's birth. A mother (housewife, aged 43), whose husband was a non-commissioned officer in the Indian Army, described her experience:

> Yes, my husband would get up during the night and comfort them. He was good on that, otherwise no ... the problem was there was only a 10 month difference between my first two. It was a very harrowing time.

A grandmother (aged 65) from a farming background explained:

> In my time I coped on my own, with no help from my relatives. I would ask my neighbours to keep an eye on my kids when I went out to the fields.... Men don't help in this country – only abroad. Not in my house, anyway. Men have to get up early in the mornings to go to the fields, how can they help? It is difficult if you are a farmer; maybe if you are in service they might lend a hand. In our country, it is considered to be a woman's job.

Traditionally, Punjabi fathers did not play any significant role in the upbringing of their babies until they grew up to the school-going age. But a recent study (Sharma, 1990), with an upper-middle income group, reports that some fathers are beginning to participate in the early infant-care practices such as bathing, feeding and changing nappies. Sharma (1990: 75) concludes: 'In general all fathers actively played with their infants and conveyed a sense of being wholesomely involved in their care.'

Then and Now

Of course, our observations are based on a small group of mothers and grandmothers from two locations. We are well aware of the pitfalls of making sweeping generalisations on child-care issues which are applicable to all Punjabis, or for that matter to all Asian communities. However, as pointed out earlier, this is a qualitative study and seeks to gain insights into the changing nature of the child-care skills of Punjabi mothers both in Britain and the Punjab. Hopefully, this should shed some light on the changing child care practices of other ethnic groups from the Indian sub-continent and elsewhere. From our interviews we gathered that, firstly, there has been a great improvement in pre-natal and post-natal care of mothers, especially among the middle-classes. Secondly, families are more aware of the hygiene matters associated with childbirth and the importance of having their babies inoculated against various diseases. Thirdly, there is more affluence in the middle-class homes and therefore they can afford modern facilities, ranging from household conveniences such as a refrigerator, a gas cooker and a TV, to children's nappies, potties and toys. This prosperity has no doubt been bought at a price. Most middle-class families are now becoming nuclear and mothers are working full-time to help family finances (see Sharma, 1990). The warmth, love and care which was taken for granted in the extended family is often absent. Apart from the few upper-class families, people cannot afford to have an *Ayaha* (nanny), and there is no such vocational occupation as registered child-minders to help look after the young babies. Lastly, as regards toilet training, encouraging independence, making children curious and making conscious efforts to lay the foundations of intellectual development, the situation has not changed significantly. Traditional values still prevail in these domains in all castes and classes. In sum, then, the physical care has changed dramatically along with the changes in the structure of middle-class families and the attendant problems which this brings, but very little has changed in the way children's attitudes and values are shaped – they are still rooted in the traditions and mores of Punjabi culture.

Sharma (1990: 76) concludes the results of her investigation on Punjabi child-rearing in these words: 'On the whole there were more similarities than differences between the kind of care given by the mothers now and the care given by the grandmothers a generation ago to their infants.' The major difference was found to be in the 'place' of deliveries: all the grandmothers in the study had their babies at home whilst only 6% of the younger mothers did so. On the other hand, the practices which were commonly employed both by young mothers and grandmothers were: massaging, bathing, dressing and sleeping with babies.

Holme (1984: 117) summarises some of the differences between the Indian and the English way of bringing up infants: 'A child in India is hardly ever alone. Babies are carried around by their mothers, and it is a common sight to see a girl, even as young as six, with a younger brother.... Children play with other children much more than they do with objects.... A regular bed-time is virtually unknown. They tend to play or sit listening to the older members of the family until they drop off to sleep, the younger ones probably in their mother's lap.... Children learn to respect their parents because they see them showing respect to their parents'.... However, we think this is more likely to be a description of the 'working-class' (lower socio-economic) rather than the middle-class families; but nevertheless it is an English perspective and should be of interest to the reader.

Another English researcher (Davenport, 1983: 133), who studied the play of Sikh children in Birmingham, England, also notes a contrasting pattern of child care with that of the English. She writes: 'Children sleep when they need to during the day rather than go to bed to suit their parents' convenience. If, during some late family celebration they fall asleep, they are made comfortable where they are rather than whisked out of the way.... Baby sitting is virtually unheard of; children are taken everywhere. They are allowed to stay late, to eat with adults, to listen to their conversation, but join in very respectfully. These children are having a wealth of experience of a special kind: they are learning by observing – a method perhaps undervalued by white Western society.' These are some interesting insights which are similar to the one described above by Holme (1984). However, the data for this study were collected sometime in the 1980s; therefore we feel her description is more relevant to the first-generation Punjabi Sikhs.

Kakar (1994: 210) summarises the nature of children as revealed and found in the sacred texts of the Hindus and their *Bhakti* (devotional) movement: '... the evidence from textual sources is overwhelming that the child in Indian tradition is ideologically considered a valuable and welcome human being to whom the adults are expected to afford their fullest protection, affection and indulgence.' He argues that the differences between the Indian and the European thinking on children's nature can be discerned from the idioms that are commonly used to describe the process of child rearing: Indian parents say: '*Palna Posna*', which implies protecting and nurturing – going with the child's nature, whereas the European use words such as 'rearing and bringing up' – evidence of a conscious attempt to shape and influence children's behaviour. The major flaw in the Indian psyche, according to Kakar (1994), is its complete omission of any consideration of baby girls.

4 Some Findings from the 1970s Research on Pregnancy and Infant Care

The findings reported in this section are based on the data collected in 1970–74 as discussed in Chapter 1. These findings should serve as a backdrop to the results and discussion of the issues addressed in the present inquiry.

Pregnancy

There used to be a belief in Punjabi villages that an expectant mother should not go outside her house after the eighth month of pregnancy; that has now changed both in Punjab and England. The other custom was that of *Reetan,* observed by a few *khatri jati* (sub-castes) such as *Chopras* and *Khoslas.* During the eighth month of pregnancy, the women in the neighbourhood would visit the expectant mother to wish her well. The mother-to-be, in turn, would go to her neighbours to top-up their clay lamps with mustard oil. This ritual is a symbolic act of giving 'light' and was intended to please the neighbours who would, hopefully, reciprocate by blessing the mother to have a healthy baby. After the ceremony, the expectant mother stayed at home until her delivery.

There were various rituals observed after the birth of a child. The nature of these rituals, however, depended on the religion of the family. Muslims observe the custom of *Azan* – the father or grandfather or any other man from the family recites, in the right ear of the new-born baby, a holy prayer from the Koran. The first line is *Allahu Akbar* (Allah is the greatest) and the last one is *La ilah illa 'Illah'* (There is no God but Allah). We were informed by a Muslim housewife (left school at 17 with matriculation):

Azan was said in her ear. The idea was that the first words she heard or went into her ear should be those of Allah. *Azan* should be said as soon as possible after birth.

All the Muslims in the sample claimed to have performed the ceremony irrespective of the country in which their baby was born or whether the baby was born in a hospital or at home. And, more importantly, the prayer was whispered irrespective of the sex of the new-born.

The ceremony of *Gurthi* or *Gothli* is popular amongst some Punjabis. The new-born is bathed and made presentable and his/her lips are touched with a piece of cotton which is soaked in honey or sugared-water. This ceremony is usually performed by a close woman relative and is a 'women-only' event. The person chosen to perform this ritual should have a good sense of humour, high intelligence and an even temperament as these attributes are supposed to be passed on to the baby. Nearly a third of the Punjabi babies – both boys and girls – were given *Gurthi*: however, a higher proportion of children born abroad (85%) had gone through this ceremony compared with children born in Britain (7%).

A Muslim housewife (literate in Urdu) explained:

> *Gurthi* was given by my grandfather. His habits were very good and he was a religious man. We thought that Allah will make this child like my grandfather, both in character and personality.

Purification Ceremony

This consists of taking ceremonial baths on certain days (3rd, 5th 11th, 21st, and 40th days) after the delivery. Also, the mother is supposed to have bed-rest ranging from three days to 40 days (and to stay indoors), depending on the state of her health. This period is called *Shilla*. Over a quarter (27.5%) of the mothers conformed to one or more of the ceremonies of staying in bed, taking ceremonial baths and staying indoors for a specified number of days. There was no social class difference in the observance of ceremonies, but more mothers (66%) with children born abroad observed the rituals than those with children born in Britain (9%). A Muslim housewife (left school at 11) described her experience:

> I got out of the bed on the 5th day. But I did not go out of the house for the first 40 days or one-and-a quarter month. I took the

ceremonial baths on the 5th, 20th, 30th days and one-and-a quarter month. These baths were compulsory. I could take baths on other days, but these were a must. Some Sikhs have a slightly different custom to other Punjabis in that a priest is invited to offer prayers and bless the family, usually 11 days after a baby's birth.

After this period, the mother's rest period comes to an end and she is 'purified' (*suchi*) to resume her household duties. Muslim women are not allowed to say prayers for 40 days (i.e. during the *Shilla*) after the birth of a child.

Naming the Child

Traditionally, the religion of the family played an important part in naming the new-born child. Names were chosen with the help of religious books: *Guru Granth Sahib* for the Sikhs, the Koran for the Muslims and *Gita* or other Hindu holy books for the Hindus. Increasingly, however, Punjabi parents are ignoring this convention and choosing names with the help of their relatives and friends. Only 10% of the Sikh families in our sample chose a name with the help of *Guru Granth Sahib*. Currently, Sikhs living in Britain and North America are prone to omit Sikh middle names (*Singh* for boys and *Kaur* for girls), and are even Anglicising Punjabi names (see Ghuman, 1994; *The Independent*, 17 April 1993). Thus Daljit Singh Gill is more likely to be David Gill and Surrinder Kaur Sandhu, Sue Sandhu!

This custom of recording a child's place, date and *exact time* of birth was considered important in Hindu and Sikh families. This was the task of a village Brahmin and was chronicled in a *Janam Patra* or birth certificate. This semi-holy document was subsequently used by *Pandas* (astrologists) to prepare an astrological chart which would predict the child's future including his/her marriage, occupation and place of residence and many other matters. A Hindu housewife (left college at 18) showed her faith in *Janam Patras*:

> We got Ram's *Janam Patra* prepared when he was about three or four years. At the time of marriage we do attach importance to them, especially if a person is born under the zodiac sign of Mars. If he marries somebody whose zodiac sign is different, then one of them will soon die. At the time of arranging marriage we use these charts to ensure compatibility between partners. In these charts the future is predicted.

In the sample of the study, only one-fifth of parents had a *Janam Patra* prepared for their child. Significantly, more middle class (40%) than working class (17%), and more parents whose children were born overseas than in Britain, engaged in this practice. This custom, however, is on its way out since a birth certificate is issued to all parents in Britain and the services of a Brahmin and a *Panda* are not easily available to carry on this tradition.

Hair-cutting Ceremonies

Hindu and Muslim parents have this ceremony performed as part of their religion – Sikhs, of course, are not allowed to cut their children's hair. The timing and details of this ritual are quite different for the two communities. The Muslims call it *Akika*. According to this holy dictate, the new-born child's head should be shaved seven days after his/her birth and money or other offerings in kind be made to the poor.

But the Muslim parents in the study gave the name *Akika* to the ceremony of offering goat's meat as a thanksgiving ceremony rather than to the hair-cutting ceremony which, according to them, can be performed at any time in one's life. An illiterate Muslim housewife told us about the significance of *Akika*:

> I liked her original hair very much, it looked so nice and she was a very beautiful child. So I didn't get her hair cut. Whenever I took her outside she suffered from fever and sometimes she would become very ill. When she was about two years old I had to get her cut, but I didn't want to. Her daddy used to tell me: 'You don't get her hair cut that's why she becomes ill and is full of fear'. I had to agree and her hair was cut. You see, whenever she became ill I suspected that perhaps this happened because I haven't performed the ceremony and I hadn't given anything away in the name of Allah.

The Hindu ceremony is called *Mundan /Mandan* or *Bhaddan* – normally it is boys who are eligible for this ceremony and it is usually carried out when the boy is two years old. A Hindu housewife (education, middle school) explained:

> We did have *Bhaddan*. We booked a hall and invited people to *Bhaddan* party. A Brahmin was specially invited for the ceremonial *puja*. He did *havan* and recited relevant mantras. A barber was brought in to close-shave the hair of my son.

Sometimes this ritual is also performed in the case of girls as it is thought to protect them from the evils of black magic. An illiterate

Brahmin housewife told us of her own daughter:

> She was *Jethi* (the first-born), so we took her to the Goddess' Mandir – *Chint purni* and had her hair shaven there and threw it into a river. Then we had no fear that somebody could get her hair locks and harm her by using it in an evil eye or black magic rituals.

Lohri Celebration and *Akhand Patth*

Hindu and Sikh Punjabis celebrate the birth of a son by distributing *Gur* and *Shakkar* (raw-sugar), maize and other farm produce to adolescent boys and girls on the festive day of *Lohri*. Also *Lohri* is an occasion for throwing 'men-only' parties where a lot of liqueur is drunk. Over a quarter of the sample said they have celebrated *Lohri* in Punjab even when a son was born in Britain.

Akhand Patth is a Sikh thanksgiving/blessing-seeking service which is performed on important occasions, such as the birth of a son; upon starting a new business; before a wedding ceremony; and before travelling abroad for the first time. The family members holding the *Akhand Patth* are obliged to listen to the non-stop reciting of the *Adi Granth* (holy book) and to give a *Langar* (free meal) to the assembled *Sangat* (congregation) and give either money or things in kind to the *Gurudwara* for the use of *Sangat*. However, only 14% of the Sikh families in the sample had held an *Akhand Patth* – another example of the discontinuation of religious ceremonies.

Superstitions

The old superstitions surrounding the birth of a baby are dying out now in the Punjab. But, in our first inquiry, 14% of the mothers who had children in Britain believed that a child born during *Katak* month (i.e., Scorpio; October–November) is likely to be affected, and that a special ritual by *Pandas* or Brahmins is to be performed to get rid of this curse. One of the suggested rituals is that water be stored in an earthen pitcher for about a month prior to the expected *Katak* birth, and the mother and her new-born baby should take a purification bath with the kept water, and then the curse would be neutralised. (But some mothers thought that such a birth can be a sign of good luck!). Other mothers (26%) had a belief in *Nazar Lagana* (evil eye): which includes, among other things, bringing about a misfortune on the object of one's praise – tempting providence. Therefore, some Punjabi mothers (15%) believed in taking actions to offset the ill-effects of the curse. A Sikh housewife (left school at 11) explained:

> I believe in the evil eye and as a precaution I take a little coal dust and put it behind the ear of the child ... I remember on one occasion when she (daughter) became victim of the evil eye. She was a very healthy baby. Someone had said: 'How beautiful she is', and she became ill. She had boils and other ailments and it took a long time to get rid of these.

An illiterate Muslim mother gave another example:

> He was victim of the evil eye on several occasions. Whenever I gave him bath and put nice clothes on him, he felt unwell. This happened many times in Pakistan, but not in this country. Whenever it happened I touched the child with chillies and threw them into the fire, and sometimes I took a little sand or dust from underneath the feet of the child and threw that in the fire.

Teething Troubles

A special ritual is performed when a baby cuts her/his first teeth. Some Punjabi mothers believe that a baby's teeth will form like those of the person who performs the special ritual. The ceremony consists in throwing chewed coconut on the baby's face by a person (other than her mother) with good teeth. It is essentially a social occasion for women folk to assert their solidarity and to give mothers recognition and moral support. At the first sign of teeth-cutting, a person with healthy teeth is chosen to throw a piece of masticated coconut on the baby's face. The rest of the coconut is given to the women present at the ceremony and sometimes it is distributed in the neighbourhood. About two-fifths (38%) of the mothers performed this ceremony. A Sikh factory worker (left school at 14) explained:

> I did perform this ceremony in the case of my eldest son, but not with others. Now things have changed. Nobody practices it in towns or large villages. It is only in remote small villages that people still engage in such ceremonies.... My eldest son was about seven to eight months old when his grandmother, who knew a lot about these things, threw masticated coconut on his face.

A slightly higher proportion of mothers of children born in Britain (39%) than of mothers of children born abroad (34%) carried out this ritual. There was a social class difference as well, more working-class mothers observing the custom compared with middle-class.

There is a superstition attached to teeth-cutting as well. If a baby is likely to cut his/her upper teeth first, that is a sign of bad omen – serious harm may come to the maternal relations. A special ritual must be performed to counteract the ill-effects of this premonition. Traditionally, to perform the ceremony the procedure is that one person from both the maternal and paternal sides of the family goes beyond the boundary of his/her village where they meet at an arranged place. The person from the assembled maternal side pours mustard oil into a bronze container and is supposed to look at the reflection of the face of the baby therein, who has accompanied the paternal relation, but who has been hidden from the maternal relative. The two adults must not converse but perform the ritual in complete silence. The bronze utensil, along with the oil, is given to a *Dukk* (a person of lowest *jati*) who accepts alms. We were given a graphic account by an illiterate Sikh mother:

> If a child cuts upper teeth first this is 'bad' for all the relations on the maternal side. One has to inform the mother's relations and not to take the child to them, as they must not see the baby's face until the special ceremony has been performed.... Narinder's paternal grandmother cut her upper teeth first when she was a baby. By chance her mother's brother's wife saw the teeth. That woman died within a few days. Shortly after her husband died – the whole family were destroyed. Although we know that whatever happens is God's will, but when the necessary ceremony is performed, then there is a satisfaction in our hearts and there is no cause for doubt or fear. My husband's sister's baby daughter was in Bradford. She cut her upper-teeth first, and we went to M1 (Motorway–Freeway to London) to do the ceremony. The meeting was arranged by phone ... though I don't believe in it, we had to do it to satisfy the maternal relatives.

A higher percentage of working-class (28%) as opposed to middle-class (5%) mothers carried out the ceremony. Likewise, a significantly higher proportion of mothers who had their children in their country of origin (45%) performed the ritual compared with mothers who had their babies in the UK (16%). But this superstition is on its way out amongst Punjabi mothers both in the Punjab and England.

There is another superstition, which applies only to a *Jethi* (first-born) child, particularly a boy, who has to be protected on the festive occasion of *Diwali* (the festival of lights). It is thought an evil-doer may clip the child's hair and use it to perform a black magic ritual which might result in a serious injury to the child. However, only a few mothers believed in this superstition, as we were informed by a Sikh mother (left school at 17 with matriculation):

> I have heard that some people get *Jetha* child's hair cut so that an evil person may not use a clipping of his/her hair, but I don't believe in these superstitions. However, I didn't allow my first-born child to go out on the *Diwali* nights. My reason was different; because people play with fireworks and the child can easily get badly hurt by fire-crackers ... the evil eye or the black magic didn't come into it.

Ghuman (1975) interviewed 32 mothers in the summer of 1974 to find out their views on child-care practices. They were absolutely delighted with the medical facilities available in England. He noted (1975: 65): 'In particular, they thought that children have such a favoured and healthy babyhood here, with all the necessary things readily available, easy access to doctor and nurse and remedies and with their mothers having so much time to look after them as a result of having household appliances, unlike the Punjab where, after the baby is few months old, the mother is fully occupied with very time-consuming cooking.' Other findings of interest included: All the babies were bottle-fed; three-quarters had no grandparents to help – a significant difference from the Punjabi situation, and nearly a third of the fathers took baby for a walk – another significant change in the fathers' participation.

Of the similarities with the old traditions, it was found that: 89% of the families lived in an extended family situation; 74% of the mothers had no plan to toilet-train their babies; 74% had no fixed hours for bed-time or for sleeping; 81% actively discouraged their children to be independent; and none of the mothers believed in smacking a child under two – in fact they were horrified that a question of this nature was even being asked. What emerged from the small-scale study was that the Punjabi parents were adopting some of the modern conveniences of the facilities available without substantially changing their traditionally held views on independence and educational training, nor their conventions regarding smacking and toilet training habits.

Conclusions

Pregnancy and child-birth evolved in most societies in an attempt to safeguard mothers' health and to protect the new-born from a variety of illnesses and physical dangers (Levine *et al.* 1992; Rice, 1988; Kakar,

1994). From the mothers' responses to our interview questions and their detailed comments, it is evident that some of the traditional ways of bringing up children were already undergoing change by the 1970s. This was particularly the case in the use of the myths and superstitions surrounding child-birth and the subsequent initiation ceremonies. Most of the mothers were happy not only to avail themselves of modern-day facilities to take the drudgery out of housework but also to eliminate some of the boring and routine aspects of baby care by using nappies, gripewater, baby-creams and other useful toiletries. Furthermore, we noticed that the child-birth rituals and ceremonies were mostly performed under the influence of an elderly grandmother or an aunt who had made a special trip from India or Pakistan for this purpose. But as the ties of kinship and the pull of 'home-country' begin to fade with the passage of time, the traditional rituals are fast disappearing. Not least, the mothers' exposure to the modern ante-and post-natal medical care services alleviates mothers' worries and anxieties about the safety and the well-being of the baby.

In the next chapter, we look at a variety of child-rearing matters by comparing and contrasting the response patterns of the 1995 sample with those of the 1970s.

5 Early Child Care

Introduction

In this chapter, we present the findings of the 1995 study on early child-care practices. The reader will recall that the sample consisted of 20 Sikh, 10 Hindu and 10 Muslim families. The proportion of different religious groups in the study broadly reflects the composition of the 1970 study's larger sample. Although a detailed cultural and religious background of the second generation was given in the first chapter, it is judicious at this point to provide a brief sketch of the changing social and economic circumstances – relevant to child-rearing – of the Punjabis as revealed by our study questionnaire. This should serve as a backdrop to the subsequent discussion on early child-care issues.

The material circumstances of most Punjabi families have changed dramatically as have those of the indigenous white population. This has been due to the rise in general prosperity as well as the special circumstances (discussed below) of the Punjabis. Although the vast majority of the Punjabi families interviewed in the 1970s felt settled in the UK, they still maintained close ties with their kinsfolk in India and Pakistan. They frequently visited their countries of origin and took generous presents and gifts for their relatives. Also, most of them felt they had to discharge their obligations to their relatives and kinsfolks. For instance, family loans had to be repaid, marriages were to be organised, *Pucca* houses to be built and land to be purchased and tube-wells to be sunk – all these enhanced the *izzat* (honour) and reputation of the joint family (see Ghuman,1975; Anwar, 1979).

These social and emotional ties with the home country provided a deep sense of security and firm identity to the newly settled Punjabis but proved to be very expensive. We were informed by a Sikh housewife (left school at 14) who was interviewed for the 1970s study:

> See, we are caught up in two customs: one of our home country's and the other of this ... we still send money to my husband's sister and perform all the customs and ceremonies required of us: marriages, births, religious obligations and other ceremonies. Also we are

trying to adopt some of the ways of the English for the sake of our children, because their schooling demands it and they have to learn to live in this country. All this is draining our money. We are in a sort of a limbo.

All the Punjabi families in the sample, except one, owned their house: 12 are in detached and 23 in semi-detached houses, four in terraced houses and one in a council house. All the families possessed most of the modern-day facilities to a varying degree. Most had a vacuum-cleaner, a refrigerator/freezer, TV and a video cassette recorder, a gas or an electric cooker, a washing machine, various kitchen gadgets, including a micro-oven, a food mixture and a toaster. We found only two families owning a dishwasher but over two-thirds of the households had central heating. The houses were well-furnished with carpets, curtains, three-piece suites, kitchen furniture and other items of furniture. A few had chandeliers in their sitting rooms, which is a sign of ostentatious wealth by Punjabi standards. Some had decorative furniture and paintings from India and Pakistan. Over half of the households had a satellite disc for receiving 'TV-Asia'. All had their own cars. Most of the drawing-rooms are organised in such a way that they can be used for receiving guests and contain family portraits, Indian or Pakistani calendars, even occasionally dolls, embroidered works and paintings of assorted type – water colours or copies of famous works by Indian/Pakistani artists. These drawing-rooms are mostly used by the elders, both male and female, except in Muslim families where they are for the exclusive use of males and their guests (see Shaw, 1988). The overall impression is that the households have come a long way since the 1970s in the ways in which they have incorporated some of the decorative artefacts of the English. The rooms reflect a kind of mixing of the East and West from decoration through to artefacts and to articles of clothing.

This is in contrast to the first-generation's taste, whose sentiments and aspirations were mainly with the country of origin. In Muslim houses, for instance, there was a preponderance of decorative articles from Pakistan. This included parchment scrolls of Muslim sacred shrines, tapestries on which *Kalmas* are inscribed, and pictures of the famous Pakistani leaders and film actors. Likewise, in Sikh and Hindu homes, artefacts relating to their religion, i.e. calendars with pictures of Gurus and holy places, predominated alongside those of famous Indian actors and actresses such as Sashi Kapor, Dharminder and Hema Melani. The bedding quilts called *rajai* (of duvet type but containing cotton), bedcovers, cotton sheets called *khesis*, embroidered pillowcases and table-cloths were all largely from India and Pakistan. Special Indian and Pakistani dolls, with suitable native dresses, were commonly used for decoration. All these items no doubt saved money, but their prime purpose was nostalgia – a sort of link to, and longing for, the homeland. These artefacts are getting scarcer now in the Punjabi homes as the tastes and flavour of the second-generation reflect somewhat different realities and situations.

The food habits of the second-generation are quite different to those of the first. The first generation mostly continued with the traditional style of food linked with the appropriate religious taboos. Thus, they mostly relied on *roti* (chappatis), lentils and vegetable curries and yoghurt. Muslims and Sikhs also had chicken and lamb or minced goat meat added to their food menus, whereas most of the Hindus were vegetarians. Very occasionally, the first generation bought fish and chips or other fast-type food, but this was invariably for the children (see Ghuman, 1980a; Dosanjh, 1975).

The second generation, however, has changed its dietetic habits remarkably (Ghuman, 1994a). Its members enjoy pizzas, fast-foods, Chinese cuisine and a variety of cooked food which is available in the high street. They are less conscious of their parents' food taboos and are willing to experiment. Most second-generation families have their main meal in traditional 'Punjabi style', but breakfast and lunch are more likely to be similar to those taken by their English counterparts – a mixture of food items; sandwiches, pizzas, home-cooked curries, pasties and salads. Of course there is a wide variation in the food eaten, but a definite trend exists towards easing the burden of time-consuming Punjabi cooking. Most women of the second generation are in full-time or part-time employment and the new trends in eating have provided an enormous relief to them.

Perceptions of Lifestyles of Two Generations

All the second-generation mothers were asked: *What are the differences between your lifestyles and that of your parents*? Without reservation all the mothers pointed to the enormous improvements in the material well-being of the present families and the range of households conveniences now available to them. A graduate Sikh pharmacist explained:

> We have a higher standard of living. My parents were very hard working but still hadn't enough money. We earn enough to be

> comfortable ... children have a lot of clothes and toys. We as a family have holiday which we never did.

Apart from the higher standard of living, mothers commented on the differences in moral and religious spheres and related problems. A graduate Hindu teacher reflected:

> One thing my parents did was to lay stress on our religious education and high moral standards. They also stressed the virtue of family life and my *Nana ji* and *Nani ji* (mother's parents) lived with us, and we learnt a lot from them about our history, language and religion. This is no more now. *(Why?)* We don't have our parents living with us. Whether I can provide my kids with the same learning environments is questionable. They had set ways, now children have input from many sources.

A graduate white teacher of French origin had very similar views:

> My grandmother was living with us. She spent a lot of time with me. I miss not having grandparents living with us. I think it is very beneficial for the children. Yes, I do. It is good for children to talk to somebody who is not directly their parent.

Some mothers touched on the subject of child-rearing when comparing the lifestyles of the two generations. A Sikh shopkeeper (left school at 16 with some qualifications) reflected:

> I think we are very more Westernised ... saying that though my Dad has become freer as he has grown older and he can relate to us better. We are a lot freer with our children than our parents ... a lot more freedom.

A Sikh shop owner (left school at 17 with matriculation), who came to this country some 20 years ago, gave her impressions of the differences between her way of life in the Punjab and here:

> Here we are in a Western culture. In India there is respect for the elders and family relationships are honoured ... say you call somebody your brother in India they would look after you. But over hear, no. They would turn around and say: 'I don't think of you that way at all'. Meaning, who wants to be your brother? I miss those relationships and respect. (*What about standards of living?*) In India we had all the facilities, including servants in the house and at the farm. Medical facilities were very good, but I suppose for most Punjabis it is better here.

This mother comes from an upper-middle class background and had attended an English-medium convent school in the Punjab. She came to this country through an arranged marriage and now runs a mini-market in partnership with her husband. Unlike the rest of the sample she has mixed feelings about living in Britain.

> A Hindu graduate trainee teacher, who was brought up in India, ruminated: Culturally completely different: here children sort of mixing with two different cultures. In India, there were different religions but obviously one language. That's it. I had an arranged marriage. My husband has been in this country since he was five. I feel settled and happy here.... I don't think educationally our children have any more benefits. My parents were teachers and encouraged us to read and achieve high. But materially we are much better off.

A Muslim housewife (left school at 16 with some qualifications) thought there has been a huge change in lifestyles:

> In every respect, it's more modern and more broad-minded. I am not very religious like my Mum and Dad. I am more liberal towards my children. My husband and I share a lot of housework, unlike our parents. We are more understanding and tolerant of our children's behaviour and try to explain more. Our lifestyle is more cushy with all the advanced technology like microwaves, fridges, Hoovers, computers, etc. It is easier for us and we are enjoying it more.

A Sikh shop-keeper (left school at 16) endorsed this viewpoint:

> Definitely different. I mean our Mum and Dad just worked. Go to work, come back and go to sleep – my Dad did three jobs to support us four kids. We work, we go out and enjoy ourselves. Them days, they never used to. It is true, isn't it?

As discussed earlier, the general standard of living has been rising steadily since the 1970s, although some social classes and ethnic groups have not had their fair share of prosperity. An indigenous white graduate, part-time lecturer, explained:

> Generally, I would say we are better off than our parents. We have more gadgets for housework and we travel more. There is far more information about diet and 'preventative' things for mothers. Fathers are more willing to help – though in all these things there are class differences.

A Hindu part-time factory worker (left school at 16) was very effusive:

If I start about it I will never finish ... I think our generation has changed. Our parents were not educated really – they didn't go to school. But at least we are. I wanted to be a nursery nurse but I had to leave school; full stop, and look for work and then marriage. So old-fashioned.... I didn't receive much love from my parents because we were a large family. I give so much more love to my daughter. My parents were very strict. But now when we talk about it, they say: 'Everybody was doing it that way and now it has all changed'.

Preference for Baby Boys

All the mothers were asked whether they wanted a boy or a girl. Nearly half the mothers (18) said they did not mind, 16 wanted a baby boy and six would have liked a baby daughter. Of those who did not mind the sex of the baby, the typical response was: 'We wanted a healthy baby, it didn't matter whether it was a boy or a girl.' Those who wanted a baby boy were mainly influenced by the traditional argument about the importance of having a son/sons in the family, although about one-third of these mothers did so to balance the family because they already had a girl/girls in the family. Likewise six mothers, including four Hindus, wanted a baby girl to have a mixed family. This pattern sharply contrasts with the first-generation Punjabi mothers, the vast majority (69%) of whom wanted a baby boy because of religious and traditional imperatives.

A first-generation Hindu couple's reply was typical:

I don't believe in Social Security. I consider my sons as my security for my old age. In our *samati* (social organisation/culture) sons are of great importance. We tell them right from the start what we are doing for them and what in turn is their responsibility. We tell N ... what he has to do for us. He has to face up to it.

Thus we see a clear shift in attitudes towards gender equality mainly due to acculturation, but also partly due to the changing attitudes amongst even the modern middle-classes in India and Pakistan. Woollett *et al.* (1991: 245) also found a similar trend in their research: all the Asian mothers in their study expressed a preference for mixed families. However, when asked whether they wanted the same number of boys and girls or had a preference for boys or girls, the replies revealed the residual bias towards having more boys.

Ante-natal and Post-natal Care and Learning of Mothercraft

There is a growing body of literature (see Woollett *et al.*, 1995; Black, 1988) on the health problems relating to pregnancy and childbirth of Asian women. There is evidence to suggest that Asian women are less likely to be single mothers, smokers and/or drinkers and tend to be younger than the indigenous white mothers (Woollett *et al.*, 1990a,b; Ghuman, 1994; Shaw, 1988). On the other hand, it has been found that Asian babies have lower birth weights and a higher perinatal mortality rate, and that young children are likely to suffer from a variety of illnesses which are unique to their *ethnic* situation (McEnery & Rao, 1986; Black, 1988). These difficulties have been attributed to the families' cultural beliefs relating to childbirth and pregnancy and diet. In our own research, we found a few mothers in the 1970s sample who also believed that an expectant mother should not go to a marriage party or to a house which is in mourning. There are certain foods which were/are considered *hot* (eggs, chicken, fish, nuts, garlic, raisins and aubergines) and which should be avoided, and *cold* foods (rice, cow's milk, lemon, peas, buttermilk) which are to be preferred by pregnant women (see Bhopal, 1986). It is argued that the situation can be improved if Asian mothers were to attend ante-natal clinics regularly and were to be given advice on diet. Most studies have found 'communication' or lack of competence in English between Asian mothers and heath care staff to be the major reason for non-attendance at ante-natal clinics (Firdous & Bhopal, 1989). In a large-scale study of Asian mothers (Mason: The Asian mother and baby campaign, 1990), Mason found that: 'The linkworkers provided a much-needed interpreter service but were less successful in imparting health education knowledge to Asian women. In fact, improvement in health education knowledge occurred in women with a good understanding of English ... there is still a very large proportion (approximately 50%) of Asian women in Leicestershire who are unable to communicate in English and are therefore not able to make full use of the available services.' Woollett and Dosanjh-Matwala (1990a,b) found that 41% of the Asian mothers in the study could speak little or no English and less than half were living in extended families. Predictably, they found mothers who spoke little English to be less knowledgeable about health care matters. McEnery and Rao (1986: 397) found that: 'Large families and poor English make it difficult for some women to attend clinics regularly.... About a quarter of all infants at the age of 1 year or more had a blood film suggestive of iron deficiency.'

Our data suggests that the second-generation mothers were more regular attenders of ante-natal clinics and this is mainly due to their ability to speak English, an awareness of health matters and a greater self-confidence. A graduate Muslim, part-time researcher, explained:

> I don't think we had any preconceived notions how we were going to look after the baby. I learnt a lot from the clinic – they gave us phamplets on different things. I did the exercises they suggested and also we read a couple of books.... But the midwife was very helpful. For the first week she came every day to check with us, then once a week and afterwards once a fortnight – a lot of help. She turned out to be a very good friend.

Some mothers relied on their own resources (Muslim housewife left school at 16 with some qualifications):

> No, not specific advice as such. It's just that I'd been through all that with my sister going into hospital and really it is in the family, you know. Asian people feel it's unnecessary because they know it and it's been passed down. So I didn't, and I really felt that way.

An Sikh shop owner (left school at 17 with matriculation) was very articulate:

> I attended the clinic and also went to the ante-natal classes. Actually I learnt a lot by doing it.... My mother-in-law was not much help. (*Books?*) I got a mother-care book and it gave you quite a bit about how to raise a small child and it was a great help. The rest from the clinics, doctors and nurses.

Contrast this with a response from an illiterate Sikh housewife of the first-generation:

> The woman isn't allowed to go out because she isn't in a fit state. She doesn't look nice. She could easily fall by tripping on the pavement ....but I don't follow it. I have been to the clinic but find it embarrassing because of the language and strange environments ... I find it difficult to open-up to total strangers. Back at home, I could confide every thing to the women of my mother's household. I suppose this is our modesty or call it shyness.

All the mothers in the present sample attended the hospital clinics regularly, whereas less than half of the 1970s sample did so. The major difficulties at that time were of communication and of deeply held traditional customs. However, only 16 mothers (8%) of the 1970s sample did not go out of their house during pregnancy. This finding is in agreement with the observation of Woollett *et al.* (1995: 66) who write: 'Whatever traditional practices may have been, Asian women now largely accept Western health care and their concern for a successful outcome ensures that they are willing to attend antenatal clinics in spite of complaints about long waits and lack of information.'

All the deliveries were in hospital. There were four caesarean births and two with complications where a long stay in hospital was necessary. It is interesting to note that, in the present sample, two-fifths (40%) of the husbands were present at the time of delivery, which sharply contrasts with the 1970s sample, where only a small minority (5%) took part. Woollett *et al.* (1995) also found that the majority of Asian mothers were accompanied by their husbands at the birth of their children.

A Sikh factory worker (left school at 16) explained:

> I wanted him to be with me; after all it was his baby too. He was little embarrassed to start with but then agreed. Everything went well.... He was very tense, but I felt good that he was there.

Nearly a third of the mothers were accompanied by a female relative and, in a quarter of the cases, nobody except the doctor and the nurse were present. The majority of the mothers were out of bed within a day or two. This sharply contrasts with the situation in the Indian subcontinent where a prolonged rest is considered essential. A graduate Hindu mother, who had her first child in India and the second in England, gave her version of events (part-time cleaner; interviewed in Hindi):

> It is all different in this country – as is the difference between the sea and the sky. When she was born (*in India*) it wasn't my husband's business to be with me. I stayed with my mother for five months; out of this two months were complete rest. Here I started work after three days. Over there I had a special *Dĥabra* made for me with a lot of *ghee* and nuts and raisins. My mother gave me plenty of milk and *Dĥabra* every day to build up my strength. Also my sister-in-law and *Bhai* (midwife) helped me in looking after the baby – massaging, bathing, feeding and changing. Here my husband helped me a lot otherwise I couldn't have coped.... I must say I like the Indian way.

It is interesting how other researchers (Woollett & Dosanjh-Matwala, 1990) also noted similar comments from Asian mothers. One of the Muslim mothers in their sample gave an illuminating reply: 'If there is someone to do it for you then you are not allowed to do it for a month and a quarter. But if you don't have anyone then you start doing it the day you arrive from hospital. If you live with your parents they won't let you touch anything for ten days. They say that if you touch anything it becomes dirty.'

As regards the special religious ceremonies connected with the birth of a baby, most of the families still performed these, although with less zeal and intensity. Thus all the Muslim families had *Azan* (special prayer) said in their baby's ears and had their head shaved (*Akika*). All, but one, had their son's circumcision done.

A graduate Muslim, part-time researcher, recounted:

> The only one my mother told me was to blow in his ear and say the *Kalma*. Really the head of the family should say it but he was not here. My parents performed it when they first saw the child. Also you have the head shaven when he was born. We did that, but a few months later. We did it for the grandparents and thought they have a right to it. We had one disagreement about circumcision. We objected to it and my mother was very very insistent that he should be identified as a Muslim, but we avoided it.

A school leaver Muslim housewife had an interesting story to tell on the salience of religion:

> I had difficulty in conceiving. I had my baby after five years. So we planned to go to this holy Mosque in Pakistan and pleaded with the Imam. He said: 'Don't eat meat till you have a baby.' I didn't eat meat for two years. After the baby was born we went to this holy place and did my prayers, they call it *Salat*, to the mosque. After that was done I could eat meat. I took his hair with me – the one we took off his head at home. Thank God (*sic*) ... thank the holy place, I mean for everything we prayed for came true.

Another CSE-educated Muslim housewife explained the nature of ceremonies:

> We had the *Azan* done in his ear, if I remember on the second day. It was the older uncle who did it. The *Azan* is the ritual of the birth ... saying the first pillar of Islam *La Illha Mhummad a Rasool Illah* into the child's ear as if to wake them to the fact that they're born into a Muslim faith.

Likewise, all the Sikh families, except two, fulfilled their religious obligations. A college-educated Sikh machinist described the influence of religion:

> We went to the *Gurudwara* for prayers when he was one-and-a-quarter month-old. Later on we had the *Akhand path* (special reciting of the holy book) and asked the *Granthi* (priest) to find the first letter of his name by the usual ceremony. Then the whole family got together and chose his name using the first letter as a guide to the full name... We did not celebrate *Lohri* for his birthday but we did it for the first one – only distributed *Ladoos* (sweets) among relatives and friends.

A Hindu trainee teacher explained what they did to mark her son's birth:

> Hair-cutting ceremony was done when he was born. We did his *Mundan* when he was three-year-old. His hair were taken back to India. There his grandmother took them to *Mata Vishnu Devi Chintpuri.*

All the mothers of the second generation in our research, except three, engaged in some form of religious observance and ceremony but these were not as intensive and prolonged as in the first generation. But none of the mothers mentioned the observances of *Gurthi, purification, Jethi* and *teething troubles,* which were performed by a significant minority of the first-generation mothers (see Chapter 4, page 58). It appears that it is the weakening of the links between the second-generation families and their countries of origin which is the major factor in the decline of such rituals. Over half of the mothers referred to the fact that their parents would have liked more religious and associated rituals in children's initiation rites, but they have simplified these due to the pressure of work and the fact that they now live in Britain and not in India/Pakistan where religious and social customs have to be observed. At any rate, some of them commented that even in India and Pakistan their relatives and friends have given up these archaic practices.

Naming the Baby

For the first-generation Punjabi Sikh parents, religion played an important part in naming the new-born babies. Thus nearly all the Sikh families had a special naming ceremony performed (*Akhand Path*) at a *Gurudwara.* The priest then found a first letter of the potential name by opening the *Granth Sahib* (the holy book of the Sikhs) at random. Thereafter, the family collectively chose the name out of all possible names which could be made up by using this first letter. This custom of naming the new-born has survived in the second-generation Sikh families: nearly two-thirds of the parents carried on with this tradition. However, just half the parents have kept the traditional middle Sikh names of *Singh* for boys and *Kaur* for girls. However, this is not the case with the Hindu and Muslim families studied: only one Hindu and two Muslim families relied on religious ceremonies, the rest chose names with the help of the extended family. But the reader is reminded that Hindu and Muslims do not have associated religious ceremonies as far as the naming of a baby is concerned. A few typical responses are presented. A university graduate Muslim teacher explained:

> It was a combined effort. There were several names suggested and I think we passed them around to the immediate members of the family and took a sort of consensus. (*Any religious ceremony*?) No religious ceremony when he was given the name but we did perform *Akika*.

A Hindu housewife (left school at 18 with advanced qualifications) told us:

> We liked Jessica, when it came to a name. We had to look in a book.We made a list of all the names we liked and my husband's sister decided.

A Sikh mother part-time office worker recounted (left school at 18 with advanced qualifications):

> We went to the Gurudwara. The letter (u) came up and my husband decided to call him Urbinder. (Are you keeping the middle name *Singh?*). Yes, of course. But as you know a lot of our kids Anglicise their names and don't use Singh at all ... sign of the times. I suppose they feel more comfortable.

Another Muslim housewife (left school at 16) described her religious sentiments:

> I always wanted to keep Mohammed as my son's name and for respect I thought I'd have another name added on to it. Because you know some children start swearing and saying Mohammed is so-and so. So I thought I'd better keep a second name so that 'He' (i.e. *Mohammed*) wouldn't be disrespected.

Breast/Bottle-feeding

It appears from the literature search that most mothers hold ambivalent opinions on breast-feeding (Garforth & Garcia, 1989). Therefore, it was thought interesting to include questions on this type of feeding. The resulting figures for the two generations are presented in Table 5.1.

An important point to note about the 1995 sample is that over a third of the mothers did not breast-feed their babies and only 10% were feeding after a year (included in this group are two mothers who breast-fed for two years.). When compared with the first generation there is an increase in the proportion of mothers who do not breast-feed their babies at all. This is probably due to the fact that proportionally more Punjabi mothers are now in employment and find bottle-feeding a convenient way of coping with their diverse commitments.

A high school-educated Sikh shop owner replied:

> Bottle right the way through. I was not successful with my first two, so I didn't go to the hassle of doing it again. I was working in a shop and this is what suited me and my situation.

A graduate Muslim mother, part-time researcher, explained:

> I had a caesarean birth and it was very painful ... Initially I was very upset because I wanted to breast-feed. My argument was that the child who is breast-fed has the immunity. Then we compared children who have been breast-fed with those who were bottle-fed in our close family and found no difference. Anyway, in the initial month the feed has the immunity and the antibodies; after that it is just milk. We also thought 99% of the population can't be wrong and

Table 5.1 Breast-feeding in the two Punjabi samples

	No breast feeding	*1 month*	*2 months*	*6 months or over*	*Total*
Second generation	16	8	9	7	40
*First generation	46	68	35	21	170

*Only those mothers who had their babies in England are included for comparison. Chi-square = 6.61 with 3 *df* is not significant the general trend is that way. The midwife agreed and the doctors were not bothered.

Some responses of the first generation are given for comparison. An illiterate Sikh housewife explained:

The nurses told me not to breast-feed the baby because my milk was 'not good'. I used to have medicine. Also my breast used to ache during feeding my first baby. Anyway, one can find plenty of dried milk in this country. So I thought it better to change to bottle.

Another Sikh woman who works in her own shop explained why she gave up breast-feeding (left school at 16):

I'd a problem. I wanted to help my husband in the shop and did a lot of housework. Sometimes, when I was breast-feeding the child, a customer would come and I couldn't feed the child and serve the customer at the same time. You've to do one thing or the other. Under the circumstances, bottle-feeding was the best solution.

Other reasons given for not breast-feeding by the first-generation mothers included: 'It would spoil my figure. If it is good for them (*meaning white mothers*) it should be good for us too; couldn't have enough milk for the baby.' Also, bottle-feeding mothers felt that it was very convenient because other members of the family could participate. They felt that powder milk of good quality is available to enable them to prepare bottle-feeds hygienically.

We now consider the responses of the 12 white mothers in our present study. Half the white mothers did not breast-feed at all, one gave up at two months, four persevered until three months and one for nine months. A graduate white mother (part-time lecturer) described her experience:

I fed her for two months only. It became very painful – I was a mess, physically. I seemed to be sensitive, but I persevered. Then it became very stressful and was affecting the baby because I was in a lot of pain and used to cry. I had a guilty feeling for a while but then I thought it through and I was OK then.

Reasons for discontinuing breast-feeding, or not breast-feeding at all, are similar to the Punjabi sample and included: 'Physical discomfort; inconvenience; had to go back to work; and it doesn't matter, anyway.'

According to one research report, Garforth & Garcia (1989: 75), only

26% of British mothers in England and Wales achieved breast-feeding for the baby's first four months. The authors argue that mothers stopped because of pain, insufficient milk and other such problems. They also note: 'Many aspects of post-natal care in the labour ward make it difficult.' Furthermore, they identify the problem of conflicting advice on breast-feeding from the health-care staff to be a contributory factor. It appears that there are several factors which are implicated for the incidence of low breast-feeding both amongst the Punjabi and white mothers: some lie within the structure of the health-care and the management of childbirth and others relate to the personal and social and economic circumstances of the mothers. If breast-feeding is considered sufficiently important, a massive campaign is necessary to persuade both health-care staff and would-be-mothers of the advantages of doing so.

Bottle-feeding and Weaning

Most of the second-generation Punjabi mothers bottle-fed their babies up to the age of 18 months and a small number recalled doing so at the age of two-and-a-half and even three years. Most of the mothers (37%) started feeding solids when their babies were about three months old and nearly all of the babies were on solid foods by the age of six to seven months (the comparable figures for the first generation are 50% and 90% per cent respectively). The most common fare was a mixture of Punjabi and English food: the mothers mentioned yoghurt, rice, chapatti, lentils, eggs and a variety of cereals. Some mothers also used tinned food and were grateful for its availability. A graduate Hindu housewife expressed her delight: (interviewed in Hindi):

> As the baby's appetite grew so he needed extra milk. But after six months I started giving him a small portion of rice, yoghurt, rice and semolina.... Then you get ready-made food here and I fed him with that. Why bother making it when it is there – all varieties, vegetarian, tinned sweets? It made life very easy – it was costly though.

A graduate Muslim mother (part-time researcher) gave an interesting account:

> Around six months ... in the beginning it was rice pudding and plain yoghurt. He rejected spicy food. He refused tin food from day one. I used to make him bland soups and liquidise it – mostly vegetarian

with cheese – and lots of porridge and Wheetabix.... He carried on with the bottle for three-and-a-half years. We tried to stop him earlier. I think part of the reason was he enjoyed his bottle and felt relaxed – very comfortable. I remember one day when we took the bottle away, the look on his face was disastrous. He was very sad so we let him continue.... Also he had a dummy for a short time.

Nearly two-thirds of the mothers (27) eschewed the practice of using tinned food and stuck to their home-made meals. Over half of the Hindu mothers (six) wanted their babies to grow up as vegetarians and most of the Muslim mothers (eight) hoped that their children would grow up to observe the food taboos of their religion, i.e. not to eat pork. From the responses of the Sikh mothers, however, we infer that they are not unduly concerned with any of the food taboos, although their parents avoided beef dishes so as not to give offence to their Hindu friends and neighbours.

As regards advice on feeding and weaning, most of the mothers received help from midwives and some from health visitors. A 'school leaver' Muslim housewife explained:

Asian midwife translated and also gave me a lot of advice. Basically it was my own knowledge – me, myself, who devised the feeding.

A Hindu mother (Certified Counsellor; runs a sub-post office) gave a very full account:

I did breast-feed for four weeks and bottle after that because we were going for business and so on. I couldn't take the baby everywhere.... The midwife said if this is what I want, it was OK. The doctor could see the reason why I had to stop ... I am a vegetarian so I give her the same food. It is only when she started going to school that we said: 'If she likes meat, it is all right by us.' We don't normally cook meat at home. So she enjoys a variety of food and it doesn't bother me.

Likewise, a graduate Sikh pharmacist explained:

I breast-fed her partially for six months and then due to my work – and it is difficult in a family situation – I had to go upstairs. I wasn't comfortable – I stopped gradually. I started on solids just after three months – also bottle till two-and-a-half years. Though she is seven she still has a bottle sometimes because of her younger sister. Actually she stopped at two and a half. I am over-anxious: wanted her to eat at the right time and the right food.

From the mothers' responses it may be safely inferred that most of them coped well with weaning and starting their babies on solid foods. And there have been no significant changes on these matters when compared with the 1970s sample.

From the sample of white mothers in the study we obtained a similar pattern of responses on the starting of solid food. Warrington and Storey's (1988: 76) in-depth investigation and their review of the relevant literature come to a similar conclusion. They write: 'Asian women appeared to follow the habits of indigenous mothers; they breast-fed less frequently, for shorter periods of time and introduced solid food earlier than they would have done in the Indian subcontinent.'

Toilet Training

All the mothers were asked at what age they started potty training. As anticipated, there were problems of recollecting the precise age due to the passage of time. But from the responses, we gather that the *Mode* (most frequent reply) is around one-and-a-half years, though two mothers started as early as three months. Most of the mothers had their babies dry during the day-time, at any rate by two-and-a-half years. Mothers were quite happy to relate events surrounding their endeavours to toilet-train their infants. A Hindu trainee teacher narrated:

> I can't remember the precise time – but it was quite early. I remember taking him to India when he was two and he had left nappies a long time before that. (*How long did it take?*) Not very long. I was quite persistent and consistent. It took two to three months at the most.

A Sikh shop owner (left school at 16) had help from her mother:

> I would say two-and-a-half years. My mother toilet trained him; I couldn't do it. I tried. She would take his nappy off and let him run in the house without a nappy on. When he wanted to do *Shee* she would say come and sit on the potty or toilet. He was dry in two months.

Another Sikh housewife (school leaver; interviewed in Punjabi) used her Indian visit to toilet train her baby boy:

> He was about two when we went to India. We didn't use nappies. He learnt it quite easily. The courtyard was quite wide and he would

run around with other children and was dry in two to three months.

A few of the mothers in the sample (five) used their visits to India/ Pakistan to train their babies. The reader may recall (Chapter 3, page 47) that so-called potty training is taken very lightly by Indian and Pakistani mothers and often nature is allowed to take its course. Our impression is that most Punjabi mothers in the sample had a very relaxed attitude towards potty training. A graduate Muslim mother's (part-time researcher) reply is quite typical:

> He was two and a half when he didn't want the nappy anymore. That was it. No accidents, nothing. He was going to nursery. He said: 'Other children are not wearing nappies'. So he decided.... I did try before that; it was not successful. He was never interested to do it on the potty. I said to myself: 'Let him carry on, he is not ready yet.'

Comparing our results with the 1970s sample, it seems that not a great deal has changed, except that disposable nappies are fully accepted now and mothers are more conscious of their responsibilities to toilet-train their infants.

Fathers' Participation

We thought it important to find out the husband's level of participation in looking after the young infant. Accordingly, several questions were asked probing this aspect of behaviour. These were: changing nappies, feeding, putting to sleep, carrying and playing with the child. Also the mothers were asked the amount of attention the father now gives to the child. We present the responses in Table 5.2.

It is clear from Table 5.2 that with the exception of 'changing nappies' fathers did play a very significant part in bringing up their child. We give selected responses of mothers to reflect the feelings of the group. As mentioned earlier, we interviewed a Hindu mother in addition to our sample (graduate; housewife; interviewed in Hindi) who had her first delivery in India and the second in Britain and was, therefore, in an excellent position to compare and contrast her experiences of child-rearing in the two milieux.

> In India husbands don't go to hospital and bother. They leave it to the women of the house. It is not his business. In this country he had to do it ... he was very good. The husband interjected: 'With my first child I didn't even wipe his nose clean, and here I had to do

Table 5.2 Husbands' level of participation – second generation

	Yes	*Occasionally*	*No*
Changing napies	5	1	34
Feeding	31	6	3
Putting to sleep	26	7	7
Carrying about	36	1	3
Playing with	37	3	0
Total	135 (68.5%)	18 (9%)	47 (23.5%)
*How much attention father gives to the child	Very high 26 (65%)	Average 12 (30%)	Not much 2 (5%)

*As rated by mothers

everything – changing nappies, feeding and playing with her. There is nobody else to help her.'

A high-school-educated Sikh shop owner had a slightly different perspective:

He did everything: nappy changing, feeding, the lot. I also work, so we share every thing... In India nowadays even they do it. My generation – my cousins and my brothers, they take full part in bringing up their children. Even when the wife is not working – it is a new thing. The mother-in-law relationship is different now. They are like friends now. Not like a queen sitting on top of you.

The women, whose husbands were not active participants, gave work as the main reason for their not helping out. A high-school-educated Muslim housewife informed us:

Occasionally he gave her a bottle. He doesn't spend much time with her. He comes home tired.... He carried her sometimes in town because of my back. She demands a lot of attention because she's quite nice sometimes. He used to give more when she was younger – she was really lovable and she was a bit of a daddy's girl. But that's as far as it is now, you know kisses and cuddles.

A graduate Sikh pharmacist also mentioned time as an important factor:

When he has time he gives his full attention: does number work,

> puzzles, stories, the lot. But he comes home late and tired and leaves early because it takes him an hour or so to travel to his work. I can only give my full attention at bed-time ... no, he didn't change nappies, but occasionally gave her a bottle and carried her about.

It is interesting now to compare our results with the first-generation mothers whose babies were born in this country. Only 11% of the fathers played a full part compared with nearly two-thirds of the second generation. Likewise, a significantly higher proportion of the second-generation fathers were feeding, putting to sleep, carrying and playing with their babies compared with the first generation. But there was little difference in the proportion of these fathers who changed the nappies of their babies. Obviously some social conventions are more resistant to change than others and nappy-changing is considered the limit. Our overall findings, however, confirm Woollett *et al.* (1995, 1992) who found Asian fathers increasingly helpful to their spouses with baby-care, household chores and by being present at deliveries. However, comments of the first-generation mothers reflect the difficulties of migrants during the 1970s. An illiterate Sikh housewife explained:

> Her daddy can't attend to her very much because at dinner time he goes to the pub. He's on night shifts and when the children come from school it is about time for him to go to work. When he comes back from work the children are ready to go back to school.

A similar explanation was given by a primary school-educated Muslim housewife:

> When her daddy is on the morning shifts he usually works overtime, but when he is on the late shifts he comes home when the children are asleep and they go to school before he gets up and he doesn't get much time on the afternoon shifts either, because he finishes round about 10 o'clock.

The second-generation families in the study, by and large, have better jobs and housing, fewer financial worries and most wives are doing paid jobs either in the house or outside compared with the first generation. Therefore these fathers are expected to help with the housework and upbringing of children. This has proven to be the case in our research.

Cot Deaths

It is an old custom on the Indian sub-continent that infants sleep with their mothers and, in modern middle-class families, the new-born baby is either in the couples' bedroom or in their bed. This is primarily to make sure that the baby is safe and is well-protected from mosquitoes and other insects at night. This custom has been carried over by the Asian families to Britain and may explain the lower rate of 'cot deaths' among Asian babies. Farooqi *et al.* (1993) found evidence which supports this contention: 94% of the Asian babies slept in their parents' room while the figure for the whites was 61%. Additionally, they found that almost three times as many white mothers as Asians placed their infants to sleep in the prone position, which is associated with an increased risk of SIDS (sudden infant cot death syndrome). We asked mothers in our sample to tell us about the sleeping arrangements when the new baby arrived. Nearly all the mothers (38/40) had their babies either in their bedroom or in the same bed. The mothers were also asked whether they would have considered using a separate room for the new-born. We give some typical responses. A graduate Muslim, part-time researcher, gave a detailed description:

> He had a cot but he never slept in it. He used to wake up every hour and it was too painful. I had to come down and feed him. Eventually I just picked him up and put him in my bed. He slept with me initially for four to five months. Then he refused to part from me. He sleeps with us even now (*7-years-old; only child*). We tease him that he will be with us till 21 ... We don't mind at the moment. We feel he is insecure and likes close touch and comfort.

A graduate Sikh pharmacist also gave a similar response:

> When she was little we were living in our parents' home so we had her in our bedroom – sometimes in our bed. She got into this habit. When her new sister arrived we had to sleep in two separate rooms to look after them.... It was inconvenient but we didn't mind. In a way it is easier than hopping in and out of bed. Anyway we have to keep an eye on her at night.

From the mothers' comments it became clear that babies are still indulged in a traditional way and this custom, according to some researchers (Farooqi *et al.*, 1993), saves many lives.

Conclusions

The following trends have been identified in this chapter. First, the material circumstances of the Punjabi community have changed and this has had a strong bearing on their lifestyles. Second, the families are becoming nuclear; but, there is still a strong extended-family-network support. Third, the Punjabi women in the study are, like other Asian women, increasingly making use of the National Health Care facilities. Fourth, with the exception of religious practices, the pattern of early-care has changed in very many ways since the first research was carried out in the 1970s.

The second-generation migrants/ethnics tend to adopt, to some degree at any rate, the ways of the host society. These include language, knowledge of social conventions and mores, dietary habits, economic and industrial awareness and the polity of the host society. The degree of adaptation appears to depend mainly on two factors: the salience and resilience of their own cultures; and the attitudes and perceptions of the host society towards the migrants' integration.

The majority of Punjabis (and for that matter all Asians) in Britain, North America and Australia are now second-generation *ethnics* (citizens) and have made many changes in their lifestyles to adapt to their country of domicile. They seemed to have integrated into British society without losing the core values of their own cultures (see Shaw, 1988; Ghuman, 1994a; Ballard, 1994b). In Britain, the second-generation Punjabis, especially of Indian origin, have higher levels of education, better jobs and housing, greater proficiency in English and are generally more settled and prosperous than the first generation. Most of the second-generation mothers in the study thought that they are really well-off now. We were told: 'I mean, my Mum and Dad just worked. Go to work, come back and go to sleep ... We work, go out and enjoy ourselves'. And 'Our parents were not educated really – they didn't go to school. We are.'. 'My Dad had to go away to earn a living and she was on her own and in those circumstances I think she did very well ... I got everything she never had.'

There has been another change in the family structure which has a significant bearing on child rearing. Most of the second-generation Punjabi families studied are nuclear and live in the outer-ring of the cities in contrast to the first generation who settled in the inner-city areas. We were informed by a mother: 'My *Nana ji* and *Nani ji* lived with us, and we learnt a lot from them about our history, language and religion. This is no more now.' Fewer grandparents live with the young families, although some families have them living nearby with a brother or sister. They have fewer children and their preference for boys is attenuated in common with the changes in attitude of the middle-classes of India and Pakistan. Most women in the study have either a full-time or a part-time job – this is in sharp contrast to the first generation where most of the mothers stayed home.

In common with the other researchers in the field (Woollett *et al.* 1995, 1991; McEnery & Rao, 1986), we found that comparatively more mothers of the second generation are attending ante-natal classes and seeking advice from health visitors and midwives. Communication is less of a problem, as most of the second-generation mothers had their full schooling in Britain. The comments of a Muslim mother illustrate this: 'I learnt a lot from the clinic – they gave us pamphlets on different things ... the midwife was very helpful.... She turned out be a very good friend.' These advances have been partly owing to the concerted efforts by various agencies to address the needs of Asian mothers and it has paid dividends (see Mason, 1990: The Asian mother and baby campaign).

Compared with the first generation, the fathers' participation has increased dramatically during pregnancy, delivery and subsequent baby-care. Significantly more fathers were present at deliveries and looked after their infants compared with 1970s sample. The mothers' responses illustrate this: 'I work in the shop with him and share everything'; and 'There is nobody else to help so he has to.' From these comments it became clear that this change has been primarily due to the fact that families have become nuclear and the help which used to be available from the extended family is restricted or is not there. Also an increasing number of Punjabi/Asian women are entering the job market or are becoming equal partners in the family business and this necessitates a change of attitudes.

The elaborate customs, superstitions, rituals and myths, which a significant number of the first generation practised, have disappeared altogether. Thus, the customs of *Reetan, Jethi, Janam Patra and Cutting of Teeth* have not been undertaken by even a single family in the study. However, the ceremony of *Hair Cutting* referred to as *Mundan/Bhaddan* by the Hindus and *Akika* by the Muslims is still celebrated as are the ceremonies of circumcision and *Salat*. Nevertheless, it must be noted that such customs are also in decline in both India and Pakistan. The majority of the Sikh families in the study still hold religious ceremonies for naming and thanksgiving (*Akhand Path*) for the new-born baby. A few Sikh families also observed the occasion of *Lohri* both in England and the Punjab. There has been little change in the feeding and toilet training of babies since the 1970s. As more Punjabi women seek jobs outside the house, there has been a slight decline in breast-feeding, but this is a wider trend as demonstrated by the indigenous white population. A research by Hackett and Hackett (1994) on child-rearing practices of Gujarati (another Asian ethnic group) and British families has also noted that a significantly higher proportion of Gujrati mothers bottle-fed their babies and had them sleeping with them until they were on average three years and three months of age. We found a similar pattern in the Punjabi sample.

A study conducted in the USA with a sample of Gujarati families (Patel, 1989: 93) found that 'Acceptance of Western values is associated with the use of Westernised child-rearing practices' (*sic*). This is rather a tautological conclusion but from the comments of our Punjabi mothers we can confirm this overall generalisation. Roopnariane and Hossain (1992: 14) carried out a research project in New Delhi to probe into the degree of participation of university-educated husbands in child-rearing. All the wives were in full-time employment. They conclude that although: '... a small portion of Indian men are more willing to embrace certain types of care giving activities, men in India are still deeply entrenched in patriarchy and still maintain good distance when it comes to the basic care of the babies.'

Our sample's educational attainment and occupational levels are broadly speaking lower than the sample in the above-mentioned study; despite this, the fathers have changed their behaviour towards the rearing of their infants. This highlights the salience of the social milieu and economic circumstances within which the family is located and thereby undertakes its socialising function. A study of Chinese families by Li-Repac (1982: 129) in the USA drew a similar conclusion to that of Patel (1989). Li-Repac concludes: 'With acculturation it (i.e. *Chinese child-rearing norms*) becomes more similar to the American norms.'

In sum, the second-generation Punjabis have changed their child-rearing practices by fathers' greater participation, the increasing use of health care facilities, the shedding of rituals which were associated with the childbirth and initiation ceremonies, and an attenuation of their diet taboos. It is not unreasonable to assume that such changes have also taken place in other Asian and ethnic minorities communities both in Britain and North America.

6 General Personality, Development of Independence and Rewards and Punishments

> Of over two hundred statements of advice on child-rearing prior to the eighteen century which I have examined, most approved of beating children severely and all allowed beating in varying circumstances except three.... (de Mause, 1974: 40)

Introduction

In this chapter we will discuss the Punjabi mothers' perceptions of their children's personality and children's special fears and anxieties. Furthermore, we will explore the mothers' attitudes to the development of independence and the ways in which they use rewards and punishment, in particular physical punishment (smacking), to guide and control their children's behaviour. As in the preceding chapters we will compare and contrast the findings of the present research with that of the first generation. Thus, the mothers' attitudes presented in this chapter should serve as a backdrop to the subsequent chapter on the development of bilingualism and bicultural identities.

Personality Development

To the question 'How would you describe to someone who does not know her/him at all?', the mothers in the study, with few exceptions, gave positive descriptions of their children. The most common attributes used to describe the girls were: gentle, loving, good, listens, lively, talkative, quiet, shy, intelligent, independent and nice. And for the boys: healthy, lively, nice, listens, shy, pleasant, fidgety, anxious, naughty, sensible, polite and easy-going. There was a tendency for the mothers to use more effusive and emotive words for the girls than for the boys. There were no marked 'religious-group' differences either in the tone or the substance of what the mothers have to say about their children. We give some verbatim replies to highlight the points made above in our narrative. A graduate Muslim part-time researcher enthused about her only seven-year-old son:

> He is lively, humorous, active and fairly intelligent. He is a very happy child.... he loves interacting with other youngsters and adults; though he gets on better with younger children and adults. He loves practical jokes and he loves his friends.

According to his parents, he seeks and gets a lot of attention from them, and they are extremely interested in his personal and social development

A qualified Hindu interpersonal counsellor gave this account of her eight-and-a-half-year-old girl:

> Well, at school she is a fairly bright child. She is on top of her class. But she has got a mind of her own and she likes to do things her own way. She could spend all day on her own, if she enjoys doing what she is doing. She can sit for hours and sew.

A Muslim housewife (left school at 16 with qualifications) was equally positive about her seven-year-old daughter:

> She's very loving, caring and very pleasant girl. I think she's got a very loving nature ... very emotional. Out of my children (*in all five*) I'd say that personality-wise she's got the best. She's the only one of my children who will notice when I'm tired, when I need rest and things like that.

A Sikh part-time machinist (left college at the age of 18) gave a candid account of her boy who had some problems in his development because of a head injury (interviewed in Punjabi):

> He is quite intelligent. But when he was about a year-and-a-half he accidentally bumped his head on a steel contraption. He was very slow in his speech. He did not talk until he was three-and-a-half. Then I took him to a speech therapist and she gave me some exercises to do with him. He now talks fluently in English but for Punjabi he has to try hard, though he can understand.... He is a very loving and good boy.

A Sikh part-time check-out operator (left school at the age of 16) described her seven-year-old daughter:

> She is so talkative. She enjoys conversation. She makes everybody enjoy her company. She is like my friend. I can talk to her about anything. She is very clever – brainy for her age.

Some mothers were mildly critical of their children. A Sikh shop owner (left school at 17 with matriculation) was open about her nine-year-old boy:

> He is very naughty – likes attention. He will do anything or everything that will get him attention. He lands in trouble for that quite often. He is not a disobedient child – a naughty child. He likes outdoor activities.

Likewise, a graduate Sikh pharmacist gave a slightly critical account of her seven-year-old daughter:

> She is a very sensitive and an observant child.... She is obstinate and can be stubborn and throws tantrum to get her own way. She likes outdoor play – football, running around and cycling as well.

On the whole, the mothers spoke in glowing terms of their children and in cases where there were points of criticism, these were balanced by positive comments. The white mothers in the study also used positive labels to describe their children, but they appeared to be less effusive and more economical in their praise. The most common adjectives used were: happy, loving, shy, fiery-temper, bright, strong-willed and out-going – a somewhat narrow range of attributes compared with the Punjabi mothers. Three verbatim extracts are given as illustrations. A graduate teacher described her nine-year-old girl:

> She is an extrovert, very bright and very warm, but difficult at times because she is temperamental.

A school-leaver cleaner described her child as 'happy, loving and affectionate' and another mother called her daughter as 'hell fire on legs with a fantastic sense of humour!'

The responses of the first generation Punjabi mothers on this open-ended question were very pithy and short indeed. The common attributes used were: shy, quiet, likes playing outside, clever and naughty. Clearly, the second-generation Punjabi mothers are far more knowledgeable and/or articulate about their children. Also they are far less critical and more positive. How far this is due to the fact that they are more tuned to answering the interview type of questions and/or are more knowledgeable about children and their needs is hard to tell. Whatever the reason(s), the second-generation mothers, broadly speaking, showed more interest in talking about their children. We will discuss this aspect fully in the concluding section of this chapter.

Specific Questions on Personality

All the mothers in the study were asked three inter-related questions: (1) Would you say he/she is placid or rather temperamental? (2) Do you find him/her easy to manage? (3) Is he/she the sort of child who usually agrees with what you want him to do, or does he tend to object to things quite a lot? The meaning of temperamental was explained invariably to all the respondents as 'opposite to placid, i.e., lively, active and a bit on the emotional side'. The responses are given in Table 6.1 along with the responses of the first-generation mothers.

The response patterns of the two samples are significantly different on all three questions. It is difficult to conjecture an explanation for the difference in responses to even the first question. At the time of writing, Dosanjh (1976) also found it hard to offer a satisfactory explanation for the fact that a high proportion of the mothers labelled their children as temperamental (the corresponding figure for the English sample was 44%). The differences between the two groups on

Table 6.1 Responses of the Punjabi samples (in percentages) to general questions on personality

Questions	*Sample*	*Yes*	*Varies*	*Temperamental*
(1) Is he placid ...?	1995	33	47	20
	1970	14	33	53
(2) Do you find him easy ...?	1995	Easy 53	22	Tricky 25
	1970	Easy 70	27	3
(3) Is he the sort who agrees with you or objects?	1995	Agrees 37	35	Objects 28
	1970	Agrees 72	25	Objects 3

Note: The chi-square test was carried out on all items and the results were evaluated with the relevant degree(s) of freedom. All the difference were significant beyond 0.05 level.

questions (2) and (3) are easy to explain. Punjabi children growing up in Britain are likely to pick up the habit of questioning and arguing from their white peers and teachers and are also likely to be less obedient than the children of the 1970s and are less easy to manage. The full discussion on this point and other emerging themes will be taken up in the concluding part of this chapter.

The second-generation Punjabi mothers gave some very interesting responses to questions (2) and (3) in Table 6.1. A graduate Muslim part-time researcher described her son:

> He is very dominant and to change his views you have to really put your foot down. He got his own mind on most issues. He does understand mostly but sometimes he is very difficult ... usually he is right about most of the issues and he proves us wrong, that is the problem!

A Sikh shop owner (left school at 17 with matriculation) used a similar tone when discussing her son's personality:

> He is not easy. You have to show him/them who is the boss in the house and they have to get along with it.... He will object – he will bring up a lot of reasons why shouldn't he do it. Why can't the older or the younger do it. But once you explain to him he will accept your reasons and do it.

A number of mothers pointed out that they have to reason with their children before they would agree. A Sikh factory worker (left school at 16) gave a warm account of her daughter:

> I find her easy to manage. She is like my friend. I can talk to her about anything. She would agree with me but I have to explain to her, and then she 'will do it straightaway. We do things together.

It is interesting to note a somewhat different perception of some first-generation Punjabi mothers, as shown, typically, by the response of a primary-educated Hindu housewife:

> Usually he agrees with me but other times it depends on the way I ask. For example, if I ask it in a loving manner he'll happily do anything for me, but if I raise my voice and tell him to do something then he will drag his feet ... he'll still do it.

Fears and Anxieties

To the question: 'Has ... any special fears or worries?' there are varied and interesting answers. Twenty-four mothers (60%) felt their children have no special worries or fears, but 16 alluded to problems of their children. The fears mentioned were of: darkness, certain films, death, going upstairs alone, nightmares, God and *Ghunna* (sin); and worries mentioned were about telling lies and not being good. Of the first-generation children, a significantly higher proportion (65%) had some form of fear or anxiety, the most frequent being the fear of dogs. The other common fears were: darkness, thunder and lightning and of certain persons such as policemen and doctors – quite a different list compared to the second generation.

A few quotes illustrate the concerns of the second-generation mothers. A school leaver Sikh check-out operator described the fear of her seven-year-old girl:

> If she does something wrong she thinks God will punish her with bad dreams. Even last night she had a terrible dream and she goes: 'Probably I never ate my food so God is punishing me ...' She got scared. So I put her with me.

Likewise a Muslim housewife told us: My son worries about God punishing him if he is naughty – he says it is a *Ghunna* (sin) not to do as you are told.'

A graduate Sikh pharmacist explained her daughter's fear:

> Yes, dying. She keeps going on about dying. I think because my mother-in-law died recently. This has troubled her a lot. Because in the first year after her *Bi Ji* passed away we had a lot of trouble at night with her. She started to have nightmares and get up ... I am going to do this drawing and leave it in *Bi J'si* room and she will see it. She has a dream *Bi Ji* is sitting in an armchair and calling her. Since her death she has asked a lot of questions: where do you go after dying? What happens? When is *Bi Ji* coming back? She is very obsessed with the subject. I have tried to answer all her questions ... She seeks comfort in her bottle.

Obviously, death in the family has affected this child deeply and she still has not come to terms with the loss of her grandmother. None of the other Punjabi mothers mentioned 'fear of death', but a white mother (graduate, teacher) gave a detailed account of her daughter's fear of it:

> She has one big fear of death. She is absolutely obsessed by that. (*How did it come about*?) Well, it has increased since she lost her little hamster – but she has always been afraid of death since she was two to three years old. She used to come and tell me after seeing a little dead bird: Can we please put a little sticky plaster on it and make it live again? I would say: 'Sticky plaster is not going to help. We are going to bury it.' 'Oh, no, no, that can't be done' ... So she did not accept it. But that is what happened and upset her. I think that was the beginning of it ... she is quite a tense person – got a nervous dry cough.

The other common fears which the white mothers mentioned were: 'Doesn't like being on her own at night, about getting lost, and spiders'. One of the mothers who mentioned the fear of spiders remarked: 'She is afraid because it is me who gave her the fear – I am afraid of them as well.' Another white mother described how her daughter felt nervous whenever she walks over a bridge: 'She goes that the bridge is going down and stands close by me'.

Three Punjabi mothers in the study mentioned that their children are afraid of going upstairs to their bedrooms on their own and are generally afraid of the 'dark', and two pointed out how horror films have scared their children and have given them nightmares.

Some Nervous Habits

To the question: 'Does ... have any odd habit you can think of?' twenty-seven (68%) Punjabi mothers said 'no' and 13 said 'yes' – the most common being the habit of nail-biting. It is interesting to note here that 25% of the first-generation children also had this habit. Other habits included stroking their cheeks and ears, twitching and scratching various parts of the body. Two mothers mentioned that when their children are upset, especially in the evening, they want their milk bottle for comfort. Three children suck their thumbs but none of the children sucks dummy now. However, the mothers of the children who sucked their thumbs were not unduly concerned. Nearly half of the children pulled their mouth or picked their faces when they were a bit strung up. Only one child in the sample had a stutter and another child, who had a head injury, was a bit slow in his speech. One out of four of the sample gets anxious or excited on 'special occasions' and half of these (i.e., five) develop a headache or high temperature as a result. Some extracts are presented to illustrate the above concerns. A Sikh check-out operator (left school at 16) described her daughter's nervous disposition:

> She tends to bite her nails a bit. She puts fingers in her mouth and I stop her. I tell her it is dirty ... Yes, she does have a temperature when excited now and then. I have to cover her up, otherwise she'll catch cold.

A Sikh teacher described her son's anxiety:

> He can be very anxious – overanxious about things and he gets worried about silly things like, for example, I have lost this at school and then he cries a bit ... He gets migraine; they haven't found the cause of it yet. It could be when he is tired or worried about something ... I try to calm him down and it does work sometimes.

A Muslim housewife (left school at 16) showed concern about her son:

> He gets nightmare sometimes about riding things.... Yes, he gets a temperature: like when someone has gone away from the family. He misses them. I try to calm him down and encourage him to play, so that he forgets.... He still uses a bottle now at night but not during the daytime. His appetite is not very good so I let him have it – he has juice in the bottle.

A Muslim housewife (left school with some qualification) showed concern about her daughter's headaches:

> She really does worry a lot; if something is on her mind she gets very worried about it. She is one of those children who let things niggle.... I've never related her anxiety or angst to excitement, but she does have headaches.

The white mothers in the study also had similar stories about their children's anxieties and worries. A Sikh teacher explained:

> She gets quite a lot of tension at school ... she daydreams a lot, so she takes a lot of time to finish her work and the teacher gets cross. She is a tense person. I talk to her to help her to cope with it. I tried to say to her that she should finish her work and then she could daydream ... she is very imaginative.

A white housewife (left school at 16 with some qualifications) described her daughter's odd habit:

> Yes, she sucks her big toe. As soon she comes in she takes her shoes and socks off. She won't walk around the house with shoes or socks on. Otherwise I don't think she gets strung up.

A white home-helper (left school at 16) told us of her daughter's anxiety:

> She bites her nails and sucks her thumb. I try to stop her when we are out or if we are in the house. Sometimes she talks with it in her mouth, which is very upsetting. So I tell her to do it at bedtime if possible.... She has been sick out of excitement once when we were going for holidays.

From the responses of the Punjabi and white mothers of the present samples, we infer that the young children suffer from similar anxieties and tensions and that most mothers are understanding and deeply caring of their young. It is not possible to draw a firm conclusion from our small samples, but we found that there is no significant differences between the two ethnic groups on such matters as common anxieties and worries of children.

As regards the first generation, i.e. the 1970s sample, we found that Punjabi children compared with white children had fewer nervous habits and tended to exhibit fewer symptoms of 'Neuroticism' and 'Neurotic behaviour'. It seems, not surprisingly, that the third-generation Punjabi children have been deeply affected by their experiences of enculturation and share both the joys and anxieties of growing up in Britain.

Development of Independence

A great deal has been written on this topic and a vast corpus of literature is to be found on this theme (Triandis, 1994). It has been suggested by numerous scholars, both European and North American and Eastern, that the emphasis on training for independence in early infancy is mainly a Western European innovation and that non-Western societies stress social conformity and obedience. Many scholars have endeavoured to link later cognitive and social development of children to this dimension of child-rearing (see Witkin *et al.* 1974; Vernon, 1968). In view of its salience, the writers investigated this topic by asking mothers several direct questions on the actual behaviour of the child under discussion. As we were following quite closely the research pattern of the 1970s study, a number of questions on 'independence' appeared to have become irrelevant as parents became very safety conscious and allowed little freedom to their children in certain activities. For instance, in the questionnaire we had items on: 'Does the child go on the bus on his/her own?' and, 'Does he/she ever go to the park by himself/herself?' All the Punjabi and white parents in the study, except one, answered these questions negatively. They stressed the importance of their children's safety in view of the recent cases of child abduction and abuse. Some mothers referred to the sad case of the toddler, James Bulger, who was abducted and killed by two primary school children.

Therefore our questions on the encouragement of independence were somewhat reduced. See Table 6.2 for responses of the Punjabi samples on the relevant questions.

Table 6.2 Responses in percentages of Punjabi parents on questions relating to independence

	Yes		*No*		*Depends*	
Punjabi samples	*(1995)*	*(1970s)*	*(1995)*	*(1970s)*	*(1995)*	*(1970s)*
Follows you around – clinging	22.5	15.0	72.5	85.0	5	–
Belongs to a club	57.5	5.0	42.5	95.0	–	
Stays over night with relatives/friends	62.5	35.0	27.5	65.0	–	
Has own pet	12.5	–	87.5	100	–	
Sleeps in his own bedroom	20.0	Not asked	22.5 (shares a room)	–	57.5 (shares a bed)	–
Choice of clothes	37.5	22.0	25.0	45.0	37.5 (joint decision)	33.0
Choice of books	100.0	22.0	–	45.0	–	33.0
Given pocket money	35.0	13.0	65.0	87.0	–	
Can earn money	30.0	4.0	70.0	96.0	–	
Helps in the house	80.0	35.0	20.0	65.0	–	
Helps with the younger sibling	42.5	49.0	32.5	16.0	25.0 (no younger siblings)	35.0

Chi-square test was used to evaluate the differences between the two samples on the raw frequencies with the appropriate degree(s) of freedom. All the differences proved to be significant ($p < 0.05$) or highly significant ($p < 0.01$), except on item relating to 'clinging', where no significant difference was found

Pocket Money and Related Matters

It is generally considered desirable that young children should be given the responsibility to handle their own money. This is supposed to give them a degree of independence and a training in rational planning. The second-generation Punjabi parents are more prone to give regular pocket money than the first-generation, but still nearly two-thirds of the parents do not do so. The comments of mothers are interesting. A Sikh shop owner (left school at 16 with some qualifications) mused:

> Yes, he gets pocket money. His Dad gives him £1.50 for working in the shop. He won't spend it. He will save it; put it in a jar at home. When he wants to buy something then he spends it. Like now he is saving for Christmas.... We are trying to get into the habit where he would appreciate the value of money.

A Sikh housewife (left school at 16 with some qualifications) gave her reasons for not giving regular pocket money to her seven-year-old son:

> No pocket money – we give him when he wants something. Usually I buy everything.... We think he will abuse it. They don't know the value of money. They are so young. On his birthday everybody gave him money and he had a bee in his bonnet about opening a bank account. He is chuffed about it. He says: 'I can buy this or that. We say you can't, till you are older. I must say he is very tight with his money.

Most of the mothers were of the opinion that he/she is too young to be responsible for his/her money. They feared children can get into bad habits and some even get spoilt. A school leaver Hindu machine operator gave her opinion:

> No, not really. I just give her sometimes, it is not fixed.... Because I buy everything for them, whatever they need. I think they might get bad habits, you never know. Going to the shops on her own could be dangerous, something could happen to them; and they don't know what they spend their money on nowadays. A lot of drugs and all that. So I have to be careful with all these things.

The first-generation mothers had similar views. A primary-educated Sikh housewife noted:

> I know that English parents give pocket money when children are about 16. They tell them also that if they want to stay with them they

> have to pay for their board. We can't do that sort of thing. Neither do we give pocket money nor do we ask for it when they grow up – they can stay with us as long as they wish. I buy everything my child wants me to buy for him, but I don't give him any money. He asks for things to eat...

In our small white sample two-thirds of the mothers gave pocket money regularly, which is significantly different from the Punjabi sample. Likewise, a positive significant difference was found in favour of the white mothers in the 1970s samples.

Therefore, we can safely conclude that as regards pocket money, Punjabi parents have not changed their views substantially on this aspect of child-rearing. A higher proportion of Punjabi children of the second generation can earn money by doing errands for their parents – a step in the direction of the indigenous norm, where earning of money for household chores is generally encouraged. But still the difference between the two 1995 samples persists: the comparative figures being 33% per cent for the Punjabis and 66% for the whites.

Own Bedroom

One of important factors in the development of independence is for the children to have their own bedrooms, which they can also use for homework and to pursue their personal interests. Only one in five of the Punjabi children in the study had a separate bedroom. Of the remainder, well over half (57.5%) shared a bed and the rest shared a room with their sibling. Two children were regularly sleeping with their parents. This is in contrast to the white children in the study, in which none of them slept with their siblings, only three shared a room and nine had their own rooms. These findings are confirmed by a larger study of Hackett and Hackett (1994) with Gujarati children – another cognate Asian ethnic group. Their sample consisted of 50 Gujarati and 50 indigenous white parents. They found that 85% of the Gujarati children shared a room, whereas the corresponding figure for the white children was only 49% – a highly significant difference. Furthermore, 25% of the Gujratis shared a bed as opposed to 3% of the whites. Also, they found that the mean bedtime for the Gujratis to be 9.15 p.m. compared to 7.45 p.m. for the white sample. Overall, they discovered radically different sleeping arrangements for the Gujrati children compared with the indigenous whites. The implications for the development of independence will be taken up later.

Choice of Books and Clothes

There is a clear difference between the two generations of Punjabi mothers. There is far more freedom given to the 'third-generation' children in their choice of clothes and toys. As for the choice of books, all the mothers allow full freedom to choose. All the white mothers in the study, except two, allow their children to choose their clothes, toys and books.

A few responses give the flavour of the mothers' views. A Muslim machinist (left school at 16 with some qualifications) remarked:

> Well, I don't buy them that so often but let him choose them as long as they're reasonable. It depends whether you can afford it at that time. Clothes? I like to put something nice on him, so I usually choose it myself because obviously he's only a child.

Another Muslim housewife (left school at 16 with some qualifications) had a similar comment:

> I couldn't really let them choose – I have five kids. It is a cross (*mixture*) between both really. I think I have persuaded her to agree with what I buy, because there are financial problems. Otherwise I would let her, but then they would get too choosy and it causes problems because there are five lots to get.

Household Chores and Related Matters

Here, again, there is a significant difference between the two generations of Punjabi mothers. A higher proportion of third-generation children help their mothers with the household chores. An important point which emerged from the mothers' responses is that there was no marked difference between the boys and girls of the 1995 sample, whereas in the 1970s sample a higher proportion of girls than boys was expected to do housework. This is another significant change in the direction of the indigenous norm of gender equality in the house. A Muslim housewife (left school at 16 with some qualifications) narrated her daughter's help:

> Yes, I make her tidy her room up. I ask her to help me tidy the room downstairs, pick the toys up, tidy her books and things, keep them in order. When she is busy I never disturb her, I never do. If she is really enjoying herself then I'll do it myself. But if there are times when I want her to know that I have make her to do something. And if I say she has to do it whether she wants to or not.

A Muslim housewife (left school at 16 with some qualifications) gave an interesting account of how her son helps her:

> With M.... I expect him to tidy his clothes and room up, and also to put his pots away once he's eaten. Besides that I don't really expect him to do an awful lot around the house because he is only a child.... Yes, it is a regular thing, but I don't object to him not doing it but it's good that he does it.

A Hindu housewife (left school at 18 with advanced qualifications – 'A' levels) described her daughter's jobs:

> On Saturdays she has jobs to do. One week she will clean her drawers out, or sorting her bookshelf out. She even dries the dishes, helps us set the table and helps to cook the dinner sometimes ... she will do it mostly, otherwise I have to remind her. I explain that the family is a whole team, if one person lets the team down, we are let down ... She also helps with the young kids and looks after her tortoise.

A Sikh part-time worker (left school at 18 with advanced qualifications) emphasised the importance of gender equality in household duties:

> He likes vacuum cleaning. He doesn't mind ironing clothes ... he doesn't do it regularly, but I encourage him. I believe in equality – he should learn do the housework.

On the whole, the replies of the first-generation mothers are in sharp contrast to the second generation as far as boys are concerned. A primary-school educated Sikh housewife explained:

> He doesn't want to do any household chores. If I say to him two or three times, he'll do a chore, but he doesn't really like to do it. He objects and says that his sister should do these tasks, not him.

Another illiterate Sikh housewife gave a different reason for not asking her boy to help:

> If he is studying we never ask him to do any household chores even, otherwise it's up to him. Sometimes he helps me in picking up things and putting them away, otherwise very little household chores are given to him to do.

On the last item in Table 6.3, relating to helping with the younger sibling where appropriate, there is a significant difference in favour of the first generation, implying that more children of the first generation looked after their siblings. This is very much as expected. The first-generation mothers were more attuned to the Indian sub-continental practice, where invariably older children, especially girls, look after their younger siblings so that mothers are free to do household chores. In Britain and in other Western countries, older children are not usually considered suitable to look after babies, although some desperate mothers resort to this practice. This was also true of the white sample in the study. The mothers did not expect much help from their children, except to play with a baby under their supervision.

In sum, the second-generation mothers give more choices and freedoms to their children compared with the first generation. These relate to pocket money, choice of clothes and books, overnight stay with family and friends, belonging to a club and allowing them to have pets. Furthermore, they give more responsibility to their children for doing household chores.

Pleasures, Pains and Discipline

The mothers were asked a general question: 'What is it about ... which gives you most pleasure?' The replies predictably varied and were most interesting. All the mothers expressed their pleasure in a positive manner. The descriptions include: being with her, affectionate and caring child, pleasant personality, happy and cheerful, smiles a lot, easy-going, beautiful and good-looking. A few quotes illustrate the warm and positive responses.

> 'He has made our family very lively. His conversations which are endless; his laughter and his happy disposition makes us all feel good.' 'He takes interest in religious matters. He reads the Koran and is a nice child.' 'She is so talkative. She enjoys conversation. She gets on very well in her school. She makes everybody enjoy her company.' 'He does not bother me and he is very obedient.' 'She is very affectionate and very caring. She asks me "Mummy, are you tired?" ... and then looks after her younger sister.'

A question probing an aggravating/annoying side of their children elicited replies which most parents/readers would readily recognise. These included: Doesn't listen; fusses over clothes; being stubborn and demanding; fighting with siblings; shouting; not taking bath often enough; too much TV; a bit *mardy* (grizzly, whining). None of the mothers mentioned anything connected with schools – the only comment in this context came from a mother who complained about the excessive zeal of her daughter's interest in reading!

A Muslim housewife (left school at 16 with some qualifications) remarked on her daughter's disagreement with her:

> Sometimes she can be very demanding. She says she wants this or that, and she'll go on and on about it. The other thing that really annoys me is that she can have a jealous nature towards her older sister.... If she sees her with something new, especially clothes. A ... always likes new clothes and she likes to look for them, everything is always too boring and she's always looking for a new outfit.

All the mothers mentioned that their children like cuddling, hugging and kissing, and they were happy to cuddle and kiss their children. As a matter of fact it was a great source of joy for most of the mothers. A few, however, remarked that their children do not like kissing and one Sikh mother did not like cuddling her children. She said: 'It would be a lie if I say I like cuddling and kissing'. We did not probe any further into the matter.

The mothers in the study were asked a number of questions relating to physical punishment, i.e. smacking. The responses are given in Table 6.3.

It comes as a pleasant surprise to the researchers that over two-thirds of the second-generation mothers do not believe in physical punishment and furthermore over half of them rarely or never use this form of punishment and doubt its effectiveness. More boys than girls are punished by smacking. Only a minority of mothers believe in smacking and its positive effect on behaviour. These findings are not significantly different from the 1970s sample. Both the substance and tone of mothers' answers are most interesting on this important topic, and we give typical responses.

A Muslim housewife (left school at 16 with some qualifications) feels ambivalent about smacking children:

> I'm not particularly for it but there again, under pressure, being a mother of five very young children, sometimes I do it without realising. I get upset afterwards myself. Otherwise, I don't think there's really any need but now and again if you hit them (*meaning smack*) I don't think it harms them either – when they really play up.

A Muslim housewife (left school at 16) gave her views:

We mustn't hit them ... Smacking is not a good idea. Children can be mentally scarred which can last for a long time.... When they grow up they will say that they won't stay with us because we have been hitting them. Occasionally, I've to smack and often I warn him. I can't let him do as he pleases ... he still remains the same.

A Muslim housewife (left school at 16 with some qualifications) is totally against this method of disciplining children:

There should be no smacking. I am against it. It's a very bad method. It's far better to make the child realise that what he has done is wrong. It is far better to make the child understand. It is better to be on friendly terms with children ... to spend time, to listen to them.

Table 6.3 Responses, in percentage, on smacking

	Samples	*Yes*	*No*	*Depends*
How do you feel about smacking ...	1995	Sometimes it is necessary 30	Disapprove 70	
	1970s	46	54	
Do you think smacking has good results*	1995	7.5	75.0	Depends/ sometimes 17.5
	1970s	2.0	73.0	25.0
Do you think parents should try to do without smacking?	1995	65	20	15 Depends
	1970s	Data not available	–	–
When smacked does she behave better?	1995	38.5	17.5	44 Not sure
	1970s	Data not available	–	–
How often does she get smacked?		Rarely or never	Once a month	Once per week 20 Every day 2.5
	1995	57.5	22.5	Once per week 11.0
	1970s	57.0	28.0	Every day 4.0

Note: The Chi-square test on the raw frequencies was performed on relevant items. The item marked with an asterisk is significant at 0.05 level.

A Hindu factory worker (left school at 16 with some qualifications) gave psychological reasons against smacking her daughter:

> There is no reason to smack – rebuke is sufficient. Children become *Dhidth* (thick-skinned and shameless) and they do not care about anybody or anything. They'll leave home as soon as they can. I have never smacked her.

Another Hindu trainee teacher gave her views:

> I don't mind giving a little smack, but I don't like it. A little peck on the cheek.... He feels this is the end. Mum has reached the last resort and this is it. If I don't, he sometimes stretches me further. I don't find any change really (*i.e. in his behaviour*), perhaps later he would be doing the same thing again. I feel really bad for a day or so and think I should not have done that. I tell him you have made me do that. He says: 'I know that, Mum.'

A Hindu Civil Servant was in two minds about it:

> I think sometimes it is necessary. Generally, it is better not to, but I think on occasions one has to. If a child gets smacked too often he gets used to it and it loses its effect.... But it hurts me more than it hurts him. (*A classic comment in its own right.*)

A Sikh check-out operator (left school at 16 with some qualifications) expressed her opinion:

> I have never physically smacked my daughter, ever. To tell you the truth, I have done it to my boy – when he gets on my nerves. If you tell a child and he doesn't do it. You tell it again and again and a child still doesn't do it, then a clip around the ear hole does not harm a child. But to be violent with children, I don't agree at all ... I feel so guilty after.

A Sikh housewife (left school at 16 with some qualifications) is very much against but feels she has to use it sometimes:

> No, I don't think it is a good way of bringing up children. It doesn't resolve anything. He gets smacked when he pushes me too far. He would carry on pushing and pushing; but I never used to. His Dad has never ever smacked him until the day before yesterday. He got smacked for taking an electric saw.... Smacking has no result on him.

A Sikh clerical officer gave an interesting account of her smacking her children:

> Last time I smacked her was when we went to the Gurudwara and I told her to sit besides me. As soon as we sat down she wanted to go to the toilet. She never returned till the service was finished. I got home and smacked her. My grandfather was there and he objected to my smacking.

Likewise the Punjabi mothers of the first generation generally disapproved of physical punishment and did so only as an expediency measure, as the following responses demonstrate. A high school-educated Sikh housewife gave her opinion:

> It depends on the child whether he should be smacked because some children become good as a result of smacking and others don't. Generally speaking, this is not a good method at all because children become *Dhidth* (thick-skinned). If they do anything of their own free will they've really learned.

A high school-educated Hindu housewife gave her considered views:

> I think it's all right to smack children a little, but you can't make children do things by hitting them, it's far better to persuade them with love, otherwise they become stubborn and fearless; they dislike their parents and as soon as they grow up they run away. Love is better than smacking.

As regards the white mothers in the study, five (out of 12) disapproved of smacking but six think it can have good results. From the style and manner of their replies, we gathered that they seemed to have more faith in smacking than their counterpart Punjabi mothers. A graduate teacher replied:

> When she was little I used to smack her – up to the age of five. Not now ... I didn't like it. I only did it when she was totally unreasonable. Got into a tantrum – say once a month.

A shop assistant (left school at 16 with some qualifications) was not entirely sure of her position:

> She does have an odd smack, but I must admit I send her up to her bedroom more and that really works better than smack. I think it is a good way in some way ... it (*smacking*) doesn't really have good results really.

A housewife (left school at 16 with some qualifications) gave a rational account of her smacking:

> Smacking is a basic animal instinct. It is along the lines of a lion and a lion cub ... It is the same with a parent, to reach forward and smack the child's hand to stop it from touching whatever it is going to hurt it. In N ... case it is there as an ultimate threat. As long as you are doing it out of discipline and not out of aggression, because the frame of mind and the emotion you are showing the child when they are being disciplined is as important as the act of discipline.

All the Punjabi mothers in the 1995 study who smacked their children felt guilty or got upset after smacking. Many of them wished they had not done it, but they felt on some occasions it is an expedient method of disciplining children. The most common offence for which children got smacked was that of fighting with siblings. The other misdemeanours included: being stubborn and disobedient, rough and noisy, messy on the dining table and for telling lies. Although less than half (45%) the mothers threatened to have their children smacked by their father, only a third carried it through. Where relevant, smacking was only carried out by parents, except in two cases, where a sister-in-law or grandparents did punish the child in this manner.

Other Rewards and Punishments

In Table 6.4 we present the responses of the mothers to various questions on rudeness, 'talking-back' and rewards and punishments.

There are both similarities and differences between the two generations of Punjabi mothers in their attitudes to children's bad behaviour and rewards and punishments. The Punjabi mothers of two generations like giving rewards for good behaviour and 'withdrawal of rewards' when necessary. This is one of the principles advocated by the experts in the field of behaviourist psychology (see Wheldall & Merrit, 1984; Fontana, 1994). But we were surprised to learn that a significant minority of the Punjabi mothers threatened to withdraw their love if their children did not behave. We did not probe into the seriousness of this threat. But this type of punishment is deemed contrary to the sound and healthy development of young children. Pringle (1974) argues that one of the fundamental needs of children is to receive unconditional love from their mothers or a mother-substitute. Any threat, perceived or real, can cause psychological problems later on during adolescence or adulthood.

There are significant differences between the two Punjabi samples on items relating to children's bad behaviour of: 'talking-back', 'being rude' and 'getting into a rage'. The explanation may lie in the parents' expectations of what constitutes a good/desirable behaviour. The second-generation mothers were expected to be very polite, respectful and obedient to their own parents and elder members of the family. However, unlike their parents, the third-generation Punjabi/Asian, and indeed other ethnic minority children, are going to be more questioning and argumentative, and this might have been construed as rudeness and 'talking-back' by the second-generation mothers. An alternative explanation may be that children of the 1995s are generally more unruly and self-willed compared with those of the 1970s. Of course, there could be elements of both in explaining this difference.

The second-generation Punjabi mothers are more prone to use 'isolating' (i.e. sending them to their bedroom) as a form of punishment compared with the first generation. This form of disciplining is very common amongst the indigenous whites. We found this to be the case in our small sample of white mothers. The first-generation Punjabi

Table 6.4 Rewards and punishments given by Punjabi mothers of two generations (in percentages)

	Sample	*Yes*	*No*
Send her out of room*	1995	32.5	67.5
	1970	17.0	83.0
Reward for being good	1995	75.0	25.0
	1970	61.0	39.0
Withdrawal of rewards	1995	64.0	36.0
	1970	58.0	42.0
Withdrawal of love	1995	22.5	75.5
	1970	17.0	83.0
Does he talk back to you?*	1995	45.0	55.0
	1970	19.0	81.0
Is he/she rude to you?*	1995	A lot 12.5; Sometimes 15 Very little 65.0	Not at all 7.5
	1970	Very little 21.0	79.0
Does he get into real rage*	1995	50.0	50.0
	1970	31.0	69.0

*Items on which significant differences were found by using the Chi-square on the raw frequencies

mothers, on the other hand, rarely use this method because they thought it can alienate their child from the family.

A graduate Hindu clerk (first generation) gave the following as an example of rudeness:

> She is a bit rude at times: For example she said to me: 'Be quiet Mum.' When I explained to her that her way of speaking was not right, she apologised to me.

An illiterate Sikh housewife (first generation) gave her interpretation of rude behaviour:

> If ever he becomes a bit rude, such as sticking out his tongue I tell him not to be silly, but to behave sensibly. He should learn good things and not bad things from other school children.

The other interesting fact to point out is that all the second-generation Punjabi mothers, except two, think that their children compared with other children are very or fairly easy to manage. No doubt there are elements of 'desire to please' and to 'feel competent' in an interview situation, but nevertheless it is a remarkably confident statement to make. In this respect they do not differ significantly from their first-generation counterparts who also thought that their children are very easy or easy to manage. Some of the responses to the questions in Table 6.4 follow. A Muslim housewife (left school at 16) talked about her daughter's anger:

> She gets angry and sulks a lot. This happens two or three times a week ... When they (*siblings*) fight. (*Do you do anything about it?*) I just ask them not to fight or argue.

A Muslim factory worker (left school with some qualifications) described her experience with her son:

> It's like if you're busy doing something and you're upset and kids come in between you. Then you say go and sit down there.

A Hindu housewife (left school with some qualifications) gave her account:

> Because of lack of time ... yes, it is, it is. You know, I did with my older daughter; there was four years between her and the next one, and poor A.... barely a year and a couple of months before the next one came along. And he had even less, you know ... and although my husband is there, when he wants to do something he creates more problems rather than help. So I do without his help, but in the long

> run I stress myself and take it out on them unfortunately.

This was a somewhat confused response, but it does show the stressful life of a mother with several children who receives little help from her husband.

A Sikh housewife (left school with some qualifications) explained how she deals with her daughter's 'talk back':

> I say to her are you trying to argue with me? She'll say ... if she is in a rage, she will argue. She says: 'It is not fair Mum, you always say that ... if she is in a good mood and she wants an explanation, I'll explain to her.

A graduate white teacher described her daughter's rudeness:

> She can be very cheeky sometimes. I'll have a sharp word with her. If she is too cheeky I punish her – send her to her bedroom. She is not allowed to come down until she is ready to apologise. I get upset but I carry it through.

A white home-helper (left school at 16 with some qualifications) gave a disturbing account of how she dealt with her son's rudeness:

> It is the ground rules; there has to be a certain amount of discipline ... we are into grounding him now and stays of the computer. Once he was being very abusive, so I told him we would put him in a children's home. I told him: 'There kids don't get loved and don't get anything. So tomorrow morning I am going to phone them up and they'll come and get you'. He cried for two or three days and he has been better ever since.

From our small group of white parents we obtained a range of replies on the questions on rude behaviour and talking back: 'Not really (3), sometimes (5) and a lot (4)'. This pattern of responses, in essence, is no different from that of the Punjabi mothers.

Discussion

In this chapter we have described the findings of our researches on children's general personalty, anxiety and fears, development of independence, and the ways in which mothers deal with unacceptable behaviour. Throughout the chapter, we have stressed the qualitative aspects of our research to tried to discern dominant trends and patterns rather than just describe their answers to our interview questions. The mothers' attitudes have been derived from their comments and narratives.

For healthy growth and development, it is imperative that a mother, or a mother-substitute, gives unremitting love and care to her young child. In addition, parents should, broadly speaking, think positively of their children so that they can develop a high self-esteem and high aspirations (see Pringle, 1974). The second-generation Punjabi mothers used very many positive idioms to describe their children's personality, which augurs well for the sound development of personality. The most common attributes mentioned included: a caring, loving child, intelligent, shy, talkative, pleasant, beautiful and good-looking and a child with a sense of humour. And again, when asked what it is they most like about their child, the responses were positive: his/her good nature, liveliness, affection, conversation, sense of humour and nice to be with. The majority of the mothers found their children easy to manage.

The first-generation Punjabi mothers were less articulate in describing their children's personality. They used attributes which included: quiet, shy, obedient, clever and naughty. We think the differences between the two generations are mainly due to their self-confidence. The majority of the second-generation mothers have been to schools in England and speak English fluently and have also received ample help from health-care professionals on matters relating to child-care. They are less inhibited and shy about talking to relative strangers (with the exception of some Muslim women) in a confident and positive manner.

The second-generation mothers described their children as more active, lively and emotional than the first generation. Furthermore, there was a significant difference between the two groups on whether their child 'agrees with them' and whether he/she is easy to manage. A significantly higher proportion of the first-generation mothers thought that their children generally agreed with them and they are easy to manage. This aspect is closely related to the development of independence in young children. Significantly more mothers of the second generation gave pocket money, allowed children to choose their books and clothes, allowed children to have pets, demanded their help in household chores and helped them to become a member of a club – mostly Karate and Brownies. Thus, there is clear evidence that the second-generation mothers are encouraging their children to become independent and self-reliant at an early age. A graduate Hindu mother, who had one child in India and one in Britain, summarised for us the striking difference between the traditional and the modern attitudes to independence training:

> My son – who goes to school here – right from the beginning, since he was four, has expressed his own opinion. I say this is a good toy, let us buy it. 'No,' he says. 'This is not good'. And tells me why he doesn't like it; and he can fully explain why. Then he says; 'If you like it you can have it, I don't want it!' In our tradition, a child will never say like this. If a mother says 'yes' a child will obey.... Then he comes home, puts the TV on and knows which programmes he wanted to watch and he has his own videos – very independent. In my days, and even now, children dared not to anything like this.

Although the sleeping arrangement of babies and children have changed somewhat, it is still radically different from the indigenous whites. We found that only one out of five children slept in their own bedrooms, the rest either shared a bed or a bedroom. Two children slept with their parents. There is a wider support for this in the study of Hackett and Hackett (1994), who found that 85% of Gujarati boys and girls shared a room or bed with someone in the family, whereas the corresponding figure for the whites was 25%. It was a common practice amongst the first-generation Punjabis to have babies sleeping in the parents' bed or bedroom, and some children up to the age of eight or nine slept either with their parents or with other family members. Ghuman (1974) found that nearly 80% of the mothers had their babies sleeping with them and the rest had their baby in their bedroom. Some psychoanalysts (Daws, 1989) have argued that sleeping alone is necessary for the development of autonomy and individuality. There is some evidence from India (see Surya, 1969) and Japan (Caudhill and Plath, 1966) which suggests a relationship between co-sleeping, on the one hand, and dependence and communal ethic on the other. Hackett and Hackett (1994: 199) argue: 'Their (meaning Gujratis) widespread use of temples, community organization, endogamy and Gujrati language at home also points to the continual importance of the community in their lives. This communal ethic could promote psychiatric well-being by ensuring a degree of joint responsibility for children.' We have no wish to delve deeper into the psychoanalytical controversy which links adult personality to child-rearing practices, but it is sufficient to note that the custom of co-sleeping with children is very much part of the Punjabi thinking and practice.

It is clear from the data that the Punjabi children of the third generation have different fears and anxieties to that of the second generation. The earlier generation of children were mainly afraid of dogs and darkness but the present generation have a wide range of fears and anxieties. These include: darkness, death, on being on their own at night, scared of TV films. Their anxieties are mainly manifested by their habit of nail-biting, striking their cheeks and ears and thumb sucking. A higher proportion of the third-generation children are perceived to have nervous habits and anxieties compared with the second generation. The plausible explanation is that the modern living has created a lot of stress on the family and children – irrespective of ethnicity – and the fact that increasingly fewer grandparents are living in the Punjabi households to support and help as they did in the previous generation.

The responses of the mothers on rewards and punishment shed light on their attitudes towards the welfare of their children. Most mothers of both the generations felt that smacking is not a good way of disciplining children and that they used it sparingly and that they get upset and feel guilty whenever they use it. So on this issue, it seems, the views of the Punjabi mothers have not changed significantly, although the second generation have slightly more faith in this type of punishment. Nearly two-thirds of the second-generation Punjabi mothers thought that parents should do without smacking. The corresponding figure for the white mothers was 50%. The research of Hackett and Hackett (1994) with Gujrati and white British mothers also found that more white mothers felt that smacking was, on occasion, necessary (72% and 91% respectively), although there was no significant difference in the frequency with which it was used.

A second-generation Hindu mother typifies the mothers' attitude to physical punishment: 'I don't mind a little smack, but I don't like it. A little peck on the cheek and he feels this is the end. Mum has reached the last resort and this is it ... I really feel bad for a day or so and think I shouldn't have done that.'

A higher proportion of the second-generation mothers think that their children are rude, talk-back, and show temper tantrums. Also mothers use 'sending them to bedroom' punishment more often than the first generation. In this respect, they are more like the white mothers in the study, which is also supported by Hackett and Hackett (1994: 194), who found the majority of white mothers (56%) used this punishment. However, only 17% of their Gujarati counterparts used it. As regards rudeness and associated behaviour, the proportion is close to the white children in the study. It appears that the third-generation Punjabi children are closer to their white peers as are the Punjabi mothers on punishment, like 'sending them to their bedroom'. Hackett and Hackett (1993: 356) make a perceptive comment on the rude behaviour of children: 'The English-born children of immigrants will inevitably be exposed to their own community's norms at home and those of the host community at school and elsewhere ... Behaviour that might be applauded as healthy self-assertion by an English parent would appear worryingly aggressive to a Gujrati.'

The Punjabi mothers of both generations used 'rewards for good behaviour' and 'withdrawal of rewards' for naughtiness – in this respect there is no difference between the two groups. In Hackett and Hackett's research (1994) more Gujrati mothers (87%) were using this type of inducement compared with the white mothers. Another interesting point regarding punishment is that high proportions (25.5% and 17% respectively) of the first and second generation of Punjabi mothers used withdrawal of love as a threat, which is higher than the white mothers in our study; and likewise, significantly far more Gujrati mothers (Hackett and Hackett, 1994) used this threat than their white counterparts. This result is quite puzzling because of our own personal experiences of the community which tells us that Punjabi mothers, broadly speaking, love their children to the point of indulgence and would not do anything serious which might hurt their children and consequently damage their relationship (see also Kakar, 1994). It is highly likely, therefore, that the notion and significance of 'withdrawal of love' is differently understood by the Punjabi/Asian mothers and their children than by their white counterparts. For the indigenous white mothers it implies a threat with serious consequences which should be sparingly used. Perhaps the writings of Pringle (1974), Bowlby (1965) and Spock (1958), who have advocated unconditional maternal love for the young child, had a serious impact on this generation of parents.

Conclusion

It is apposite now to draw final conclusions from the data presented in this chapter. Firstly, it is abundantly clear that the second-generation Punjabi mothers have changed their attitudes to the development of independence in the sphere of 'management of money', letting children choose their books and clothes and generally in helping them to develop their personal interests. However, they are more like their first-generation counterparts in giving and receiving a lot of affection, in giving rewards and praise, in the dislike and disapproval of the use of physical punishment and in the 'co-sleeping' arrangement of babies, infants and children.

Secondly, their thinking and attitudes are closer to indigenous white mothers in 'sending children to their bedrooms' as a punishment, encouraging boys and girls to help in housework and in joining clubs. Thirdly, the third-generation Punjabi children have acquired anxieties, fears and behaviours which are closer to that of their white peers. Lastly, it appears that the Punjabi mothers are beginning to strike some form of synthesis between the two differing cultural traditions and beliefs about child-rearing and that they are trying to get the best of both worlds for their children.

Researchers (Kelly & Tseng, 1992: 444) studying the children of Chinese origin in America have also identified such a trend: 'Results related to terms of the need for immigrant Chinese to maintain ties to their culture of origin and to accommodate to the socialization practices of the host culture'. Such a message also flows from the study of Lin and Fu (1990: 429), who conclude: 'Chinese parents are also increasingly adapting to the necessary changes while holding on to certain traditional family values.... These values would possibly facilitate "bicultural" socialization in that these immigrant children would be able to function effectively in both...' The discussion on this and related matters will be taken up in the final chapter of the book.

7 Bilingualism, Religion, Identity and Racism

Introduction

The processes of formation of the personal identities of ethnic-minority young children are necessarily far more complex than those of the dominant indigenous group. Such a complexity arises due to forces which are both internal and external to minority groups. Internally, in some domains, the values of an ethnic minority may be at variance, if not diametrically opposed (such as with arranged marriages versus love marriages and freedom of speech versus religious sensibilities), to those of the mainstream and this can cause anxiety and tension in the family and the growing child. On the other hand, the majority group might employ procedures and practices – either intentionally or unintentionally – which lead to the exclusion of some minority groups as in the case of discrimination against Asian and black people by the white British in the UK. This could be an additional source of worry and distress to ethnic-minority families and their children. As these worries and concerns are bound to affect the ways in which Punjabi and Asian parents bring up their children, these are fully explored with the help of our interview data.

This chapter describes in some detail the attitudes of Punjabi parents to the two core values of their community – namely religion and the mother tongue – which are deemed to be crucial in the identity formation of young children. Further, it explores the parents' attitudes to racism, inter-racial marriages and gender equality. These issues as such are inter-related and have important bearings both on the theory of acculturation and the practice of bringing up third-generation ethnic minority children. From a theoretical perspective, it is imperative to know whether the acculturation process is a linear or a multifaceted one, i.e. could there be a full integration (assimilation) or is the process of integration going to be fundamentally different in the public and the private domains? Rex (1985: 5) has made this distinction explicit in his seminal writings on the nature of a multicultural society: 'One might envisage a society which is unitary in the public domain but which encourages diversity in what are thought of as private or communal matters.' Our findings on these issues are analysed within the context of existing research.

Migrant communities tend to recreate the social and religious institutions of their country of origin. These institutions serve two main functions: they provide psychological security and stability; and thus establish mechanisms to transmit their core values to the next generation. The first-generation migrants usually have to endure many hardships in order to accomplish this objective and the Asian migrants to the UK, North America and Australia are a prime example of this process (see Chapter 1).

The first generation of Punjabis in our study successfully reunited their families in the UK and also established *Gurudwaras, Mandir* and *Mosques* for collective worship. These also served as meeting places for their respective communities. The second-generation Punjabis/Asians thus have an enormous advantage over their first-generation counterparts in that they are spared the agony of being temporarily rootless and the need to create a myth of return (see Anwar, 1985). Their task of socialising the young into the social and cultural mores of their community becomes relatively easier.

Maintenance of Mother Tongue and Development of Bilingualism

The Punjabi mothers were asked eight questions concerning the languages spoken at home. Their responses are given in Table 7.1.

It is clear from Table 7.1 that English is increasingly becoming the first language of the Punjabi homes in our study. A significantly higher proportion of the third-generation children use English with their mothers, fathers and siblings compared with the second-generation counterparts. Furthermore, 85% of the children mostly speak English at home This is despite the determined efforts of a significant number of mothers to encourage their child to speak Punjabi. The dilemma of the parents is lucidly described by a perceptive owner of a shop (left school at 17 after matriculation):

> He only talks to grandparents in Punjabi. Basically it is our fault. We made life too easy – we live in the Western world and have been educated in English-medium schools and speak English fluently. When we talk to our children it comes easy. We don't try to make the

effort to speak Punjabi. So I blame myself and my husband. By the time we decided to do that (*meaning to use Punjabi in the home*) they were grown up and didn't feel the necessity to learn it. Now with the baby I am making the effort.

The decline in the use of Punjabi in the homes is quite marked since the earlier 1970s research. A significantly higher proportion of children of the 1995 generation use English with their mothers, fathers and siblings. However, it is interesting to note that over three-quarters of children in the present sample still use Punjabi with their grandparents.

We will discuss the ensuing parents' linguistic concerns in some detail presently. In Table 7.2 the responses of the mothers on the questions relating to the use of Punjabi in nurseries and schools is presented.

It is clear from Table 7.2 that very few educational institutions have

Table 7.1 Responses of two generations of Punjabi mothers on language(s) spoken at home

In what language does he/she talk to ...	*Sample*	*English (%)*	*Punjabi (%)*	*Bilingual-Mixed (%)*
you?*	1995	58.0	22.0	20.0
	1970	8.0	72.0	20.0
his/her daddy?*	1995	67.5	12.5	20.0
	1970	11.0	55.0	34.0
his/her siblings?*	1995	95.0	–	5.0
	1970	73.0	9.0	18.0
his/her grandparents?	1995	8.0	78.0	14.0
	1970	Not asked	–	–
relatives?	1995	55.0	27.5	17.5
	1970	Not asked	–	–
Other Punjabi children?	1995	95.0	None	5.0
	1970	92.5	None	7.5
Language mostly spoken at home by the child	1995	85.0	None	15.0
	1970	Not asked	–	–

*Denotes statistically significant differences

Table 7.2 Mothers' responses on the provision of community languages in schools*

Was there any provision for the use of Punjabi in:	*Yes (%)*	*No (%)*
Play group (if attended)?	17.5	82.5
Nursery school (if attended)?	17.5	82.5
Infant school?	12.5	87.5
School which he/she attends now?	7.5	92.5

*Data for the 1970s sample is not available

a provision for the use of Punjabi. On further probing, we found that there was either a nursery helper or a teacher of Punjabi origin who spoke Punjabi, but none of the schools had a formal provision for the teaching of Punjabi or, indeed, any other community language. Regrettably, the present organisation of nurseries and schools does not take serious account of the arguments advanced by very many academics, (see Baker, 1993, 1994; Tomlinson, 1984), who argue that there should be a degree of continuity between home and school life in order to achieve an all-round social and intellectual development of children. (Baker, 1993: 197) writes: 'A mismatch between home and school can be positively addressed by strong forms of bilingual education for language minorities.' Some academics (see Vedder *et al.*, 1995) also advocate a multicultural approach and multicultural curriculum to the teaching and learning in nursery and infant schools. Such an approach should enhance the self-image of ethnic-minority children and also should lead to better communication between home and school.

All the mothers were asked whether they are in favour of the teaching of reading and writing of their mother tongue. The responses are given in Table 7.3.

Before we fully discuss the contents of Table 7.3, it is important to put the reader in the picture regarding the status of Punjabi as a mother tongue. This digression will, hopefully, place the ensuing issues in their proper perspectives. Although Punjabi is spoken universally by everybody living in the 'Indian' and 'Pakistani' Punjabs, very few Hindu and Muslim families would consider teaching it to their children. Instead, Hindus prefer to teach the national language of India, *Hindi*, and, likewise, the Muslims prefer *Urdu*, the national language of Pakistan. These preferences are firmly retained by the Hindus and Muslims when they emigrate to other countries. Therefore, it is mainly the Sikh

Table 7.3 Mothers' responses on the teaching of mother tongue

	Yes (%)	*No (%)*
Are you in favour of the teaching of reading and writing of mother tongue?	92.5	7.5
Does he/she go to any community/religious school?	55.0	45.0
If not, do you intend sending him/her to one?	85.0	15.0

Punjabis who want their children to learn Punjabi at community schools in the UK and North America.

This situation is further complicated because of the legacy of the colonial era. Socially aspiring parents in the Punjab, irrespective of their religion and social class/caste, send their children to English-medium private schools where Punjabi is rarely taught. Such a situation also colours the perceptions of Punjabis living in the UK and underlines the complexity and the politics of community language teaching in the UK, America and Canada.

All the mothers, except two Hindus and a Sikh, were in favour of teaching their community language, whether it be Punjabi or Hindi or Urdu. Of the 40 mothers, 22 already send their children to a community school, and a further 13 intend do so in the near future. Two mothers in the sample mentioned the speech difficulties of their children (one due to injury and another due to slow development) and were advised by their speech therapist not to teach them Punjabi in case it should confuse them. In the 1970s study, 97% of the mothers wanted their children to learn their community language, which is slightly higher, but not significantly so, than the present sample. The comments of the mothers are most interesting as these reveal the underlying attitudes and value orientations.

A university graduate Sikh housewife, who preferred to be interviewed in Punjabi, was very keen for her son to learn Punjabi:

> Yes, I want him to learn Punjabi. He talks to me in English. But I answer him in Punjabi. Then I tell him to speak with me in Punjabi. He tries, but after saying a few words he begins to laugh.... Yes we will send him to a Punjabi school. But it should be taught in schools.

Another college-educated Sikh, who is a part-time teacher in a Gurudwara and runs a Punjabi school, predictably supported the Punjabi cause (interviewed in Punjabi):

> My parents always say that S … must learn our language. He must learn to read and write. That way he be able to read the *Granth Sahib* (the religious text of the Sikhs) and communicate with them.… He goes to the community school twice weekly – Saturdays and Sundays for an hour.

Some Muslim parents want their children to learn Arabic in addition to Urdu as it is the language in which the Koran is written. However, they are also conscious of the excessive academic workload on their children. A school-leaver Muslim housewife showed her enthusiasm and caution:

> He talks to me in Urdu/Punjabi … hopefully we'll send him to an Urdu school next year. At the moment he goes to an Arabic school twice a week. It would be too much for him now. He gets tired in the evenings.

A Muslim housewife (left school at 16), who was involved in setting up a community school, and is well aware of the difficulties of securing the co-operation of white parents:

> We've set up a school and I've been involved with that, so that I have a lot to do with the Section 11 funding (Central Government funds to support inner city schools).… There is no provision in the school because it is predominantly a white area. Sadly, I'm barred from driving so I can't take him for his Urdu lessons.… But it's very slow trying to change English attitudes towards the teaching of our languages.

A university graduate Sikh pharmacist pointed out some of the difficulties in retaining Punjabi:

> She understands Punjabi and occasionally says a few words. But there is no way she will hold a conversation with anyone. I want her to read and write desperately because I missed out. It is part of our religion and culture.… She is not willing to go to a Punjabi school, but I make her.

The first-generation mothers had a different motive for the teaching of their mother tongue. An illiterate Sikh housewife explained:

> He should learn Punjabi, not only to speak but also to read and write.

> I keep telling him that he should learn this language because if we have to go back (*meaning return to the Punjab*) he would look blank when they speak in Punjabi as we do when our children speak English.

The first-generation migrants often face this dilemma of 'going back' to their roots – some academics have referred to this as the 'myth of return' (Anwar, 1979). However, it is interesting to note that a vast majority of the 1970s generation Punjabi and Asian children did not have the opportunity to learn their mother tongue. The main reason seems to be that ethnic communities were not fully established in the UK and did not have the facilities and resources to set up week-end community schools on their own. Ghuman (1995: 38) interviewed Asian teachers for another project and was informed by a respondent:

> It has gone through several phases; in the 1950s the main emphasis was on the teaching of English. No attempt was made to do anything about minority languages. The shift came about in the late 1970s, with the publication of the Bullock report – but then it was do with the European languages. I think it was the early 1980s when the minority languages were considered.... Asian children began to feel important about their culture.

Another teacher amplified the situation by giving an anecdote:

> I recall in the mid-1960s my sister's children came to the UK to join their father, who came in 1960 ... We start a big drive to teach them English. They were told off speaking Punjabi with one another and with the elders, except with their grandmother and mother. We thought somehow Punjabi will interfere with the learning of English – that was the wisdom of the time. At any rate Punjabi was, and regrettably still is, considered to be a low status language in India – Hindi is more prestigious and English speakers are thought to belong to the elite class. So there were all sorts of misguided reasons for abandoning Punjabi. Now they don't speak Punjabi at all. And they can't read or write. We all have come to regret this.

The first-generation Asian parents were perhaps not as anxious about the teaching of the mother tongue and were satisfied if their children could just speak it. This was partly due to the prevailing *Zeitgeist* of that time, which cast doubts on the value of being bilingual (Baker, 1994; Bellin, 1995), and partly due to the colonial mentality of the Punjabi parents. It was widely believed that the Indian languages are inferior to English and other European languages. This negative attitude was reinforced further by the fact that the elite of India and Pakistan still sent/send their children to English-medium public schools and that the language of the top civil servants, military generals, high court judges and barristers and university professors was and still is English. Stubbs (1985: 111), in the first important publication on minority languages in the UK (*The Other Languages of England*, 1979–83), underlined the importance of the colonial past on the status of minority languages. He wrote: '... The relationship between English and many minority languages in Britain today, both new and old, is embedded in a long history of colonisation, with English as a language of the rule.' Furthermore, the attitudes of the majority of white teachers in the UK at that time were entirely negative, if not downright hostile, to the teaching and learning of community languages (see Ghuman, 1995). A residue of such attitudes is still to be found amongst a few Punjabi parents in our study. A graduate Muslim father, who was present when his wife was being interviewed, touched upon some of the typical reasons:

> I think it is an obsolete exercise, to be honest, when we are living in this country. It may be a temptation. But it is not going to produce an explosion of intellectual activity. It would be more beneficial if he were to do French. One has to be realistic.... If he shows interest we'll help him. But now we are quite happy for him to be able to speak English language to his fullest potential.

The first-generation Punjabi parents were also ambivalent about the relevance and economic benefits of community languages. An illiterate Sikh housewife explained:

> He should learn Punjabi and speak with others in a respectful way. We don't emphasise the Punjabi language too much at this stage because we want him to be successful in his education by learning English.

There is yet another dimension to the teaching of community languages as highlighted by the comments of the above two parents. A lot of Punjabi/Asian parents are, and were, anxious about their children's future in the UK. These fears and anxieties arise mainly due to the awareness that their children are going to face racial discrimination in all walks of life (see Brown, 1984; Smith, 1977). To allay their anxieties, the parents would like to ensure that their children are given as many advantages as possible to compete successfully with their white counterparts. Consequently, some Punjabi and Asian parents have become very instrumental in their approach to education: they encourage their children to study subjects such as physics, chemistry and maths and a European language, which would prove more beneficial for entry into higher education and, later, into employment. Also, for this very reason, an increasingly large number of middle-class Punjabi/Asian parents are sending their children to fee-paying private schools to give them a head-start in life. In this context, it is interesting to note the comments of Vedder *et al.* (1995: 90) on the language shift of ethnic minority parents in the Netherlands for a variety of reasons: 'In the Netherlands, an increasing number of immigrant parents, themselves born and raised in the Netherlands, make a choice to speak Dutch to their children.... A simple belief in the first language maintenance rule may be valuable, but only in particular settings.'

Religion: Its Importance and Teaching

Religion has always been an important part of the Punjabi migrants' way of life. It provides them with security and a firm identity in a country whose racism is embedded in its institutions. The first-generation Punjabis, and other ethnic minority groups, had to put in an enormous effort and resources to establish their places of worship. It was not an easy task as they faced a considerable degree of racial prejudice and bureaucratic hurdles. We considered it imperative to find out from the second-generation mothers how they view the relevance and salience of religion in their children's lives. We asked several questions on this theme. The answers are tabulated in Table 7.4.

The overwhelming majority of the second-generation mothers wish to retain their family religion; in this respect, they are not different from the first generation. Over two-thirds of them think this is very important or important, although a small number feel it 'doesn't matter'. Some illustrative comments follow. A Muslim housewife commented (left school at 16; interviewed in Punjabi):

> It is very important for us Muslims. Allah is one and the Koran tells us to listen to and respect our elders. She is beginning to learn to love her brothers and sister and be good. Then Allah will like her very much. We want her to learn to recite the holy Koran.

Another Muslim housewife was very committed (left school at 16):

> Religion plays an important role in our lives. Without religion everything in one's life is destroyed. It guides you on the true path and you can distinguish between the good and the bad, sinful and the virtuous.

Table 7.4 Responses of two generations of Punjabi mothers on questions on religion

	Sample	*Positive response (%)*	*Negative response (%)*
How important is religious education?	1995	Very important 62.5 Important 25.0	Not important/ doesn't matter 12.5
	1970	Very important 70.0 Important 14.0	Not important/ doesn't matter 16.0
Does she/he go to temple/mosque/ Gurudwara?	1995	Regularly 36.0 Sometimes 59.0	5.0
	1970	Data not available	–
Do you ever talk to him/her about religion?	1995	Yes 87.5	No 12.5
	1970	Data not available	–
Does he/she say prayers at home?	1995	Yes 47.5	52.5
	1970	Data not available	–

A university graduate Sikh teacher gave her opinion:

> ... I think is quite important from my point of view. Then, of course, they are given English RE at schools and we normally don't object to that because we provide our own education at home or at the Punjabi school. I do *Japji Sahib* (Sikhs' morning prayer) and then he goes to the Punjabi school where they also teach our religion.

A graduate Sikh part-time lecturer in computer studies further elaborated the role of community schools:

> Sometimes we tell him he is a Sikh and what does it mean, but not very much. He does go to a Punjabi school on Saturday mornings. He learns there, too ... I am sure they do teach religion and that's why we send him. It also gives him a chance to meet other Sikh children.

Many Sikhs say prayers at home as their religion is not dogmatic about the time and place of worshipping the omniscient and omnipresent *Wheguru*. A liberal Sikh co-owner of a shop explained:

> It is very important that he should know our religious teachings. They attend *Satsang* (prayer meetings) and these are not to be in a

> *Gurudwara* – it can be in our house or our friends'. They listen to the tapes with us. They follow our way of life. We are vegetarians and we have to explain to them the reasons why ... We tell them God is everywhere and it doesn't matter where they pray.

Hindu religion is pantheistic and has several gods and goddesses for the devotees to worship. Most Hindu families in the study had a shrine with their own personal deity, the popular ones being: *Hanuman, Ganesh, Sasrsawati, Mata Durga* or *Kali* and *Navratri.*

A Hindu housewife gave an account of her daughter's religious education (left school at 18 with 'A' levels-entry qualification to university):

> She has been a couple of times to the Nottingham Forest temple, but we say prayers at home to our deities ... Grandma does more than I do. She is very religious; she reads (*religious*) books all the time and tell them stories. She says prayer at home with Granddad. We go to the temple on special occasions: *Janam Asthmi,* festivals of *Holi.*

A Sikh and two Hindu mothers, who felt that their family religion is not that important, argued that: 'It is up to her to decide when she grows up; and, we are not practising Sikhs. I think I'd be a hypocrite if I said it is important'. It became quite apparent from the interview data and our personal impressions that the Muslim families were the most committed to the transmission of their faith, while the Hindus, on the other hand, were quite relaxed.

Compared with that of the Muslims and Sikhs, Hinduism is an ancient religion (precise date of its origin is difficult to trace, see Nehru, 1946) and there are very wide variations in its practice and interpretation (Jackson & Nesbitt, 1993: 6). The two most holy books of the Hindu religion, *Mahabharata* and *Ramanya,* are accounts of wars resulting from the internal family feuds with little in the way of explicit theology and dogmas (*Bhagvat Gita* is an exception but, again, it takes the form of Lord *Krishna's* sermon to an army-chief *Arjuna* who refused to fight his kith and kin in the war of *Mahabharata*). Therefore, most Hindus feel that their religion is more a way of life than of theological dogmas and strictures. What follows from this is that Hindus, in general, believe that their religion is transmitted to the next generation through the medium of their day-to-day living. As we were informed by a university graduate Hindu housewife (interviewed in Hindi):

> My mother never told me what to worship, but when I saw her

> watering *Tulsi* (*a holy relic*) daily, since I was a child, then I took it in. So sometimes when my mother couldn't do it, she would send me to water *It* and put *Haldi* (yellow powder) on it. This is how children's religious education goes on.... When I am praying I ask my children to join me and when I am reading a *Pothi* (a holy book) she (her daughter) sits with me and when I fast and so on.

According to Jackson and Nesbitt (1993: 9), who have surveyed the literature and carried out an in-depth study of Hindu children in the UK, religion is transmitted through the family mainly by women. They write: 'For many parents in India, the religious upbringing of children is a natural and partly unconscious activity, centred in the home but fostered by many aspects of cultural life....' It is also worth quoting their conclusions from research conducted in Coventry (Jackson & Nesbitt, 1993: 180). 'While language classes teach their pupils an elementary literacy, oral language is primarily passed on in the home. So too with the other two strands of Hindu traditions which emerged prominently from our research, namely the expression of the values underpinning family life and the emphasis on vegetarianism.'

The Muslim parents in our study tended to lay emphasis on their children's ability to recite the holy Koran, and this can be better accomplished at the Mosque rather than at home. The Muslim mothers in the research have either made arrangements for this or intend to do so in the future. This, in our view, explains the differences between the Muslim and Hindu parents in their attitudes to regular visits to a temple or a mosque. The Sikh parents' attitudes lie somewhere between that of the Hindus and Muslims.

Identity and Racism

The quest for a personal and social identity is universal, although it is closely interwoven with one's national identity. For the second-generation ethnic minority parents, the dilemma is what are they going to tell, teach and inculcate in their children right from the beginning? Several questions were included in the interview schedule in order to find basic value orientations of the Punjabi parents and their attitudes to this vexed question of identity. However, these questions were not part of the 1970s research because it was considered that the main concerns of the first-generation parents were somewhat different. The responses to these questions are presented in Table 7.5.

The data in Table 7.5 tell us a great deal about the Punjabi parents' thinking on their children's identity. It is important to note that only a small proportion of mothers consider themselves to be anything but Indian or Pakistani, but when conjecturing on their children's identity only under half of them think he/she would take on her (mother's) national identity. Over a third of the mothers think that his/her identity would be a mixed one: British Muslim or Indo-English. Only three mothers think that their children would have English/British identity. It is most encouraging to note that all the mothers, except six, think that their children will be accepted by their white peers at schools, and later at work and socially. On the question of inter-racial marriage, the opinion is more evenly spread. Most Hindus would accept one in their families whereas the Sikhs and Muslims would

Table 7.5 Responses of second-generation mothers on identity questions*

	Hyphenated/ Mixed (%)	*British (%)*	*Indian/ Pakistani (%)*
What do you consider yourself?	17.5	–	82.5
What would be his/her national identity?	40.0	15.0	45.0
Do you think he/she will be accepted by the whites?	Yes 85.0	No 15.0	
Are you going to talk to him/her about racism?	Yes 57.5	No 42.5	
How would you react if he/she decides to marry someone of different race?	Disapprove 32.5	Object but accept 37.5	Approve/ depends 30.0
If facilities were available would you send her/him to Muslim/Sikh/Hindu religious school?	Yes 45.0	No 47.5	Depends 7.5

*These questions were not part of the interview schedule with the first-generation parents

disapprove. On the question of schooling, the sample as a whole is evenly divided between those who would prefer to send their child to a school which is run along the lines of their family religion and those who would prefer the mainstream schooling. However, It is interesting to point out to the reader that nine out of ten Muslim mothers preferred 'religious schooling' and in contrast only one Hindu mother did so. The mothers' views on racism vary between those who would talk to their child about racism and those who would prefer to ignore it. The comments of mothers on these issues are presented below.

Identity

A Hindu housewife explained (left school at 18 with 'A' levels):

> I am English with Indian origin. Our food and part of the language and custom I'd like her to keep. I don't mind British food, music and things like that ... I think her identity is going to be British.

A school-leaver Hindu machine operator gave a more precise analysis of her situation:

> I am Indian but my nationality is British; well I am no less Indian than I am British – I am both. My daughter always says she is British.

The theme of biculturalism cropped up several times. A Muslim housewife felt very much in this situation and articulated her views with vigour (left school at 16 with some qualifications):

> My identity? Pakistani-British-Muslim. I don't mean that I am born here, I actually do belong – part of me is from this culture. When I went to Pakistan I missed England; the weather (*sic*), the simple everyday things that you wouldn't think of – the milkman, the postman and the TV – although television is there. My brothers and sisters laughed at this – So I can't say I'm not British.... I don't want my children to grow up in this society feeling second-class citizens. I want them to be proud of being a Muslim – their culture and heritage. I want them to be positive, not negative and confused.

Likewise, most of the Sikh mothers put their faith in a varying degree of biculturalism and in 'hyphenated' identities for their children. A university graduate Sikh teacher commented:

> Indian, I suppose. But I suppose most of my expectations are English.... There is hardly any difference between middle-class

> British and middle-class Indian ways. (*His identity?*) British with an Asian bias.

However, there were several mothers in the study who wished to lean more towards their family cultural roots. A Sikh pharmacist explained:

> I told her we are different: our colour, food, religion and language. And there is nothing wrong in that, you should be proud of it. I try to instil this...she doesn't get anything from the school about Sikh culture. The only thing she does get is from the Punjabi school in the Gurudwara. I insist on her going.... I'll object to mini-skirts, low-cut dresses and smoking and drinking in pubs. I am putting in a lot of time on her.

A qualified Hindu inter-personal counsellor made a detailed comment:

> I am Indian. Because at the end of the day we are Indians and they should be proud of it and value our culture ... I pray everyday and they see me; I cook vegetarian food at home; we feel peace within ourselves. So in a way, I am passing my religion and culture on ... She would be Indian though holding a British passport. I wouldn't like her to be fully westernised.

A Sikh shopkeeper was slightly hostile to the English (left school with some qualifications):

> I want him to grow up as a Punjabi person. He is not going to live like the *Goras* (whites). I like him to learn Punjabi later on like his cousin who has passed his 'A' (Advanced) level in Punjabi. (*His identity?*) Both really!

And finally, a Muslim housewife's comment is relevant (left school at 16; interviewed in Punjabi):

> We live here – one can say that we are British but English people don't regard us as British. They consider us second-class citizens, so we regard ourselves as Pakistanis Muslims. We don't want to be like a 'washerman's dog', who neither belongs to home nor *Ghat* (*washing place – this is a popular saying on the Indian sub-continent to describe alienation*) ... (*His identity?*) Pakistani.

English customs and habits

We have not quantified the data on these matters but present a selection of mothers' views. A Muslim housewife gave this description (left school at 16 with some qualifications):

> I'd like her to be very physically active in school and to enjoy the pleasures that school offers. I'd like her to take part in musical activities and drama. Sadly, our children don't seem to participate in that kind of fields. I like her to go to Brownies.

A university graduate Muslim part-time researcher was very warm in her appreciation of English ways but with some reservations:

> Fairness, good manners, international language and freedom, I'd say are some of the good qualities. On the negative side I'd mention two things: maybe there is coldness – I don't like that, and obsession with sex.

A 'Hindu housewife was very matter of fact (left school at 18 with 'A' levels):

> I don't mind British food, music, drama and art and things like that but I don't want her to roam around and get into bad habits like drugs and mess around with boys.

An owner of a shop gave her appreciation and reservations (left school at 17 with matriculation qualification):

> I was brought up in the old English environments (*She attended a convent school in India*) – respect for your elders; love and affection for the younger ones. These I find lacking in a modern-day English environment. I can never think of calling my parents the 'old-man' and the 'old-woman'. There is no respect for women anymore; I suppose we have spoilt it ourselves by asking for too much equality.... Everything is for yourself.

Regrettably, most mothers in the study picked out the negative stereotyped images of English children and consequently were on their guard to protect their own children from such things as: roaming and loitering, drugs, smoking and drinking, shop-lifting, girls wearing provocative clothes, being rude to parents, and uncalled-for quarrels with parents and leaving home at the slightest pretence. These negative images are held partly due to the fact that most Punjabi mothers (34/40) in the study do not socialise with whites and have little first-hand experience of the latter's family life, especially that of the middle classes. A typical remark in the interviews was: 'Gora (*white*) friends are my 'work-mates' and that we do not visit each other's house.' Their negative descriptions are mostly picked up from the TV programmes and tabloid newspapers. A Sikh mother's remark was characteristic:

> I have English friends but nobody I feel comfortable inviting to my house ... only one English person – an old school friend of mine used to come to my father's house. Now girls go to the white neighbours but we don't. Our visiting is with our relatives.

White parents, in turn, also hold mostly negative images of the Asians' parents. These include: being too strict with their children, especially with girls; too money-minded; overcrowding their houses; wearing outlandish clothes; and being very clannish. Obviously, there are some deep inter-cultural misunderstandings between the two ethnic groups and positive policies on multiculturalism are needed to bridge the gap.

Racism

Asian and black parents in Britain are well aware of the fact that racial discrimination is going to adversely affect the life chances of their children. There is a significant body of research data on the existence of racism in British institutions and public life (Brown, 1984; Jones; 1992: Troyna & Hatcher, 1992), which very often goes to reinforce their personal experience. The first-generation ethnic minority migrants, which included a large number of professionals such as teachers and doctors (see Ghuman, 1995; Anwar & Ali, 1987), were led to believe that their disadvantaged positions in employment and others walks of life were mainly due to both their deficiencies in spoken and written English and their supposedly sub-standard professional qualifications. The second-generation Asians and blacks, who have gained their qualifications from the British institutions, still face a similar degree of racial discrimination as did the first generation (see Cheng & Heath, 1993; Brown, 1984). Under the circumstances, the only reasonable conclusion the ethnic communities can draw is that their children are going to be discriminated against. Most Asian parents, therefore, will like to open their children's eyes to the fact that they have to compete at some disadvantage with their white peers in employment, housing and the pursuit of the good life. With some, over half the Punjabi mothers said that they talk to their child about racism in general, and how to cope with the racism which they are likely to meet in their daily lives. Some comments should illustrate the mothers' concerns: A Sikh shopkeeper described her son's first encounter with racism (left school at 16 with some qualification):

> Yes, he did get a bit when he went to a local school in D.... He had few people say to him Paki. And he said to me: 'Mum, am I a Paki?'

> I said: 'No, you are not a Paki.' I went to his school and saw his teacher and told him: 'He is not a Paki; he is a Sikh (*sic*).' That is when we took him to a private school – there is no racism or bullying. I know the headmaster. He will stop it.... He was really upset – he was only four.

The reader will no doubt detect the irony in this mother's remark. Psychologically, she wanted her son to be spared the agony of the label 'Paki', and the associated abuse which is implied without, perhaps, realising that it is a generic word of abuse meant for all the Asians living in Britain.

A university graduate part-time Muslim researcher gave a disturbing example of her seven-year-old son's experience at school:

> There is a slight element of racism/prejudice in school. He does know and acts in a way that he is different. This is as a result of comments by white children.... This child called him 'pooh-coloured' and told him to play with the same colour children. As a result of comments by white children, you know at school, he is beginning to find partners who are of related colour. He is constantly fighting it; he had it since he was five. We keep on telling him to ignore it. We told him to play with the ones who want to play with him; and keep on saying he has to work very hard to succeed.

This young boy seems to be trying very hard to make sense of his experiences. During the interview he made a remark, which reflects his state of mind: 'I talk like the whites but I am like you, Pakistani'. And again to the interviewer: 'You are married to a white woman but you are brown'.

A university graduate Sikh teacher described her experience:

> Yes, for example my daughter came one day and said that her teacher says: 'All the Asian girls are alike in that they do this and that' – generally negative things, you know.... So I went to the school and had a word with her teacher. I told her my daughter wasn't happy about your negative comments about Asian girls. The teacher said: 'It was a misunderstanding.' ... I have asked my children to come and tell me if they have been discriminated in school. I talk to them about racism and how to deal with their feelings when upset. I say put it to their ignorance; that it is a minority of people who do that ...

A Muslim housewife (left school at 16 with some qualifications) was very balanced in her approach:

> I'd like her to be aware. I'd like her to be tolerant, though. I don't want her to grow up with anti or negative views about the whites. I want her to be strong and positive. I want her to enjoy the multicultural society that she lives in and appreciate the different religions.... We can live together.

A university graduate Muslim part-time researcher also stressed the importance of understanding:

> We'll explain to him the historical significance of why we came to Britain. We'll teach him to be proud of his colour and that we are not inferior. We have our own customs and way of life as good as any other. We have rich culture and civilisation. We'll take him to India, Pakistan and Kenya and broaden his outlook. Make sure he has a firm identity rooted in his culture.

However, a different viewpoint was expressed by a shop owner (left school at 17, matriculated):

> They don't bring it up as an issue because it hasn't come up. The school is multicultural really. There are pupils in the school from all over the world. If they don't have any problems why start putting ideas in their heads that this sort of thing can happen really?

However, this mother subsequently gave an account of how her elder son, who was called a Paki, resolved his pain and hurt feelings:

> ... His father came to the conclusion that he is going to be in trouble one day. So he said: 'Next time he call you Paki, just thump him.' So he did.... Teachers didn't do anything. He has not been abused since.

Another Sikh mother described a similar incident in which her son hit a white boy who called him a Paki (he got into trouble with the teachers) and after that incident he had no problems. Instead, according to the mother, he made a lot of white friends.

Regrettably, very many teachers in the UK schools still tend to ignore the verbal racial abuse, which is quite common in most primary and secondary schools, and let the children sort out their own problems. This is an old-fashioned view, which advocates that adults should interfere as little as possible in children's play and quarrels. It is supposed to be character-building. An old adage sums it up: 'They have to stand up to the bullies for themselves.' There is evidence to show that in schools where teachers take racist bullying seriously and make determined efforts to combat it, such incidences are reduced drastically (see Verma *et al.*, 1994). A Hindu student teacher wanted to deal with her son's problems only when these arise:

> Yes, I would when he faces that situation. But I don't want to make a big issue of that: sometimes you can make a big thing for them rather than it is being there and tackling it sensibly. If it comes up, then I'll definitely.

A Sikh clerical officer had a strategy to talk to her son (left school at 18 with advanced qualifications):

> Yes, they got be aware of it. (*When?*) Possibly within the next few years, I should talk to him. I think I'll use examples and incidents which have happened in the past or things which we confront day-to-day and read about.

Over a third of the mothers were of the opinion that raising problems – when their children have not faced them – would only add an extra burden on their minds. A Sikh university graduate teacher explained:

> No, I shall leave it to him. If he wants to talk about it. I really do not want to pre-empt the situation and I don't want him always to be on the look out for it.

Thus we have a range of opinions on the subject from the mothers in the 1995 sample. The first-generation parents were, in our judgement, not willing to fully admit and accept, for all sorts of reasons, that their children were going to encounter a high degree of discrimination. For instance, Ghuman (1980a: 128) found Punjabi parents to be a little more optimistic about their children's future as far as racism was concerned. A Punjabi father remarked: 'I have not met discrimination at a personal level – probably I am lucky. I have heard stories from my friends alleging discrimination in jobs. A friend of mine who wears a turban and keeps a beard has been refused several times.'

Of course, the mid-1980s recession in Britain has made both the intensity and extent of racism far worse. On average, the ethnic minorities are twice as likely to be unemployed as their white counterparts and the situation of the young people, irrespective of their qualifications, is far worse (Jones, 1993).

Inter-racial marriages

No other issue has caused more misunderstanding between the Asians and the indigenous white population than that of the arranged marriages. To most white parents, it is an anathema: an archaic feudal practice which denies young people their fundamental right to love and to self-fulfilment. To Asian parents, on the other hand, this is one of the fundamental social mores which will ensure survival of their religion, family traditions and the life of the community. We have fully discussed the background to this topic in Chapter 1. However, we wish to remind the reader that Hindu and Sikh parents arrange marriages which are based mainly on the *Jati* (castes) but are outside their family network. The Muslim marriages, on the contrary, are normally made to first or second cousins and, therefore, are within the family or extended family network. The caste of a family is one of the most important considerations in arranged marriages. The caste system is still very much part of the Hindu psyche and the Indian social system. Indeed, it has also deeply affected the followers of the Muslim and Sikh faiths, who are supposed to be free from its shackles. Nearly two-thirds of the mothers in the study (see Table 7.5) do not like the idea of inter-racial marriages, but half of these would object but accept it grudgingly, as it will become clear from their comments. A Hindu mother gave an ambivalent answer (left school at 16):

> Times have changed. We've to accept (*meaning inter-racial marriages*) but our children must not become whites, except their skin. They should remain Indian. We want her to marry in our own culture, but we know we can't stop her marrying anyone.... But we will try our best.

A Muslim housewife explained (left school at 16):

> I don't want him to be white inside and brown outside and want him to remain in his religion and culture. I like to take him to Pakistan every two or three years to see our family so that he sees who are his relations.... I would disapprove him marrying outside the family. It would hurt me in many ways.... I'll hate it.

A Muslim housewife showed confidence in her ability to influence her children:

> ... They need to be brought up to be positive and if I fail in my duty and bring them up confused then she'll take a step like that. Fortunately I know I'm good as a mother. I don't need to worry on that respect. But if she did something like that, I think you just grin and bear it.

A Sikh shopkeeper is willing to accept inter-racial marriages (left school at 16 with some qualifications):

> Well, I would say I am Indian but our lifestyle is more British ... I would accept if he marries outside the Sikh community. He had never any problems with the English. It is ironic that only problem he had was with a Muslim girl.

A Sikh owner of a shop was more realistic in her appraisal (left school at 17 with matriculation):

> We always talk what would happen on this front. It works sometimes and doesn't work other times. I won't strongly disapprove or object. I'll advise him that we choose a girl with our way of life. But at end of the day, yes, I have to accept his decision. If he is happy with a person – he has to live with it.

A Sikh nursery-nurse gave an ambivalent answer (left college at 20 with some qualification):

> (*A long pause*) I would object but probably accept. Even in English culture it does not always work out. I don't know really. There are good and bad in all cultures.

A university graduated Sikh administration assistant had a list of priorities:

> If she wants to marry someone after leaving school at 16 we'll totally disagree ... I am more likely to 'yes' if he's a Punjabi even an Indian, Gujarati etc. To an English or West Indian I'll say no, first. To Pakistanis – they are better than West Indians and English – Asians after all.

A couple of Sikh mothers said they would prefer an English to a Muslim person as a partner for their daughter because they feared Muslim families would be too orthodox and strict. Most Hindu and Sikh mothers felt that it is likely that their son/daughter may not accept the traditional pattern of an arranged marriage but might accept a modified arrangement, in which boys and girls are given some freedom to choose from within their own community. However, we feel certain that the first and second-generations' custom of bringing brides/bridegrooms over from the Indian sub-continent is going to become obsolete by the third generation. The first-generation mothers in the study overwhelmingly (93%) expressed their belief in arranged marriages. Their comments are revealing of their strict attitudes. A Sikh shopkeeper (left school at 17) argued:

> It's very difficult to keep Punjabi customs here. We're losing them

and we can't expect our children to keep them, but he must marry according to our customs.

A Hindu *Brahmin* housewife was very caste-conscious (left school at 17 with matriculation):

I don't want my daughter to marry outside our caste. It is all right if my son marries just below caste, he may marry a girl of the *Khatri* caste (*lower than Brahmins*). I wouldn't mind that.... She must marry within our own caste and according to our custom.

In sum, it became clear to us that the second-generation Punjabis have moved a long way towards accepting a modified system of arranged marriages and over a third are willing to accept, if somewhat reluctantly, marriages outside their community. Their attitudes are far more tolerant and understanding of their children's predicament, who often have to reconcile the differing demands of home and British way of life.

Gender equality

Traditionally, Punjabi parents, in their socialising practices, have tended to favour boys over girls in assigning household chores, access to education and employment opportunities and in generally giving them more freedom and choice. We asked mothers several questions to discern their attitudes on this topical issue. The responses are tabulated in Table 7.6.

Table 7.6 Mothers' responses on gender equality – in percentages*

	Yes	*No*
Should girls be treated the same as boys?	95.0	5.0
If yes, do you treat your daughter the same as your son:		
In education?	95.0	5.0
In going out?	12.5	87.5
Household chores?	95.0	5.0
Opportunity to work away from home?	0	100.0
In choice of clothes?	36.0	64.0

*These questions were not included in the 1970s interviews

All the second-generation mothers, except two, agreed with the general principle of raising their boys and girls on the basis of equal opportunity and treatment. But when it came to specific spheres of activity, it was only in the domains of education and household chores that the mothers conceded parity. Most of the mothers in the study are very protective of their daughters as will become apparent from their comments.

A Hindu bakery worker qualified her stance on equality (left school at 16):

> (*Opportunity to work in another city?*) If there is a job problem we'll have to send her away. We'll have to make certain that everything is OK where she lives. (*Going out?*) No, neither son nor daughter.

A Hindu machine operator explained (left school at 16):

> At the moment I am not treating my son any different to my daughter. I will treat them little bit different when they grow up. Only when the boy grows up, he'll want to go out with his friends, whereas, my girl – especially when she is 16 – it is more dangerous for her.

A Muslim housewife (left school at 16) gave a very detailed account:

> I think household work should be equally shared. Girls have not to do the cooking and cleaning whereas boys just sit about and eat. This is what usually happens in our culture.... We have to protect our daughter because if she makes a mistake she can be landed with a baby but boys do not have this problem. We do not want either our son or daughter to go out: evil is evil for both boys and girls.

There were a lot of comments on the question of the choice of clothes. Most of the mothers stressed the importance of modesty in clothes for girls. Their comments included: 'girls should not to wear skimpy clothes'; 'should wear Indian clothes at home'; and 'should not wear low-cut dresses and mini-skirts.'

A Muslim housewife was rather strict in her attitudes to clothes (left school at 16):

> She should dress like a Muslim girl. But it does create a problem if our daughter is the only one in *Shalwar and Kameez*. We don't want her to wear jeans and pants or skirts.

It is a well-established fact that Muslim parents tend to be stricter than Hindu and Sikh parents on dress matters (see Stopes-Roe and Cochrane, 1991; Anwar, 1985). We found a similar trend in our research.

A Muslim housewife, who does not believe in equality of opportunity, argued (left school with some qualifications):

> I don't really believe in this equality. I'm sorry, I don't. I'm a bit old-fashioned. I agree that women should have the respect and confidence.... The ignorance is there in men, because there is equality given to women in our religion. I don't like all the new things.

This mother went on to explain, at some length, that the holy Koran has ordained full equality to women but men in their machismo have distorted its writings to their own advantage. At the same time, she said disapprovingly that the modern women are far too forward in demanding sexual freedom, sharing household chores with men and the like, and this has created problems of divorce and family disintegration.

In sum, the second-generation Punjabi mothers are happy to give their daughters equal opportunities in the sphere of education and generally at home but are still very protective of them as far going out and seeking a job away from home are concerned.

Discussion and Conclusions

We have successfully probed the attitudes of the Punjabi mothers on a variety of important subjects, ranging from bilingualism through religion to identity and racism. The third-generation Punjabi children are increasingly becoming English speakers despite their mothers' attempts to maintain their mother tongue. Many of them are bilingual, albeit at a spoken level only in the mother tongue. The presence of grandparents is helping to maintain the community languages as has the establishment of week-end schools at community centres, Mosques, *Mandirs* and *Gurudwaras*. There is no provision for the teaching or use of the community languages at either nurseries, infant or junior schools. A few nurseries and schools did have a Punjabi-speaking teacher or an assistant, who helped with communication between the parents and teachers. Almost all the parents were making efforts to send their child to a community school for learning the mother tongue.

The second-generation of the 1970s missed out on this facility as the Punjabis and other Asian communities were then in the process of establishing these institutions (see Anwar, 1978). Unfortunately, in England and Wales, due to the implementation of the National Curriculum and deep cuts in the Section 11 funding (Central Government funding mainly for inner-city schools), which was partly used by some authorities to provide facilities for the teaching of community languages, any hope of including the minority languages in the primary school curriculum has been dashed.

However, according to Vedder *et al.* (1995: 49–60), there are some laudable initiatives in some pre-school education centres, at Coventry, England, where both Punjabi and English are used for teaching and learning and attempts are made to involve parents in a cognitively orientated curriculum. Vedder *et al.* also visited many such centres in Western European countries and found a variety of multicultural initiatives in place. The authors conclude (1995: 79): 'In terms of ideologies or goals, most of the centres we visited stressed the importance of building positive relationships between children from different cultural and ethnic backgrounds, whereas very few promoted submersion in mainstream culture and language.'

All the mothers, except three, stressed the importance of religion in their family's lives and expressed a deep desire to pass it on to their children. In this respect, they do not differ from the first-generation parents. The Hindu families stressed the importance of the religious ethos at home in order to pass on the rituals, customs of fasting, vegetarianism and prayers. The Muslim families, as found elsewhere (Stopes-Roe & Cochrane, 1991; Ghuman, 1994), were more committed than the Hindus and Sikhs in sending their children to their Mosque to learn to recite the Koran. The Muslim communities in Britain are better organised than any other Asian community. They even have a central body for co-ordinating the teaching of Islam which publishes material for the use of parents and teachers (see Akhtar, 1993). We felt there has been a resurgence of interest amongst parents, especially Muslims, and they are extremely keen to transmit the moral codes and spirituality associated with their religions to the third generation.

For most Punjabi families, religion is the key element upon which their personal identities are formed. However, they are also conscious of the fact that their children are going to live and work in Britain and will acquire at least some of the social mores of the host society, while over half of the mothers think that their children will have either a 'hyphenated' identity or a British one. But nearly all the mothers think that their children will be accepted by whites socially and in their places of work.

Although over half of the Punjabi families live in white neighbourhoods, very few of them mix with whites; their social life is confined to either their relatives or friends from within their community. This has led to many misunderstandings between the two communities regarding their respective-child care practices. For instance, the Punjabi parents' negative and stereotyped images of whites are that they are not very caring and do not impose much discipline on their children. Whites, on the other hand, think that Punjabis/Asians are very strict, especially with girls, overburden their children with Urdu and Arabic and have too many children. These, of course, are our impressions based on a small sample and it would be interesting to explore this topic further to enhance better understanding between the two communities.

Most Punjabi, and indeed Asian and black, parents in the UK are well aware of the fact that their children are going to face racism in their lives. In the expression of the Home Affairs Committee, racist harassment is one of the most 'frightening realities' for black citizens and their children (Home Affairs Committee, 1989: xv.) Over half of the parents in our study talked to their children about racism and some children had encountered verbal abuse both at school and in the neighbourhood. This is confirmed by other research studies (Kelly & Cohen, 1988; Troyana & Hatcher, 1992). However, a significant minority of the mothers did not want to discuss race-related matters because they thought it would place an undue burden on their growing child. A few said that they would deal with it when, and if, the matter arises.

Nearly half of the parents (nine out of ten Muslims) would like to send their child to a school run along the lines of their own religious affiliation. This finding supports other researchers in the field who have found a demand for religious denominational schools amongst the Muslim parents (Akhtar,1993; Anwar, 1985). The vast majority of Hindu and Sikh parents are content with the mainstream schooling as they feel they can meet themselves the religious needs of their children at home and in *Mandirs* and *Gurudwaras* (see Ghuman, 1994, 1980c,d).

On inter-racial marriages, a surprisingly large of number of mothers were willing to accept, if somewhat grudgingly, this possibility within their own families. It seems to be that most Punjabi and Asian parents of the present generation have moved away from the strict orthodox custom of arranged marriages and are allowing a degree of freedom to their young people to choose partners from within their own community. This new outlook now extends to giving equal opportunity to girls in various ways, but they still remain protective of their daughters.

To conclude, there has been a mixture of continuity and change in the child-rearing practices of our group of Punjabi parents. The parents still highly value their religion and would like to pass it on to their children. Most of them are determined to provide facilities for their young to learn their mother tongue and yet they realise it is extremely difficult for children to sustain motivation because, with the exception of a few nurseries and playgroups, infant and primary schools do not support their efforts. So some parents are content to see their children acquire competence at a spoken level only, and a few think that their children would be better off concentrating on a mastery of English rather than expending their energies on Punjabi or Hindi. A further change of attitudes has come about in the sphere of equal treatment of boys and girls and on arranged marriages. All in all, most of the Punjabi and ethnic minority parents are in the process of developing and shaping a new form of culture, which combines elements of British and their own culture. In their view, this form of biculturalism will provide an enriching experience for their children.

8 Home and School, Interests and Friendship

Introduction

It has now become firmly established that the educational progress of the young child is very much contingent upon the active co-operation between home and school. Unfortunately, there has been a great deal of misunderstanding between Asian and other ethnic-minority parents and the school in the realms of school curriculum, teaching methods, children's food, school uniform, co-education and the teaching of religion (see Tomlinson, 1984; Ghuman, 1980a,b). In the first part of this chapter our aim is to present some findings on our Punjabi children's schooling, with special reference to the learning of the 3 Rs. We also discuss parental involvement in their children's education and the children's likes and dislikes of school. The findings are compared with those of the first-generation Punjabi parents and conclusions drawn about the changes which have taken place since the 1970s.

It was considered important to find out about the interests, hobbies and play activities which young children pursue at home before being able to fully understand their all-round development. Therefore, in the second part of this chapter, the aim is to describe these activities of the children in our study and to include an assessment of their friendship patterns. To assist in this, we discuss the mothers' attitudes to their children's friendships and the ways in which they guide and monitor their behaviour during this period of development. Such a comparison of two generations of Punjabi mothers' perceptions should throw light on the changing nature of the children's interests and friendship.

Home and School

For the successful scholastic achievement of ethnic minority students, it is desirable that there should be a degree of cultural continuity between home and school (Ogbu, 1994; Baker, 1994). It is quite well documented

Table 8.1 Responses of two generations of Punjabi mothers – in percentages – on their level of satisfaction with schooling

	Sample	*Yes*	*No*
Which school does he/she			Fee-paying private
attend?*	1995	85.0	15.0
Local Education Authority	1970	95.0	5.0
Are you aware of any			
difficulties which he/she faces	1995	10.0	90.0
at school?	1970	9.0	91.0
In general, would you say you			
are pleased with the school ...	1995	95.0	5.0
because it suits him/her?*	1970	73.0	27.0

*Items on which significant differences were found with the Chi-square test

(Smith and Tomlinson, 1989; Ghuman, 1980c; Gibson, 1988) that Punjabi students, both in Britain and the USA, achieve at least on par, and in some cases significantly better, results than their white counterparts. This is despite their difficulties with the English language and the degree of racism which they encounter in British and American schools (Swann, 1985; Gibson, 1988; Ghuman, 1994a). This success has been mainly attributed to the high aspirations and positive attitudes and outlook of Punjabi parents – irrespective of their social class – when it comes to the education of their children (Bhachu, 1985a,b).

In view of the importance of home–school links, it was considered imperative to ask mothers their views on their children's progress at school. We included several questions in this domain and present the responses in Table 8.1.

Second generation

It is quite clear from Table 8.1 that the present generation of Punjabi parents is well pleased with their children's schooling. The general level of satisfaction is somewhat higher than that expressed by the first generation. However, this may be because a higher proportion of the second-generation parents are sending their children to fee-paying private schools. The mothers' comments are most revealing of their attitudes. A university graduate Sikh teacher explained why she sends her son to a private school:

> We think there is a better education: smaller classes, good discipline and teachers really care. Before that he went to our local school – it was not satisfactory.

The other parents who sent their children to private school echoed these sentiments. A few of the other mothers expressed their disquiet at large class sizes and also wished to send their children to a fee-paying private school. A graduate Sikh pharmacist explained:

> She was in a class of 20 and now she is with 33 – the number has been going up. I'm very troubled by that and I'm seriously considering of private education. Basically it is the cost. For two it would be difficult ... maybe tuition, but then tutors have their own way and that might confuse them.

However, all the mothers, save two, were generally satisfied with the school which their children attended, whether run by a local authority or private fee-paying. The mothers offered a variety of reasons for this, including: 'teachers care', 'standards of attainment are high', 'can talk to teachers', 'child is well-adjusted'.

The reasons for dissatisfaction were well-articulated by a university graduate Sikh information technology manager:

> No, I am not pleased. They are in a mixed-age group. She is eight years old and there are children seven or nine years old. She is not stretched. Teacher says she'll have to set extra work for her. And the class size is too big.

A Hindu restaurant owner (left school at 17 with some qualifications) was concerned about her son's special needs:

> No, I think class size is too big. He needs special attention (*her child is asthmatic and according to her lazy*) which he is not getting. There should be special needs provision in school.

Although only these two mothers were overtly critical of the schools their children attended, a few other mothers expressed concern over such matters as homework not being set and marked and class size.

First generation

Those first-generation parents who sent their children to private schools also gave similar reasons to those of the 1990s sample. A factory worker (left school at 17 with matriculation) gave her reasons:

> I'm fully satisfied with the school. Our children go to private schools. In local authority schools the classes are large. The proportion of children who succeed in studies is much higher in private schools than in state schools.

A Sikh housewife (left school at 16) made an interesting comparison with her own education in the Punjab:

> I'm satisfied. Here education is practical. In India we put education into the child; here they take education out of the child!

It is interesting to note that one of the main sources of dissatisfaction amongst the first-generation was also homework, i.e. it was not set and marked regularly. Others included: 'Would like more English children in school', 'teachers are too friendly', 'lax discipline' and too 'much drawing'. A comment of a Sikh housewife (left school at 17 with matriculation) illustrates:

> I'm not satisfied. Teachers are too friendly. They don't bother much whether the children study or whether they understand. They don't give children any homework. I asked the teacher if she could give my son some homework and she said to me that she doesn't care whether or not we help him at home ... I intend to send him to a private school.

But even in this generation nearly three-quarters of the parents were happy with the way their children were being educated at school. Ghuman (1980a: 130), in his pioneering research with Punjabis, also found the majority of the parents in his study to be satisfied with English schooling, but concluded: '... they would like teachers to be more strict and demanding, set homework regularly, and check and monitor children's progress more frequently and on a realistic basis'. Some of these sentiments were echoed by our second-generation parents.

White mothers

All the white mothers send their child to a school run by the Local Authority and are satisfied with it. But two of the mothers had complaints about certain aspects of their child's schooling. A white domestic helper (left school at 16 with some qualifications) described an incident:

> We are very happy with the way the school deals with A...., but not with certain things in the school. He bumped his head the other day

> and they didn't tell us. He nearly knocked himself out. He had a bump on his head the size of an apple.... They didn't take him to hospital. He had migraine and felt sick when he came home. This is not good enough.

The other white mother complained that her child gets headaches because the class is too noisy and her teacher is not very understanding. Overall, there are no significant differences between the second-generation Punjabi and white mothers on their respective levels of satisfaction with their child's schooling.

Parental Involvement

We asked several questions on parents' involvement in the education of their children. In Table 8.2, we summarise the responses.

On all the questions on which data is available, the second-generation parents, predictably, are more participatory in their child's education than their first-generation counterparts. In this respect they are very close to the white parents in our study. The explanation probably lies in the fact that not only are the second-generation mothers more educated and competent in English but they also understand the importance of helping their child at home and of getting involved in the educative process. Most of the Punjabi second-generation fathers helped with maths and the mothers helped with reading. As regards the mothers' occupational aspirations for their children, these have changed somewhat since the 1970s in that a lower proportion of the second-generation mothers nurture high professional aspirations for their children. But there is no change between the two generations in the dimension of 'educational aspirations' for their children. The comments of mothers give a taste of flavour of their attitudes.

Second generation

A Muslim housewife (left school at the age of 16 with some qualifications) commented:

> I'd like her to make something of herself. She can study as far as she likes ... definitely up to the age of 18 ('A' Advanced levels for entry to university). I would like her to be a teacher or a nurse. I know English people think all Asians want their children to be doctors! But really anything successful, like the law, medicine.

Table 8.2 Responses of two generations of Punjabi mothers on parental involvement in education

	Sample	*Yes (%)*	*No (%)*
Did you ever do anything like telling a story at bedtime?	1995	50.0	50.0
	1970	Data not available	Data not available
Do you still do that?	1995	35.0	65.0
	1970	Data not available	Data not available
Do you or anybody else often read to him/her?*	1995	70.0	30.0
	1970	12.0	88.0
Is there anybody who has tried to help with reading out of school hours?*	1995	92.5	7.5
	1970	75.0	25.0
Do you or his Daddy or anybody else ever help him/her with school work?*	1995	95.0	5.0
	1970	66.6	34.3
Have you ever taken him/her to pictures?*	1995	75.0	25.0
	1970	68.0	32.0
What about museums and art galleries?*	1995	62.5	37.5
	1970	46.0	54.0
Are there any other exhibitions or shows to which you have taken him/her?*	1995	33.5	66.5
	1970	11.0	89.0
Has he/she ever been to a zoo or a circus with you?*	1995	90.0	10.0
	1970	75.0	25.0
Does he/she ever go to a football match or another sporting event?	1995	32.5	67.5
	1970	Data not available	Data not available
If he/she showed ability how far would you like him to go with his education?		University	As far she/he would like to
	1995	25.0	75.0
	1970	27.0	73.0
Have you any idea now about what would you like him/her to do when he is grown up?*		Professional	Depends
	1995	28.0	72.0
	1970	34.0	66.0

*Significant differences were found on these items ($p < 0.01$) with the Chi-square test

Another Muslim housewife (left school at 18 with qualifications) echoed the above sentiments:

> I mean, we have got high hopes of my son and daughter; we treat them all equally and we're here to support them every single step of the way ... Something like a doctor or an engineer. My husband has always wanted one of his children to go into engineering.

All the mothers (except one Muslim mother who wanted her daughter to leave school as soon as she is 16) want their daughters to have the same educational opportunity as their sons, and they are willing to support their child as far as he/she can go on the educational ladder. As regards future occupation, well over three-quarters of the mothers said that it all depends on the child's progress with his/her studies. Comments such as: 'I don't mind as long as she is happy,' and 'If he wants to be a builder/plumber, it is OK by us' were frequently made. These responses are close to those of the white mothers, all of whom wanted to leave the decision to their children.

First-generation

The parents in the 1970s had a very traditional outlook as far as the education of girls was concerned. They tended first to seek the approval and affirmation of their kith and kin in India and Pakistan, whereas the present generation is more oriented towards their relatives and peers in this country. A Sikh factory worker (left school at 11) explained her views:

> I would like her to study as much as she can, it is our duty to help her. It is only in India that some people are against the education of girls, but there is no difference in this country.

An illiterate Muslim housewife commented:

> If she turns out to be clever then we'll continue with her education. We don't want her education to stop as soon as she finishes school, and if we can trust her we'll send her to college. We have to consider family honour. By the grace of Allah my other two daughters have kept our *izzat*, and if she remains good like my other daughters I'll send her to college.

The mothers, however, were all in favour of the best possible education for their sons. An illiterate Sikh housewife (interviewed in Punjabi) explained:

If he turned out to be brilliant we'll want him to go on studying at a higher level. He can study as much as he wants to and can do any job he wants to, although we would prefer him to be a doctor.

The 3 Rs

The importance of reading and writing in the early stages of a child's development cannot be overstated and, in this process, the role of parents is crucial. In Table 8.3, we summarise the responses of our samples on the reading and writing habits of their children.

There are a number of points which emerge from Table 8.3. Proportionally, fewer of the present generation children read at home, but a higher proportion belong to a library and are considered better readers than their 1970s counterparts. The former predictably also have more books at their disposal. Over two-thirds of them do writing for their own pleasure, but less than half of the children are in the habit of writing letters. The reading and writing of the white children, judging from their mothers' responses, is significantly better than that of their Punjabi counterparts. All of them read at home and most of them enjoy letter writing and writing for pleasure. Furthermore, all the white mothers helped their children with reading whereas less than three-quarters of the Punjabi mothers do. This may be due to the lower level of interest in reading generally amongst Punjabis. There is some evidence to suggest that Asian people are less likely to read books regularly compared with their white counterparts – the corresponding figures are 28% and 49% per cent respectively (see *Social Trends*: HMSO, 1995).

Children's Adjustment at School

For the child to sustain his/her motivation, it is important that he/she should enjoy school and feel part of its community. We asked several questions on this aspect of the children's schooling and the results are presented in Table 8.4.

From the data presented in Table 8.4, it is clear that the Punjabi children of both generations like their English schooling. A significantly higher proportion of the present generation is willing to take things to show to their teachers and to talk about school to their parents. This shows a high level of interest and involvement in the school. Because the school catering services have changed beyond recognition and now provide a variety of vegetarian and pasta meals to cater for the needs of ethnic minority children, we see a significantly

Table 8.3 Responses of two generations of mothers on reading and writing

		Sample	*Yes (%)*		*No (%)*	
*Can he/she read well enough to enjoy a book for its story?		1995	90.0		10.0	
		1970	80.0		20.0	
*Does he/she read much at home?		1995	75.0		25.0	
		1970	91.0		9.0	
*When he/she is reading a book, does he/she say the words aloud, mouths or reads silently?	Aloud	1995	32.5			
		1970	39.5			
	Mouths	1995	12.5			
		1970	14.5			
	Silently	1995	55.0			
		1970	46.0			
*Does he/she belong to a library?		1995	87.5		12.5	
		1970	67.0		33.0	
Does he/she ever write letters to people?		1995	47.5		52.5	
		1970	Data not available		Data not available	
Does he/she do any writing for his/her own pleasure?		1995	66.0		34.0	
		1970	Data not available		Data not available	
*Approximately, how many books he/she has of his/her own?			No of books		No of books	
			50+	25+	12+	<12
		1995	37.5	23.5	24.0	16.0
		1970	–	–	5.0	95.0

*Items on which significant differences were found. The Chi-square test was used on the raw frequencies with appropriate degree(s) of freedom

higher proportion of these children staying for school meals. It is interesting to note that nearly three-quarters of the present generation children enjoy their lessons and the remainder at least enjoyed games and physical activities and their peer contact. The mothers' comments included such gems as: 'He enjoys chips and fish fingers, maths and colouring'; 'playing with friends and chips and cheeses'; and 'videos and history'. Three mothers mentioned their children's dislike of maths

Table 8.4 Responses of two generations of mothers on their child's interest in his/her school

	Sample	*Yes (%)*	*No (%)*
Does he/she ever say that he/she does not want to go to school today?	1995	12.5	87.5
	1970	8.0	92.0
Does he/she get on well with his teachers?	1995	95.0	5.0
	1970	96.0	4.0
*Does he/she stay for school dinners?	1995	85.0	15.0
	1970	62.0	38.0
Does he/she ever complain about school?	1995	17.5	82.5
	1970	17.0	83.0
Does he/she like school?		Very much / Well enough	
	1995	77.5 / 20.0	2.5
	1970	Data not available	
*Does he/she often take things to show his/her teacher?	1995	Often 7.5	17.5
		Occasionally 75.0	
	1970	Often 00.0	58.0
		Occasionally 42.0	
*Does he/she naturally come and tell you about school, or do you always have to ask him/her?	1995	Loves telling 37.5	**Have to ask 32.5
		Sometimes 30.0	
	1970	Sometimes 32.0	Have to ask 68.0
Do you know what he/she enjoys most at school?	1995	Academic 47.3	
		Everything 26.3	
		Games etc. 21.3	
		Friends 5.0	
	1970	Data not available	

*Items on which significant differences were found ($p < 0.05$). The Chi-square test was used on the raw frequencies with appropriate degree(s) of freedom.
**Mothers have to ask their children about school

and school puddings – certain things do not change, a fact to which many readers will readily testify! A Muslim housewife (left school at 16) exemplifies:

> That was the problem. He hated his dinners and came home hungry. He doesn't like the smell. He is very shy so he would go all day without food. It took us a long time to say to dinner ladies to give him an extra packet of crisps for break time. So I now prepare him a lunch-box of things he likes.

Children's complaints

The same proportion of children in both Punjabi samples had complained in some ways about their schools. In both the groups, the majority of grievances (five out of seven in the present sample) related to the misbehaviour of other children and three children in the present sample had encountered racist abuse from their white peers.

A university graduate Muslim part-time researcher explained:

> There is one boy who used to bother him – the only one in his class. He used to call him: 'Black and pooh-coloured'. He certainly didn't like that. That is when he began to realise and play with children of the same colour. I didn't worry about it a couple of times and then I told the teacher. Now he (*her son*) stays away from him. He wasn't happy at school then. He would be better off with more Asian children.... On the other hand, I don't want him to find protection in that kind of area. Because he must, at the end of the day, interact with all kind of people.

There is a difficult decision to make when an Asian parent faces this type of situation. But it is important to point out that it was not always white boys and girls who were the offending parties, as a Sikh shop owner (left school at 16 with some qualifications) explained:

> Last year this Muslim girl was hassling him a lot. I have to go to school. I said to the head move them. She was moved and it was OK then... That's why he didn't want to go to school and pretended he was not well.... He enjoys sports, PE and computers. He writes his journal and writes letters to his *Masi* (aunt). We help him with his homework. We are pushing him to do well and want him to go to college.

Two white mothers in the study also mentioned a complaint made by their child. One was to do with the noise level in the class and the other with the school meals. A university graduate teacher explained:

> She doesn't enjoy school. She rather stay at home with me and read. She hates talking about school; it is like getting blood out of a stone. It is the noise in the class which gives her headaches. She also day-dreams and takes a lot of time to do things. That makes her tense and anxious. She likes her own pace.

On other aspects of schooling, a significantly higher proportion of the white children are reported to: love talking about and taking things to school; asking questions about something which was shown at school; having a magazine or comic bought for them, than do their Punjabi counterparts. Moreover, it was evident from these interviews that, in general, the white mothers felt more confident in approaching teachers about their children's education and gave more help to their young children in reading. The Punjabi mothers, on the other hand, seem to be instilling, both overtly and covertly, high educational and occupational aspirations and the Punjabi fathers are more involved than their white counterparts in the education of their children. The reader is reminded, however, that these inferences should be accepted only with a great deal of caution in the event of there being only 12 white mothers in the study.

General Activities

The mothers were asked a general question about their children's activities when they are not at school. This was followed by a more specific question: 'When he/she comes home what does he/she do with his/her free time until bed-time?' The responses to the first question were varied, but one of the activities often mentioned was watching TV and playing out in the garden, especially in summer. A few typical responses of the mothers are presented. A Muslim housewife (left college at 20 with qualifications)) gave an interesting account of her daughter's activities:

> On Saturday, first thing after breakfast she goes to an Urdu school. Then we do shopping and after there is usually time to read the Koran – they should be reading it now. Because it is in Arabic they need to recite it. So she'll do that. She helps me and then watches TV, and loves reading.

A Hindu trainee teacher also gave a very full picture of her son's spare time:

> He goes to a Karate club and Hindi school and then *Tabla* (Indian drums) classes. He does band practice – he is in the school band and he does a recorder in. He got activities everyday: scouts, Tai Chi. So in between the times he would play with his brother and sister or watch TV depending on his time.

However, the spare time of most of the children in the study was not spent as gainfully as the picture painted in the above two descriptions. A Sikh secretary (left school at 16) described her daughter's weekend:

> On Saturday, she goes shopping with me. Then we have a snack; put away the articles we've bought and then she watches TV. On Sundays, morning is taken up getting ready for visiting relatives or going to the *Gurudwara* (Sikh temple). In the afternoon she does her homework. Twice a week she goes for tuition in maths and English to a private school.

Several mothers mentioned watching TV, playing outside and taking part in sports, the latter especially for boys, as the favourite pastimes of their children. The mothers' comments included: 'Playing outdoor, running around, cycling'; 'Indoors we have to work hard to stop her watching TV cartoons – they are the bane of our lives'; 'Playing football with other children, reading'; 'He likes swimming and physical sports, likes going-out to a cinema'; 'Plays with her dolls or her friend next door, likes reading, she doesn't enjoy TV too much'.

On the specific question: 'What do children do after school?' the responses included: doing homework, watching TV, playing outside, especially in summer, reading, helping in clearing up, eating and so on. A few responses should illustrate the nature of these activities. A Sikh owner of a shop (left school at 17 with matriculation) lists her daughter's pursuits after school:

> When she comes home from school she washes her face, gets changed, have her tea, watches TV and helps in the kitchen, if I need it. She does writing and reads and plays with her dolls.

A Muslim housewife (left school at 15) had this to say about her seven-year-old son:

> At 5 o'clock, Monday to Friday he goes to an Arabic class – it has just started. He reads a book which he brings from school everyday. He is enjoying his bike at the moment.... He has got his bedroom and his things, but by the end of the day he likes to sleep with his Mum and Dad – he is not ready to sleep on his own.

A Sikh housewife (left school at 16) talked warmly of her daughter's afternoons:

> ... They have something to eat straightaway and then watch TV for half an hour until 5 o'clock. She would take out her books and draw and read for two-and-a-half hours. She would be very busy – won't bother us. Then has a bit of break and talks to me or her father about what she has done at school or what games she has played.... She loves reading. She has more brains than I have already!

Another question asked concerned children's special interests and hobbies – i.e., what they most liked doing. The responses to this question and to whether they watch Asian films are presented in Table 8.5.

As is clear from Table 8.5, the modal response to the hobby/interest question is playing with computers closely followed by reading. The

Table 8.5 Responses of second-generation mothers on interests and 'Asian films'*

Activities		*Responses (%)*
What does he/she most like doing after school?		
Playing with computers		35.0
Reading		22.5
Drawing		7.5
Playing musical instrument		2.5
Gym		2.5
None/Mixture		33.0
Does he/she play imaginative games? e.g. role-playing, acting	Yes	57.5
	No	42.5
Do you have *Asia TV*?	Yes	10.0
	No	90.0
Do you have a video cassette recorder? Yes		100.0
Does he/she watch Asian programmes?	Yes	22.5
	No	77.5

*Detailed data is not available for the 1970s sample.

first generation of Punjabi mothers also gave reading as one of the main interests of their children. It is disappointing to note that nearly a third of the children, according to their mothers, have not developed any specific interest. However, nearly two-thirds of the children in the sample like role-playing and acting. A couple of responses are illustrative. A Muslim housewife (left school at 16) talked about her daughter's imaginative play:

> You just like role-playing Ansia ... Anisa says: 'We sometimes play witches, goblins and ghouls.' Then she plays Mums and Dads and sisters with her dolls. She is full of ideas.

Several mothers described their daughters' role-playing of teachers, Mums and Dads, shopkeepers, and their play-acting and dressing up. More girls than boys engaged in imaginative play but boys preferred football and rough and tumble games, like climbing and chasing. A Muslim housewife (left college at 19 with qualifications)) described her son's interests

> ... He likes to do a variety of things, it's not just one particular thing he does. Sometimes he'll play on the computer or play outside hammering, you know what children are like, especially boys. Besides that he's very creative and outgoing

A Sikh owner of a shop (left school at 17 with matriculation) described her son's interests

> He likes drawing a lot. Give him a paper and coloured pencils. He can draw for hours. But his favourite pastime is playing outside, if it is nice, or watching TV ... the programme he likes – the more fighting the better.

The white mothers in the study also described their children's main interests to lie in the field of computers while television viewing emerged as one of the most common pastimes of the children in the present Punjabi and white samples. But, surprisingly, only a few mothers complained about its excessive viewing. Less than a quarter of the third-generation Punjabi children watched Asian programmes on TV. A Sikh shop owner (left school at 17 with matriculation) explained:

> They don't like Indian films because they don't understand the language and they are quite fake, really. They laugh at them and give me a lot of stick for watching them as well. (*What sort of programme do they like on TV?*) The more fighting the better it is. The only thing I stop them is watching WWS wrestling. I would not

accept that. They try doing the movements on each other and end up hurting themselves.... No TV after eight; they are not allowed. They got computer games and their books.

A minority of children were cited as watching Indian/Pakistani films, the Hindu epic *Mahabhrata* and a family saga (*Insanieet*), originally produced for Pakistani television, on the two BBC mainstream channels. But the BBC has now discontinued broadcasting special programmes for Asian viewers and the only alternative left open to the potential viewer is the new commercial channel *TV Asia*. From the interviews we gathered that the third generation has little interest in events happening in India and Pakistan, despite the fact that over a third of the children have enjoyed their holidays there. The typical comment, according to the mothers, was: 'It is nice for a visit, but we don't want to live here'.

In contrast to the first generation, none of the mothers in the present study allow their children to walk or 'bus' to or from school whereas, in the 1970s study, two-thirds of the mothers did so. As discussed in the previous chapter, this seems to be due to the parental fear and anxiety caused by recent attacks and abduction of young children. Most mothers/ fathers accompany their children to and from school and this was also the case with the white sample. Those who could not do so made very firm alternative arrangements with relatives/neighbours or a baby sitter.

Friendships

Several questions were included in the interview schedule to find out as much as possible about children's friendship and their mothers' attitudes towards it. The responses to some of the questions are given in Table 8.6.

From Table 8.6 it may safely be inferred that the Punjabi children's play and friendship patterns have changed since the 1970s in certain important respects. First, their choice of playmates now extends far more widely. Second, there is less fighting amongst the siblings but, surprisingly, more with friends. In addition, significantly more second-generation mothers intervene in their children's quarrels than did their counterparts of the 1970s. We cannot, however, offer any satisfactory explanation for the shift of maternal opinion on children's quarrels. We illustrate these differences by using the mothers' own comments.

A Sikh shop owner (left school at 16) described her son's friendship:

His best is friend is Italian. He comes to our house and R.... goes to his. He has got a wide circle and quite happy to play with all the other children in his class. He has no dislikes: all ages, races – he is comfortable.... He fights with the older one quite often. They have a strong character; first, boxing, kicks and punches fly out. Luckily they don't hurt each other. (*Do you stop them?*) No, not physically, I can get hurt. I let them get on with it. It helps to work out their aggression.

Table 8.6 Responses of Punjabi mothers of both generations to friendship questions

Questions	*Sample*	*Yes (%)*	*No (%)*	*Others (%)*
*Likes to play with other children	1995	67.5	10.0 (Alone)	Both (22.5)
	1970	83.0	4.0 (Alone)	Both (13.0)
Plays mainly with siblings	1995	72.5	5.0 (Alone)	Friends and siblings (22.5)
	1970	79.0	4.0 (Alone)	Friends and siblings (17.0)
Mothers happy with his/her friends	1995	95.0	5.0	
	1970	84.0	16.0	
*Do you intervene in their quarrels?	1995	55.0	45.0	
	1970	27.0	73.0	
Are you happy with his/her friends?	1995	90.0	10.0	
	1970	84.0	16.0	
Have you ever tried to discourage any friendship?	1995	28.5	71.5	
	1970	28.0	72.0	
*Fighting with siblings	1995	67.5	32.5	
	1970	87.0	13.0	
*Fighting with friends	1995	55.0	45.0	
	1970	38.0	62.0	
*Plays mostly with Punjabis/Asians	1995	22.5	Mixed ethnic 77.5	
	1970	64.5	Mixed ethnic 35.5	

*Items marked with an asterisk are significant at 0.05 level

A university graduate Sikh pharmacist described her daughter's play friends:

> She plays more if we invite her friends over. She will also play with her younger sister and then she will go off and do her own thing ... She has no black friends, but English friends from school. We call over once or twice in a month ... but mostly Asian relatives' children.

A few mothers, although allowing their children to play with children of other ethnic groups, tend to encourage friendship from within their own ethnic group or families. A Hindu bakery worker (left school at 16) commented:

> We do not like that she plays with children other than Punjabis.... Times have changed but our children must not become white persons, except their skin.... (*Discourage friendship?*) Yes, I do. The reason was that the other child ordered things from the catalogue. I do not want my child to have such ideas and that she should ask me to order things for her.

A qualified Hindu counsellor had this to say about her daughter's friendship:

> She has a lot of friends ... I suppose close ones are Punjabis and English. She normally plays with her sister.... Sometimes they fight a little, nothing serious, it's all part of growing up. (*Do you interfere?*) On two occasions I did; she would come home and complain and moan and use bad words. Her friend tried to dominate her and she was picking up bad habits, so I stopped that.... But again I'll explain giving her the reasons why she should not mix with bad children.

A Muslim housewife (left school at 16) described why she had to intervene in her son's friendship:

> ... He was a half-caste boy. Mum is English and Dad is an Afro-Caribbean. But there was some sort of conflict in their family.... They (*meaning her boy and his friend*) had a fight over something and my boy is small and he is very big and he can get hurt. So after that we didn't let him go to play with him.

A Sikh housewife (left school at 16) explained why she would interfere in children's quarrels:

> She plays hopscotch and on their bikes outside and scrabble and other games insides. She plays both with English and Punjabis ... I

try not to interfere but sometimes if she is very upset or there is a fight then I'll stop it. Generally, I try to find the reason why it happened and let them tell me what the whole story is.

Thus we had a range of responses on this important dimension of personal friendship. It seems to us that the second-generation mothers are far more satisfied with their children's friendship and feel confident enough to interfere when necessary in their children's quarrels and even to stop friendship when it is deemed to have undesirable effects.

Discussion and Conclusions

Since the 1970s, the interests and friendship patterns of the third-generation Punjabi children have changed considerably. The present generation has access to computers with which they tend to spend a great deal of their spare time. Reading is less popular than computer games, but the watching of TV is still one of the major pastimes. Our own impression is that the viewing of Indian/Pakistani films and the listening to songs of Asian origin have, predictably, suffered a decline.

As regards inter-ethnic friendships, it is heartening to note that three-quarters of the mothers report mixed friendships as judged by their description of their children's play activities. However, the previous research in this field (see Smith & Tomlinson, 1989; Thirkell & Worrall, 1989) has shown that the overriding factors in determining young children's friendship tend to be those of sex and ethnicity. But these studies dealt mainly with second-generation children, whereas we are more concerned with the third generation. The parents of the latter are generally more sympathetic than the former when it comes to inter-ethnic friendships and even inter-racial marriages, as can be seen from our discussion in Chapter 7.

Education researchers have consistently found that Punjabi parents tend to have high aspirations for their children as far as education and occupation are concerned. These high aspirations are independent of social class, caste and the religion of parents (Bhachu,1985b,c). Penn and Scattergood (1992: 92) carried out a comprehensive study of the career aspirations of young South Asian people in the north of England. They conclude their research: 'Asian respondents had very high aspirations. This confirmed previous research by ... 77 per cent of Asian respondents desired higher education compared with 55 per cent of non-Asians.' Our present investigation confirms these conclusions.

A few Punjabi mothers in our study mentioned racism as one of the factors which made their child unhappy at school. There is a whole body of research which supports such a contention (see Milner, 1983; Kelly & Cohn, 1988; Troyna & Hatcher, 1992). For instance, Moran *et al.* (1993: 431) found that: '... significant difference by ethnicity was found for racist name-calling.... One-half of the bullied Asian children, but none of the bullied white children in the sample, were called names about their colour'.

Wright (1993: 12) reports the results of an extensive ethnographic research on the interaction between Asian, black and white pupils. She concludes: '... They were concerned (*meaning Asian children*) that this often exacerbated the teasing, ridicule and harassment which they felt they received daily, particularly from the white children'. Racist name-calling and the hurts and pain it causes is still very much a part of the experience of a minority of third-generation children. Indeed, as discussed in the previous chapter, nearly half of the mothers are taking it seriously enough to discuss it with their growing child.

The majority of mothers, both Punjabi and white, in the study, helped and supported their child in the 3Rs. This is in line with a very large-scale research (Tizard, *et al.*, 1988: 83) carried out in the inner London area, where some 90% of the mothers were found to be supportive of their children's learning. The second-generation Punjabi mothers are even more supportive and involved than their first-generation counterparts. This is mainly attributable to their knowledge and experience of the English education system and greater competence in the English language. However, there remains a quarter of the mothers who do not help with the 3Rs due mainly to their poor command of the English language.

Several primary-school headmasters in the city of Birmingham, England, have mentioned the low scholastic achievement of young Asian children (7- to 11-years-old) in conversation with one of the authors. A large-scale research by Smith and Tomlinson (1988:136) has empirically confirmed this low achievement pattern. The authors summarise the situation in these words: 'It is clear that on entry to secondary school at 11 both Asian and West Indian children tend to be achieving at a lower level than white children, even if comparisons are made with children from comparable social backgrounds.... Asian children catch up during the secondary school years in terms of test scores, and in spite of scoring much lower than white children at the age of 11, they obtain similar examination results.' Indeed, there is some research evidence to show that South Asians of Indian origin could even be 'over-represented' at the British universities (see Ballard & Vellins, 1985). We think that the main reason for this delayed academic success lies in the fact that most Punjabi/Asian parents generally instil in their children the importance of gaining good qualifications in order to secure jobs in a very competitive and racist environment. Thus, high aspirations ('N'ach' – need to achieve, see Musgrove, 1970) are internalised in early childhood and sustain students' motivation in school and later on in their youth and adult life. This complex interplay of several factors thus accounts for the slower start but later, accelerated development of Punjabi/Asians in British schools. Kysel (1988: 88) did an in-depth analysis of the extensive data published on the achievement of ethnic minorities students in the UK. His findings reinforce the conclusions reached by Smith and Tomlinson (1988). He writes: ' ... This is a transient problem which has been largely overcome by the time they reach the fifth year of secondary school' (Kysel, 1988: 88).

In the USA, Ogbu (1994, 1988) has used a comparative anthropological approach to unravel some of the factors implicated in the scholastic attainment of ethnic-minority students. Some initial disadvantages, and the poor performance of the Punjabis in the USA are, according to Ogbu, due to the primary cultural differences between home and school, which are eventually overcome to some effect. He cogently argues (1994: 367): ' ... Voluntary minorities do not perceive learning the attitudes and behaviours required for school success as threatening their culture, language, and identities. Instead, they interpret such learning (e.g. English) instrumentally and as additive, as adding to what they already have (their own language), for use in the appropriate context. They also believe that the learning will help them succeed in school and later in the labour market.' Ogbu's analysis is also relevant to the predicament of our own Punjabi/Asian students. Moreover, such an analysis also explains why two Asian sub-groups, namely, Pakistani and Bangladeshi, do less well academically at the end of their schooling than their Asian and white peers. Broadly speaking, Muslim parents in the UK perceive schooling to be a threat to their religion and identity. Ghuman (1995: 68) was informed by the white headmaster of a multicultural school:

> ... But older generation of leaders within Mosques – very encapsulated and in a narrow Islamic tradition – had a strong influence on the local Muslim community. Parents of the 60s were persuaded to ask for a *Mullah* (priest) to be in the school. Lurking behind this

worry lies this unease that their *children are being corrupted; and this is not too strong a word.*

In this context, the research of Gibson (1988: 170), who carried out an intensive study into the social adjustment and academic achievement of Punjabi Sikh high-school students in California, is also relevant and interesting. She argues: 'The Punjabi's success in school appears to stem less from cultural attributes *per se* or from conformity to the majority culture than from diligence and persistence in their schoolwork, combined with a strategy of accommodation and acculturation without assimilation.'

We contend that, in general, Punjabi families in our study are also adopting such an approach. They are encouraging their children to acquire competencies (knowledge of computers, for instance), social skills and interests which will ensure their success in wider British society. At the same time they are doing their best to pass on the family values and traditions in order to ensure a degree of continuity of the home culture. Such adaptive strategies have been noted by other researchers studying ethnic minorities in a variety of social and political contexts (Bhatnagar, ed., 1981; Gibson, 1988).

9 Continuity and Change: Some Reflections

Introduction

We set out to compare and contrast the child-rearing practices of two generations of Punjabi parents in Britain – who are separated by almost a generation. At the same time we attempted to discover links with the indigenous white and the native Punjabi mothers' ways of rearing children and their corresponding attitudes. For methodological reasons, we selected Punjabi families only for our research (see Chapter 3) and although this is the focus of the study, our findings have relevance for other Asian groups and ethnic minorities in Europe, North America, Australia and elsewhere. We have eschewed the use of existing universal models and excessive theorising because the project has an essentially empirical orientation. Roopnariane and Carter (1992: 250) gave us a timely reminder: 'As such existing theories and frameworks have become outmoded and have always been culturally limited. To continue to push traditional theories as universalistic in their application my be erroneous.' Our approach to data collection – through semi-structured interviews and systematic personal observation – was more akin to an ethnographic perspective rather than a quantitative one.

Serious doubts have been cast over the building of universal child-rearing models which do not take into account the cultural imperatives, history and the social context within which parents rear their children (see Levine *et al.*, 1994: 273–4). We did not plan to test any explicit hypotheses nor probe into definite research questions as such; rather our predilection and subsequent stance was to discern patterns, to look for insights and illuminations and to learn from the mothers in our study. To this end, we feel we have been amply rewarded both in gaining a mine of relevant information on topics we chose to investigate and about mothers' concerns and worries for their children.

We have made extensive use of extracts from the interviews –

verbatim as far as possible – in order to convey to the reader both the substance and nuance of the mothers' opinions. Our selection of quotes is necessarily selective but an attempt was made to be as comprehensive as possible and to avoid bias. We have, of course, analysed and interpreted the interview data and made cautious generalisations in the light of our findings and the research extant in the field. However, we concede that alternative explanations are possible. The number of white and indigenous Punjabi mothers in our study is small but we have tried to complement our analysis, wherever relevant, by using existing literature on child-rearing practices. Separate analyses of the data by religion and social class were not undertaken because the numbers involved were too small and any ensuing generalisation could have been misleading (see Chapter 2).

First Generation

The lifestyles of first-generation migrants are usually very close to those of the people of their countries of origin. They tend to retain their food habits, dress styles, social interactions and, moreover, their family religion and language. Their motivation for migration, which is often economic, dictates their patterns of settlement in the country of their adoption, and because their aspirations are often modest they tend to cling to their own traditional way of life. Their interaction with the people of the host country tends to be functional, often requiring minimum adaptation to their lifestyles. The first report on race relations in the UK (Rose *et al.*, 1969: 25) analysed the migrants' predicament as 'the process of adaptation may be slow and the degree of adaptation may be the minimum required to get employment and shelter; it may be met by a minimal amount of acceptance. This minimum *modus vivendi* between host and immigrant has been termed a state of *accommodation*'. In our view, the first-generation Punjabis and other Asians of the 1970s generation made just such an accommodation to the British way of life. This same type of adaptation was also made (in the 1960s and 1970s) by the first generation of: Algerians in France (Charlot, 1981: 109); Turks as *Gastarbeiter* (guest-workers) in the former Western Germany (Raoufi, 1981: 109); Moroccan, Turks and Surinamese in the Netherlands (Eldering, 1995, 1994); and people of Chinese origin in America, Canada and Australia (Lin *et al.*, 1990; Li-Repac, 1991; Taft, 1966).

Second Generation

Second-generation ethnic minorities tend to move towards *integration* into the mainstream way of life and culture, but the extent to which such a move is made is contingent on a variety of socio-political factors in the country of domicile. Integration here is taken to mean (Rose *et al.* 1969: 24): 'a process whereby a minority group, while retaining its own culture and religion, adapts itself to and is accepted as a permanent member of the majority society in all the external aspects of association'. The second-generation Punjabi families in our study have moved in this direction, particularly those of Hindu background. There is wider evidence to support this conclusion (see Stopes-Roe & Cochrane, 1991; Jones, 1993). However, the Muslim communities in Britain and elsewhere in western European countries are finding it somewhat difficult to integrate into the host society of their adoption for reasons both of their own internal religious imperatives and the external wider political situation (e.g. the Rushdie affair and the emergence of Islamic fundamentalist groups such as *Hamas*). In this context, Berry's (1994: 129) model may be useful to explain the adaptation process of some minority groups. He postulates that where an ethnic community chooses to retain its own culture but considers it of little value to maintain relationships with the dominant group, the adaptation process may be described as separation and not integration. We have no conclusive evidence to enable us to say that the Muslim families in our study were adopting this strategy, but from the comments of Muslim mothers on retention of their religion, language and separate schooling, it appears that they are approaching the British way of life with a great deal of scepticism (also see Shaw, 1988, 1994).

The present generation of Punjabis, and indeed other Asian groups, in Britain have made modifications to their lifestyles in order to accommodate such factors as the growth in awareness of individual personal identity and the adoption of fast foods and the European style of dress. Most second-generation Punjabi parents are fluent English speakers and they have also maintained their mother tongue at least at a spoken level. The vast majorities of marriages are still arranged and are endogamous, i.e. within religion and caste, thus ensuring the continuity of family culture and the perpetuation of *Biraderi* (kinship) (Nesbitt, 1994; Ballard, 1994) for, unlike the white family, the Asian family is closely interconnected to a *Biraderi* which plays a vital role in the primary socialization of the young (Rex, 1985: 13). Such a social arrangement provides a degree of stability and security for its members and is considered to be of immense value in the healthy development of young children (see Bronfenbrenner, 1994).

The educational and occupational levels of second-generation Punjabis and Asians in Britain, with the exception of Pakistanis and Bangladeshis, are higher than those of their first-generation counterparts and are almost on a par with those for whites (Jones, 1993), despite the level of discrimination they have to encounter. Cheng and Heath (1993: 164) carried out an in-depth analysis on social mobility of a number of ethnic minority groups by using comprehensive nationally representative data for residents in England, Wales and Scotland. They conclude: 'Despite the differences in their histories of migration, their cultures, their internal differentiation, the Indian, African, Pakistani and West Indian men all suffered an *ethnic penalty* of some size, irrespective of their level of education.' (Italics added).

Compared with their parents, the financial position of the second-generation families have improved dramatically. The second-generation mothers' comments included: 'Ten times better than my parents – more money'; 'We live in a land of milk and honey'; 'We have microwaves, fridges, washing machines, computers and holidays.' There is little doubt that the present generation of Punjabis and the majority of other citizens in the UK enjoy a very high standard of living compared with that of their 1970s counterparts. This affluence, however, has been bought at a price. Some second-generation mothers in our study felt obliged to go out to work in order to sustain their high standard of living. Consequently they have less time than did their mothers to spend with the children. But all agreed that working outside the home has enhanced their social standing, both within the family and in the community as a whole, and has given them a degree of freedom.

Pregnancy-related Rituals and Early Child Care

The second-generation Punjabi parents have fewer children than those of the 1970s sample, but still, on average, have more than do whites. Fewer of them live in extended-family households and all of them, except four, speak English fluently. None of them are single-parent mothers, and all of them, except one, own the house they live in. Some of these changes discussed above in family size and structure have also taken place in India and Pakistan amongst the middle classes; but the degree and intensity of change is much less (see Chapter 3).

Expectant mothers in the Indian sub-continent and African countries (see Levine *et al.*, 1994) learn the craft of motherhood mostly from their own mothers or women of their kinship. The young mother acquires the skills by imitating and emulating, rather than explicitly being taught (at school or in the popular women's magazines) physiological functions such as menstruation, lactation, pregnancy and birth. Furthermore, all these bodily functions are surrounded in rituals, mythologies and dietary taboos (see Kakar, 1979, 1994) and were originally meant to protect and safeguard the expectant mother and her vulnerable new-born baby. For a fascinating portrayal of these practices among the mothers of South Asian origin, the reader is referred to an anthology: *Asian Mothers, Australian Birth: Pregnancy, Childbirth and Childrearing* (Ed. Rice, 1994). Manderson (1994: 7) writing in this volume, describes some of the rituals: '... certain behavioural prescriptions pertain throughout pregnancy in all Asian cultures. Some of these draw on metaphor, analogue or sympathetic magic: woman should not eat "twin bananas", for example, lest she give birth to twins; her husband should not kill animals or the child might die; she should avoid funerals ... In China ideas of *yin* and *yang* are not dissimilar and there is good evidence of people borrowing theories from different sources.' According to this writer a lot of these practices are predominantly either of Unanic (Iranian) or Ayurvedic (Indian) origin. Gusii mothers, in Kenya, observe many rituals associated with childbirth and for the protection of their new-borns. Levine *et al.* (1994: 92–135) describes in vivid detail many ceremonies and rituals. For instance, if twins are born the family must go through a protective ritual (p. 134): 'In the case of Gusii, the sense of dangers is also present but the spiritual peril is symbolically embodied in the physical vulnerability of the mother-child unit, which requires procedures to enhance physical strength and foster healthy growth.'

Nearly a quarter of our 1970s Punjabi mothers practised some of the taboos and rituals which are linked to their own Punjabi upbringing. These relate to confinement (*Reetan*), eating *hot* (eggs, chicken, garlic) or *cold* (rice, lemon, peas) food as appropriate, rituals surrounding teeth-cutting and *Bhaddan/Mundan* (hair cutting) ceremonies. However, except for the hair-cutting ceremony, none of the other rituals and ceremonies have survived into the 1990s generation. But religious ceremonies related to childbirth are still very much part and parcel of the present generation's beliefs. For instance, the majority of the Sikh families in our study still hold special religious ceremonies for naming and thanksgiving (*Akhand Path*). Likewise, most Muslim and Hindu mothers have continued with their respective religious ceremonies of *Akika*, *Salat* and *Bhaddan*. That these celebrations are widely observed is confirmed by our personal experience of the communities both in Britain and North America (see Ghuman, 1994). Moreover, the importance of religion in the formation of young children's personal identity cannot be overstated and we will return to this theme presently.

Like other researchers in the field (see Woollett *et al.*, 1995, 1991, 1990a; McEnery and Rao, 1986), we found that second-generation mothers are beginning to make use of health-care facilities offered by the National Health Service, by attending ante-natal classes and by seeking help from midwives on diets, feeding and matters relating to hygiene. This has come about because most present generation mothers, being fluent in English, do not have to rely on interpreters (which tended to be either their husbands or an older child to add to their embarrassment) to explain their problems of a very personal nature.

Role of the Father

A major change has taken place in the role played by the Asian father since the 1970s. The second-generation fathers are far more helpful during pregnancy, delivery and subsequent baby-care. Their support takes the form of sharing in the household tasks, shopping and looking after the young baby. To our surprise, we found that a large number of fathers were present in the delivery room. This is a significant departure from the traditional Punjabi practice where childbirth is largely the concern of the womenfolk of the family. We were told by a Sikh mother: 'He would pull his weight. He found little babies too small to handle. But he would do the rest of the housework – cooking, cleaning, washing and ironing. With this one he changed nappies, and I could leave the baby with him. Remember, I share with him the work in the shop, I believe in equality and so does he.' There has been little change in India on this aspect of child-rearing. Roopnariane and Hossain (1992: 14) found that even the highly educated middle-class Indians in Delhi 'still maintain good distance when it comes to the basic care of the babies'. Our second-generation Punjabi families' attitude to preferring baby boys to girls has attenuated as has the desire to have large families. This has also happened with the middle-classes of India and Pakistan (see Chapter 3). Other researchers in the field have found a similar pattern (Woollett *et al.*, 1990b).

General Child Rearing

There was a general level of confidence shown by the second-generation mothers in the way they talked with deep knowledge and affection of their children. They were mostly positive about their children's personality, describing it in glowing terms. For girls these descriptions included: gentle, loving, good, listens, lively, talkative, quiet and intelligent. And for boys: healthy, nice, shy, pleasant and polite, naughty and easy-going. The majority of mothers of both generations claimed their children to be easy to manage. There is evidence both from the mothers' responses to our factual questions and from the attitudes thus displayed that those of the second generation are generally giving more freedom to their offspring than did their first-generation counterparts. A significantly higher proportion of the third-generation children attend clubs and activities intended for junior children (e.g., Karate classes), choose their clothes and books and are allowed to have pets to care for. Furthermore, they tend to question their parents' opinions, as exemplified by the comment of a Hindu mother: 'I say this is good toy, let us buy it. "No", he says, "this is not good" and tells me *why* he doesn't like it; and he can fully explain why. Then he says: If you like it *you can have it*, I don't want it! In our tradition, a child should never say like this.' Overall, the third-generation children perforce are given chances to take some independent decisions – which is a significant advance from the freedoms accorded the children of the 1970s.

A higher proportion of the third-generation children have nervous habits and anxieties than those of the second generation. The explanation for this increase in anxieties seems to lie, in part at least, in the lack of the full support of the extended family and maybe also in the stress of modern living – the latter independent of ethnicity. Also, partly it may be due to the increase of racism (or their awareness of it), which they meet in their daily lives (Troyna and Hatcher, 1992). The Punjabi mothers of both generations do not approve of physical punishment (smacking) as a way of disciplining their children, although a minority use it as a last resort. A Hindu mother explained: 'I don't mind a little smack, but I don't like it. A little peck on the cheek and he feels this is the end ... I really feel bad for a day or so and I think I shouldn't have done that.' Nearly two-thirds of the second-generation mothers thought parents should manage without smacking. The corresponding figure for the white mothers is 50%. The research of Hackett and Hackett (1994) with Gujarati and white mothers found a similar pattern of attitudinal difference: 91% of the white mothers felt that smacking was, on occasion, necessary, whereas only 72% of the Gujarati did so. But there was no significant difference in the frequency with which it was actually used by both groups of mothers. Like their white counterparts, the second-generation mothers use isolation (sending them to their bedroom) as a way of punishing their children for misdemeanours – a significant difference from the first generation. In this context, it is important to note that three-quarters of the second-generation Punjabi mothers give rewards for good behaviour, and two-thirds believed in the withdrawing of such rewards for misdemeanours. Both these practices, incidentally, accord with the thinking of the school of Behaviourism, which advocates that rewards and punishments should be contingent on the production of a desired response (Wheldall and Merrett, 1984).

A higher proportion of the second-generation mothers think that their children are rude, that they talk-back, and that they show temper tantrums. In this respect, the third-generation children are closer in behaviour to their British counterparts. The explanation for this perceived rudeness lies in the fact that norms of behaviour tend to vary from one culture to another and behaviour which is applauded as self-assertion by an English parent might appear rude and aggressive to a Punjabi parent. The third-generation children are absorbing the norms and values of the host society from their attendance at British schools with the result that the traditional norms of respect and obedience to parents are therefore under challenge.

However, the sleeping arrangements of babies and young children have not changed significantly since the first research was carried out in the 1970s. Only one in five children sleep in their own bedrooms, the rest either share a bed or a bedroom – two children are sleeping with their parents. This is reinforced by the research findings of Hackett and Hackett (1994) with another Asian ethnic group, the Gujaratis. They report that 85% of boys and girls shared a room or bed with someone else in the family; the corresponding figure for the white sample was only 25%.

It has been suggested by some psychoanalysts (Daws, 1989) that sleeping alone is a prerequisite for the development of autonomy and independence in young children and empirical evidence is cited from India and Japan to support this contention. Such an arrangement of sleeping is widely practised in parts of Africa (Levine *et al.*, 1994), and in many other countries. In our view, to link the development of autonomy to independent sleeping would be to impose a Eurocentric view of the world on other cultural groups.

The psychoanalytical theory is very much based on Western European notions of man's repressed sexuality and his ensuing predicaments and problems in inter-personal and sexual relationships. More recently, the writings of Freud and of other scholars of this school of thought have come under renewed scrutiny and have been found wanting in objectivity and scientific rigour, not the least because their theories were based on highly selective and biased samples and made wide generalisations (see Webster, 1995). Extended discussion on this topic is beyond the scope of this book, but the reader is referred to the works of Kakar (1994, 1992) and Kurtz (1992). Kurtz writes (1992: 30): '... where traditional psychoanalysis focuses on a child and its mother, we must learn to understand children who live amidst the complex but unified array of caretakers in the Hindu joint family. As currently constituted, however, psychoanalysis is ill suited to such an approach, its intellectual framework having been shaped by our Western individualism.'

From the responses of the Punjabi mothers of both generations, we gathered that they were in favour of encouraging their children to be conscious of, and appreciate, the custom of familial interdependence rather than follow and absorb the Euro-American style of rugged individualism. Witness the comments of two mothers on the question of 'giving pocket money to their children':

> A Hindu mother reflected: 'No I wouldn't. We got a shop, they can do a little bit work for me. Then they understand they are helping the family and getting some reward. Even then I won't give the money in the hand – buy them something or it goes to their building society accounts.'
>
> A Sikh mother elaborated: 'I know that English parents give pocket money when children are about 16. They tell them also that if they want to stay with them they have to pay for their board. We can't do that sort of thing. Neither do we give pocket money nor do we ask for it when they grow up – they can stay with us as long as they wish.'

The sentiments expressed reveal 'togetherness' or interdependence which are deeply embedded in the Punjabi and Asian psyche (see Shaw, 1994). The second-generation Chinese in America also stress the importance of family interdependence and mutual support (Lin & Fu, 1990). And likewise one of the major goals of African-American families in the USA, according to Carter and Middlemiss (1994: 115), is the 'socialization toward interdependence'. In a comprehensive review of literature on ethnic minorities' practices of child rearing, they conclude: 'Extended family patterns and philosophy of familism also appear to typify the families of other minority groups. For example, Hispanic-American, Asian-American, and Native-American families emphasise family loyalty and interdependence of family members.' Japanese society also places a premium value on interdependence where 'the emphasis on *amae* dependency in the structuring of social values and social roles differs from Western practice, where parents try to make their children independent as early as possible' (Azuma *et al.*, 1981: 8).

A related concern of Punjabi and other Asian groups is that of arranged marriages. Although the second generation in our sample has shown more tolerant attitudes to marriages formed outside the caste and religious spheres, they would still prefer the old system in a modified form (see Ghuman, 1994a,b, 1995; Bhachu, 1985a). This custom is essential to ensure the continuity of family culture and to affirm the primacy of social kinship and networks. A Sikh mother opined: 'It's very difficult to keep Punjabi customs here. We're losing them and we can't expect our children to keep them, but he must marry according to our custom to carry on the family traditions.'

Once again, the threat of 'individualism' is in at the forefront of the mothers' thinking. In general, they are of the opinion that individuals have to make compromises in favour of the primary needs of the family to ensure its continuation in traditional form. Rex (1985: 10) has analysed the situation in a succinct way and touches upon the anxieties of Asian parents: 'Indeed it can be said that the whole system gives the bride more rights than does the notion of marriage upon random selection and romantic love. Much more than this however, the assertion of freedom in sexual matters is bound up with a whole set of values about the marketability of sex which is reflected in the media and sex-shops.'

Transmission of Mother Tongue and Religion

The first generation of the 1960s and 1970s had to struggle hard to reproduce its institutions of religion and family and its community networks. The second generation is subsequently in an advantageous position to transmit its cultural heritage because the necessary social structures are in place to do so. Most mothers of the second generation believe in the teaching of the mother tongue and make arrangements for their children to attend community centres for lessons either at the week-ends or after school. However, it is regrettable that there are no formal arrangements in pre-school education institutions (play groups and nurseries) in Britain for the teaching of community languages so that the parents have to struggle hard to maintain their mother tongue without the support of the school system. A comment of a Sikh mother is illustrative: 'Yes, I want him to learn Punjabi. He talks to me in English. But I answer him in Punjabi. Then I tell him to speak to me in Punjabi. He tries, but after saying a few words he begins to laugh.'

In previous decades, owing to the legacy of British colonialism both internal and overseas, the learning of the mother tongues, e.g., Welsh, Punjabi, was considered to be a disadvantage. The teaching of mother tongue was supposed to interfere with the learning of English and generally hampered scholastic achievement. Migrants face similar situations in all the western European countries to a varying degree (see Bhatnagar (ed.), 1981). Charlot (1981: 107) analysed the predicament of Arab children in France and concludes: 'However, the same is true neither for Portuguese and Arabic, which denote populations previously colonised and held in low regard ... to become like the others, to forget and make others forget his origin, the immigrant child refuses to learn or to speak the language of his parents. This refusal is a sign of the desire to assimilate, often shared and encouraged by the family.'

The educational and social benefits of bilingualism are only just beginning to be appreciated. Baker (1994: 129) has comprehensively reviewed the research extant in this area and concludes: 'However, to conclude that all research is invalid, fails to acknowledge that the judgement of the clear majority of researchers tends to be that there are positive links between bilingualism and cognitive functioning.' Baker (1994: 94) is optimistic about the revival and maintenance of minority languages: 'For example, amongst Punjabi, Italian and Welsh communities in Britain, there are groups of "fourth generation" individuals who wish to revive the language of their ethnic origin.'

However, some Punjabi parents in our study are taking a more pragmatic view of the teaching of their mother tongue which is similar to that of their counterparts in California of whom Gibson (1988: 194) writes: 'Most Valleyside Punjabis were opposed to bilingual instruction for their children as part of the formal school program and were quite specific in their preference for an all-English curriculum, for in their view school hours devoted to Punjabi were school hours taken away from mastering English.' Our own personal knowledge of upwardly socially-mobile Punjabis in the Punjab confirms this contention. The vast majority of middle-class parents there send their children to English-medium schools, where Punjabi is often assigned a third place (after English and Hindi), if at all, in the school curriculum.

Vedder *et al.* (1995: 45) also report this type of pragmatic attitude to the learning of Dutch rather than the mother tongue by the Surinamnese migrants in the Netherlands. Moreover, the writers found the attitudes of care-givers to the development of mother tongue to be ambivalent: 'More than half the centres are convinced that stimulating children's first language proficiency is an important goal for multicultural education, whereas the other centres are convinced that this is not so.'

The predicament of a Sikh teacher in our study highlights the situation in which ethnic minority parents find themselves: 'When I had my first child I used to speak Punjabi to her all the time and thought she would learn English at school. But when I found out that she had problems at school because she didn't know a word of English I was very upset ... with my second daughter now I speak English.... It is difficult to know what to do?'. In our view, a range of solutions to this problem will probably emerge depending upon the interplay of many factors among which cultural, contextual and situational predicaments of ethnic communities will be foremost.

Like their first-generation counterparts, most of the second-generation Punjabi parents want to pass on their religious codes, spirituality and morality to the next generation. A Muslim mother's commitment is typical: 'Religion plays an important role in our lives. Without religion everything in one's life is destroyed. It guides you on the true path and you can distinguish between the good and the bad, sinful and the virtuous.'

However, the Punjabi and other ethnic communities in Britain have to make their own arrangements for the learning and teaching of their respective religions because the school system only caters for the needs of the mainstream Christian faith. This is in spite of strong demands from the Muslim parents to make some formal provision in those schools where the vast majority of students are from their faith (see *The Times Educational Supplement,* 1 March 1996). In the UK, the demand of Muslim parents for denominational Government-funded schools (known as Grant Maintained), on a par with those already established for other religions, e.g. the Roman Catholic schools, has met with little success. Therefore, Muslim parents are becoming more vociferous in demanding the teaching of their religion where there is a high proportion of children of their faith. For this reason, all the Muslim parents, save one, in our study would like to send their children to an Islamic school. However, emanating from our research and that of others (Smith & Tomlinson, 1989; Gibson, 1988), we can safely generalise that Hindu and Sikh parents in the UK and elsewhere are generally content with the mainstream schooling. They think they can themselves effectively meet the religious needs of their children, and that it is good for their children to mix with their white peers in multicultural schools. A Sikh father's comment about segregated schools is illustrative: 'My own view is that they'll become ghetto schools and this would have a negative effect. And we haven't got a black university ... and it is against integration. We should stay within the mainstream and demand our just rights, like single sex-schools.'

The Hindu families emphasised the importance of a religious ethos at home in order to pass on the key principle of vegetarianism, the customs of fasting and their prayer rituals. The Muslim parents, on the other hand, are keener to send their children to a local mosque to learn to recite the Koran and to pray communally.

Formation of Identities and Racism

All our second-generation Punjabi mothers, save two, think that their children will not be fully accepted as English/British. Consequently, most mothers are encouraging their children either to develop bicultural 'hyphenated' identities or to consider themselves as Indian/Pakistani and thus remain rooted in their family culture. A Hindu mother opined: 'I am Indian. Because at the end of the day we are Indians and they should be proud of it and value our culture ... she would be Indian though holding a British passport.' A comment of a Muslim mother further illustrates: 'We live here – one can say that we are British but English people don't regards us as British. They consider us second-class citizens, so we regard ourselves as Pakistani Muslims.'

These perceptions are affirmed and reinforced by the extensive evidence of both a well-researched and anecdotal nature that racism is embedded in all the British institutions of the police, education, the law, the health service, civil service and the armed forces (see, Anwar & Ali, 1987; Brown, 1984, Jones, 1993,). Most minority groups from the former colonial countries now living in western European countries are aware that their children are going to face racial discrimination in all walks of life (Miles, 1994; Wrench, 1992). This is also true in the case of African-American and Mexican-American and other visible minorities in America (see Carter & Middlemiss, 1992: 115).

Over half of the second-generation Punjabi mothers have discussed racism with their young children once they became aware it had been encountered in schools. A Muslim mother gave an example: 'This child called him "pooh-coloured" and told him to play with the same colour children.... He is constantly fighting it; he had it since he was five.' There is evidence from other researchers to confirm the prevalence of racial abuse in British primary and secondary schools (see Troyna & Hatcher, 1992; Kelly & Cohn, 1988; CRE, 1987). However, most Punjabi mothers were very balanced in their approach when they faced this topic. One Muslim mother's comments are typical: 'I'd like her to be aware. I'd like her to be tolerant, though. I don't want her to grow up with anti or negative views about the whites. I want her to be strong and positive. I want her to enjoy the multicultural society that she lives in and appreciate different religions.... We can live together.' In this context, it is interesting to note that all the mothers, save five, thought that their child would be accepted by the whites both socially and at work. However, we think the mothers were mainly thinking about economic integration because it became clear when they were asked the question about their own personal friendships and social visiting that only a few of them were on visiting terms with their white neighbours, the majority having their social mixing with relatives or friends from within their own community.

Treatment of Boys and Girls and Friendship Patterns

The Hindu parents generally have always taken a liberal attitude towards their daughters' education and social ambitions (see Nehru, 1946). The Muslims, on the other hand, have usually been more circumspect, and the attitudes of the Sikhs have been somewhere in between these two perspectives (Stopes-Roe & Cochrane, 1991).

The second-generation Punjabis are in favour of giving girls and boys equal opportunities in education and even in demanding help in household chores but still cautious of their daughters working away from home, going out and choosing clothes. A Hindu mother's comment illustrates: 'At the moment I am not treating my son any different to my daughter. I will treat them a bit different when they grow up. Only when the boy grows up, he'll want to go out with his friends, whereas my girl – especially when she is 16 – it is more dangerous for her.' Overall, then, we found that the second-generation is moving towards the European norm on gender equality but with some reservations on going-out and dating for girls.

The friendship patterns and interests of the third-generation have changed quite dramatically. The present generation have access to computers and, according to the mothers, they spend a great deal of their time using them. Reading has become less popular as a pastime than computer games for this group of children. However, the TV is as popular as it was with the children of the 1970s, although the viewing of Asian programmes and films has declined in a marked way. This is in part due to the discontinuation of ethnic programme broadcasting by the main channels and a general fading of interest in Punjabi/Asian affairs.

There has been a marked proportional increase in the formation of inter-ethnic friendships by the third generation; three-quarters of the mothers reported out-of-group friendship. The previous researchers (Thirkell & Worrall, 1989; Smith & Tomlinson, 1989) have noted the overriding salience of ethnicity and sex in young children's friendships. As we are dealing with the third-generation children, it is likely that the situation has changed somewhat and both ethnic and white parents are encouraging mixing. We feel that the balanced ethnic mix of neighbourhood and of pre-school centres and primary schools are important factors in inter-ethnic friendship as Verma *et al.* (1994) discovered in their research in secondary schools. Further research on this topic should clarify a changing situation.

Home and School

We found that a higher proportion of second-generation mothers help their children to read and are, in general, more involved in the education of their offspring than those of the first generation. The explanation lies in the fact that the majority of the former have been educated in British schools and thus realise the significance and the value attached by teachers to active parental involvement. However, there remains a quarter of mothers who do not help actively to support their children. If this finding were to be extrapolated to apply to a wider population, it might partly explain the initial lower achievement of Asian children compared with that of their white peers in reading and maths in the early years (see Chapter 8). There is a further general point to be made concerning reading as a leisure-time pursuit as the Asians in Britain read less frequently than do whites – the comparative figures for the two groups are 28% and 49% respectively (HMSO: *Social Trends*, 1995).

We have alluded to the interesting phenomenon in which Punjabi and some other Asian children (with the exception of Bangladeshis and Pakistanis) have a lower level of achievement in their early years (7–11) but catch up with their white peers and achieve on par with them by the end of their secondary education (Smith & Tomlinson, 1989). Some researchers have also reported over-representation of South Asian students at British universities and polytechnics (Ballard & Vellins, 1985). But a comprehensive research on this topic by Modood (1993: 181) shows that the pattern of admissions to British higher institutions is a complex one, and concludes: 'Yet it is striking that most ethnic minority groups have worse class (*social class*) profiles than whites, but produce much larger proportions of applications and admissions in the national higher education system' (our italics). This conclusion confirms both British and North American researches (Verma *et al.*, 1987; Ogbu, 1994; Gibson, 1988) which suggest that migrants' children tend to have higher educational aspirations and a greater motivation to achieve than their white counterparts. Indeed, some groups, notably students of Chinese and Japanese origin in the USA, out-perform their white peers (see Trueba *et al.*, 1993).

Our interview data shed some light on this phenomenon. A higher proportion of the 1970s mothers had higher expectations of their children than did those of the second generation – although the latter still harbour far greater expectations of their children than do their white counterparts. The first-generation migrants often tended to find employment on the lower-rung of the occupation ladder even when their qualifications were cognate with those of their native counterparts (Anwar & Ali, 1987). For instance, during the 1960s a very large number of Indian graduate teachers could only secure jobs as bus conductors in the English Midlands despite their best efforts to find employment in schools (Ghuman, 1995). Consequently, they became very determined to secure a better future for their children and instilled in them the need to achieve. In the migrant parents' view, the best escape route from lowly paid jobs is through the gaining of recognised qualifications (the often given advice to children is: you have to be twice as good as the white man). A Sikh mother's comment is relevant here: 'We are professional people ... we also worked hard to achieve. That has been passed to us from our parents to do well for ourselves.'

The second-generation parents are a bit more relaxed about their upward social mobility and are increasingly taking into account their children's interests, feelings and aptitudes – which is more akin to white mothers' attitudes. The white mothers in our study when asked: 'What would you like him/her to do when he/she grows up?, invariably responded: 'It depends on him/her'. And this child-centred approach to career aspiration is also being adopted by some of the second-generation Punjabi mothers in our study.

A child's progress at school, initially at any rate, depends upon the extent to which the school's cultural and social forms are closer to those of the home. This is a pressing concern of most ethnic-minority parents in western European countries and elsewhere. Vedder *et al.* (1995) carried out a survey of the provision for multicultural education in nurseries and playgroups in several Western European countries and conclude by postulating three important conditions for consensus-building across the relevant professionals, namely: 'These three conditions (anti-discrimination, family involvement and responsivity) are closely interrelated. We consider responsivity to be of permanent importance to quality education, irrespective of which multicultural model of education is adopted' (Vedder *et al.*, 1995: 115). According to the authors, the concept of responsivity requires self-reflection 'in order to be able and willing to be responsive with children and parents from a variety of cultural backgrounds'.

We have amply alluded to the first two concepts identified by the authors in our discussion of Punjabi children. In our view, as far as the 'responsiveness' of school and nursery staff is concerned, it is axiomatic that in order to be effective any institution has to be sensitive to the needs of its children as well as to those of parents. A British Government-sponsored report on the teaching of English in schools (Bullock Report; HMSO, 1974: 286), published some two decades ago, made a plea, which has been often quoted in the literature on ethnic-minority children: 'No child should be expected to cast off the language and culture of the home as he crosses the school threshold, nor to live and act as though school and home represent two totally separate and different cultures which have to kept firmly apart. The curriculum should reflect many elements of that part of his life which a child lives outside school.' Another Government-sponsored report in the UK, compiled under the chairmanship of Lord Swann (*Education for All*: 1985: 317), endorsed such sentiments and went further in arguing that multicultural perspectives should inform and permeate the whole school curriculum and that such curricula should be for *all* children in multicultural as well as in all-white schools. Such a plea has also been made by educationalists in Australia (Caldwell & Berthhold, 1995), Canada (Skutnabb-Kangas & Cummins, (eds), 1988) and the USA (Yee, 1991).

Mothers' Childhood: A Comparison

In the concluding part of this last chapter of the book, we think it is apposite to present the views of the second-generation mothers on one of the most important topics in the interview schedule, namely: asking them to compare their ways of raising children with those of their mothers. All the second-generation Punjabi mothers, except two, conceded that there have been radical changes in their child-care practices since their own mothers' time, and these are mostly in the direction of Euro-American norms. A selection of responses is offered to give the reader a flavour of the freshness of the mothers' thinking on this theme. A Sikh mother, who was brought up along with her four sisters and two brothers, felt deeply about her experiences:

> If I start about it, I'll never finish. It was different in every way. We (*meaning girls*) were treated so different. We couldn't wear trousers at all. My daughter can wear skirts, we were not allowed to. We never had no pocket money – even though we were grown ups. We have to learn to do the housework. We have to ask if we wanted something ... I give far love to my daughter, I received not that much love because we were a big family. I left school at 16 because my parents won't let me study, I wanted to be a nurse ... now I say to them why didn't you let me go out and choose clothes which we wanted, and why there was so much difference between us and my brother.... It is all very different for my daughter.

The above comments highlight some of the key areas in which changes in child-rearing have taken place. Another Sikh mother strongly affirmed some of the points:

> It is totally, totally different for my children. Children have so much more freedom, especially girls. I was never allowed to go on school trips – never abroad. We were first-generation Asians born in England. They are basically allowed which we were not allowed – we are a lot freer with our children. We are very much Westernised and my Dad has become freer as he has grown older.

This theme of freedom and independence runs through most of the comments made by the second-generation mothers. A Hindu trainee teacher, who was brought up in the Punjab, added a cultural perspective:

> Culturally completely different. Here children are sort of mixing with two different cultures. It can cause a lot of conflict and confusion. In India there were different religions but one culture really.... I had an arranged marriage but I don't think my children are going to go through it.

A Hindu bank clerk provided another dimension:

> We are not at home all the time. My Mum was at home all the time cooking, washing and cleaning. We both work full-time and only see them (*children*) for two or three hours or so in the evening so that's different. With food, we have English and Indian – I had Indian only and had to cook ourselves. I take more interest in them, I think my parents were more interested in settling down. She (*meaning her mother*) was not educated so she couldn't take an interest nor help in what I was doing, whereas I do.

Increasingly, affluent Asian parents now prefer to send their children to fee-paying schools. A Hindu civil servant explained:

> They (*her parents*) came from India with nothing and worked their way up. Now I just sort of tend to go out and buy a lot of things without thinking about it too much. I drive a car; they only had a car in the last ten years. I have a lot better life, and this is what they worked for to improve our lives ... got a big house and children go to private school.

A Muslim housewife talked about the maintenance of Islam:

> My mother was illiterate – she was not educated, I am. I am giving my children quite a lot which I didn't get. I am giving Islamic education and teaching them right from wrong. I take them to Church and to Gurudwara so that they don't think they are different – all are the same but we worship in a different way.

A Muslim shop owner also touched upon religion:

> Very different; more broad-minded as I have been brought up here. I impose different views on children. I want equal opportunities for my girls and boys. I am not very religious like my Mum and Dad, so I am more liberal towards their religious education. We are more for understanding and tolerant of our children's behaviour and try to explain more.

A Muslim housewife was nostalgic for the old ways:

> My Mum had to go out and work in the fields; she had to make mudpacks and she had to milk the cows, cook and all that. And we got everything – we take it for granted. She valued food, money, loyalty and the elderly. So do I, but it is diminishing in our society. We're not holding onto standards like they did and I really feel saddened by that. I really wish I could go back in time and bring my kids up where they were morally strong and fit in that respect.

Two other mothers in our study were lyrical about the old-times, in particular about the extended family network they experienced in the Punjab where they spent their early childhood. A Sikh shop-owner, who belongs to an upper-middle class family and went to a fee-paying convent school, ruminated:

> Our childhood was much more relaxed and easier. My mother didn't work and she had time to devote to us. At the moment, I work and my husband works. So we have a little time left for children.... Here they learn self-reliance at an early age; they learn to do things and grow up more quickly as well.... I would have liked to bring up children in India – oh yes, children would have been children for longer and all the aunts and uncles to love.

A Sikh pharmacist tried to be objective in her comments:

> I would say our parents were very hard-working but had not enough money; they earned enough to be comfortable. One thing my parents did was to give us religious and moral education. Also we had a full love and support of our grandparents. Whether we can provide it to our children, is questionable? They (*meaning parents*) had set ways. I was brought up the Indian way, for my children it is not clear-cut.... I am pushing them to be English. Identity maybe a problem with them? It was never with me.

The comments of most of the mothers embraced the sentiments and notions contained in the responses presented above and in addition included: 'More opportunities now', 'No differences between boys and girls', 'My parents didn't have time to read to us', 'We obeyed our parents and were afraid', 'We shared things, now they own their own', 'Want my daughter to go as far as possible, it was not in my *Kismet*', 'Respected my religion, was obedient and accepted arranged marriage' and 'my children have to face drugs and racism which I didn't'.

At this juncture, it is apposite to present a summary of the opinions and attitudes of the native Punjabi mothers so that the opinions of the second-generation Punjabi mothers can be evaluated against the background of those changes that have taken place mainly due to the march of time rather than due to acculturation (see Chapters 3 and 4 for details). Likewise, the opinions of white mothers should be considered in order to provide a fuller picture of the context in which the attitudes of our second-generation Punjabi mothers are changing.

Indigenous Punjabis

From our interviews, we were able to infer the following. Firstly, there has been a great improvement in the pre-natal and post-natal care of mothers, especially in the middle-classes. Secondly, families are more aware of hygiene matters associated with childbirth and also the importance of having their babies inoculated against various diseases. Thirdly, there is more affluence in the middle-class homes and therefore they can afford a range of modern facilities like their British Punjabi counterparts. Most middle-class families – which may be considered to comprise a cognate group for comparison with our British Punjabi mothers – are now becoming nuclear and mothers are working full-time to help family finances and thereby facing similar problems relating to child care and housework as the British Punjabis (Sharma, 1990). The support of grandparents and an extended kinship is now often absent. Fourthly, as regards toilet training, babies sleeping with their mothers, views on training for independence and father's non-participation in baby care, the situation has not changed significantly. Fifthly, the middle-class and higher caste families generally tend now not to have more than two children and there is less prejudice against having a baby girl than used to be the case a generation ago. Finally, although the rituals and customs surrounding pregnancy and childbirth are rarely performed, the role of religion is still paramount in these matters (for details see Chapter 3).

White mothers

In contrast, the white mothers when answering this question on change seemed restrained and hesitant as if they were searching hard for something significant to say. The Punjabi mothers we have listened to came gushing out with long anecdotes and examples of change and turbulence in their way of raising children compared with that of their own mothers.

A teacher (living in Britain but of French origin) gave her considered opinion:

> It was a stricter childhood and education, but on the other hand for more freedom to go out and roam about. We had fewer books at home. My mother worked full-time and my grandmother was living with us ... I do miss that. I think it is very beneficial for the children.... Now children have more facilities: far too much TV, computers and toys. We have more presents for children. We ask too many questions whether we are doing the right thing or the wrong thing and we discuss things about children.

A single mother gave a somewhat detailed account:

> I had a father who favoured my brother. That was not fair. So my mother was for me to even it out. I found it caused problems. Treat them the same.... Children are more advanced now and there are many facilities which my Mum didn't have. Children are a lot of work, I would not recommend bringing a child on your own, and then again I don't want to bring her up with a person I don't want to be with. Her (*child's*) Dad doesn't pay her. He has no comeback in months and years to come (*meaning responsibilities*) ... if it is a woman she gets branded.

These comments illustrate the different set of problems facing single-parent families which an increasingly number of second-generation Asian mothers are going to have to face.

A part-time lecturer made some interesting points:

> I know I had lot more support than my mother did because my father was in the forces. She was totally on her own.... I think possibly we are more affluent even taking into account the inflation and the rest of it. There is more know-how about children. I don't believe it was available then. A lot of emphasis now on pre-natal care such as exercises.

A part-time teacher gave her reflections on the matter:

> I would say probably raise my children in a similar way to the one in which I was brought up, although there are practical differences.... I tend to be more lenient when it comes to choosing their hair styles and clothes for the day.

Two-thirds (eight out of 12) of the white mothers said that there has been no major change in the way they are raising their children compared with their own upbringing. The comments included: 'Not any different', 'Not a lot has changed – material things' and 'Very similar'. Two mothers spoke of how their own mothers had an easier time rearing them because they had little fear of their children being kidnapped or abducted.

Conclusions

For the sake of simplification, we have attempted to summarise the changes in the child-rearing practices of Punjabis since the 1970s in a tabular form (see Table 9.1). The white mothers of our study are excluded from comparison since there have been so few significant changes in their style of parenting. In our view, the valid comparison is the one between the second-generation Punjabi mothers living in the UK and middle-class Punjabi mothers in the Punjab. Although we had only a small number of native Punjabi mothers available to study, we have complemented our sources from the published research and our own personal observations.

From the complexity of child-rearing practices we have investigated, our findings unravel the concurrent themes both of continuity and change, and of biculturalism and bilingualism . We have alluded to these themes throughout and it is apposite now to draw the various strands of the inquiry into a coherent whole. We find the second-generation Punjabi and Asian parents to be shedding most of the traditional rituals, myths and superstitions relating to childbirth. There is plenty of evidence (Woollett *et al.*, 1995) to suggest that Asian mothers in Britain are using the health-care facilities provided by the National Health Service in both pre- and post-natal periods. They are tending to have smaller families and the traditional attitude of preferring baby boys to girls is radically changing as is the involvement of fathers in child care and general help in the house. There is an enormous change in that girls and boys are treated on a par at home and girls are given equality of opportunity in education and other walks of life, although parents still remain somewhat protective of their daughters. The importance of religious ceremonies to mark the rites of passage of the young infant has only slightly attenuated and the parents are as keen as the first generation to impart the piety, devotion, morality and spirituality of their respective religions to the next generation. This desire to preserve their religion is so strong amongst Muslim parents that most of them prefer to send their children to Islamic schools whenever these are available.

The first language of the second-generation families tends to be English, although the mother tongue is being continually used by

Table 9.1 Summary of changes to modernity – since the 1970s – in child-rearing of second-generation British Punjabis and native Punjabis identified as radical (major)/moderate/no change, i.e. still traditional

Domains of experience	*British Punjabis*	*Native Punjabis*
Rituals surrounding pregnancy and childbirth	Radical	Radical
Father's help	Radical	Very small change
Availability and use of medical care	Radical	Radical
Massaging and bathing in traditional way	Radical	No change
Bottle-feeding	Radical	Moderate
Toilet training	Moderate	Moderate
Baby's sleeping arrangement	No change	No change
Preference for boys	Radical	Moderate
Family structure – become nuclear	Radical	Radical
Family size	Radical	Radical
Religious ceremonies	Moderate to small	Moderate to small
English spoken by children	Radical	No change
Mother tongue spoken by children	Radical	No change
Bedtime stories and reading	Radical	No change
Inter-ethnic friendship	Radical	Not relevant
Parental active involvement in education	Radical	Moderate
Independence – assessed by such items as pocket money, etc.	Moderate	No change
Identity – from Indian/Pakistani to a hyphenated one	Radical	Not relevant
Physical punishment	No change	No change
Parental awareness of racism	Radical	Not relevant

grandparents and by many mothers. Despite the strenuous efforts by the Asian communities in Britain to teach their respective mother tongues, most third-generation children can only understand their mother tongue at best although a small minority do speak and read and write. Here the reader is reminded of the wide variations within the Asian community: Muslim parents generally have been more successful in retaining their children's interest and motivation in the learning of the mother-tongue Urdu. But even with others, the mother tongue still provides a continual link, if somewhat tenuous, with the family traditions and religious teachings of the country of origin.

Asian families still tend to emphasise inter-dependence rather than the independence that is valued in western European countries. This is supported by the mothers' comments and their corresponding attitudes on different aspects of child rearing. Stopes-Roe and Cochrane (1990: 159) summarise their research findings on the comparative child-rearing practices of Asian and white families, in England, in a succinct way: 'The prediction that ethnic background would have an effect on the evaluation of conformity and self-direction was strongly supported; Asians were more in favour of conformist and less in favour of self-directing qualities than were the British.' The Chinese ethnic groups in the USA also seem to have retained some elements of the Confucian ideals of conformity and duty to the family but have adopted some aspects of the American way of life (see Chieu, 1987; Li-Repac, 1982; Lin & Fu, 1990). Lin and Fu (1990: 433) write: 'The Chinese and immigrant Chinese parents are also increasingly adapting to the necessary changes while holding on to certain traditional family values.' This traditional outlook on family unity, cohesion and stability has distinct advantages for the healthy development of young children, as noted by Bronfenbrenner (1994: xvi) in his comments on the way Gusii people in Kenya bring up their children. He writes: 'Today, the hectic pace and increasing chaos of contemporary American life undermine the evolving consistency and continuity that are essential for psychological growth.... Therein lies perhaps the most important cultural lesson from us to them and from them to us.'

As we worked our way through the interview data and searched the literature extant in Britain and elsewhere, we became convinced that the second-generation Punjabi parents – and other Asian groups for that matter – in Britain and elsewhere, are evolving new cultural patterns which are built out of the threads of both the home and host cultures. These patterns, of course, differ in form, hue and texture and depend upon the individual family and its religious and social orientations. Such new idioms are emerging in the field of literature (*Bhudda of Suburbia*: Haniff Quarshi – 1984; V.S. Naipaul and S. Rushdie's prolific writings), in religion (the practice of Yoga and meditation and the popularity of vegetarianism), films and theatre (*Tara theatre, Bhaji on the beach*), classical music (Menhuen and Ravi Shankar's rendering of: *East meets West*; and Indian *Ragas* with classical music) and in popular songs (*Punjabi Bhangra beat*), in food (*Samosa*, fish and chips with curry sauce) and in many other walks of life. It is a mixture of the old and the new which Asian parents are passing on to the third-generation children in the hope that they will live in peace and harmony with their own community and will be tolerant, and respect the ways, of society at large.

We let a Hindu mother have the last word:

> I'd like him to take the best out of both cultures. The British are really good to communicate with, their language, freedom and fair play; we would like him to have that; ... he believes in Christmas. Our culture comes from the heart and I want him to appreciate that. I'd like him to be caring, which is a big part of Indian culture, to be aware of his family and respect his elders and things like that, which tended to be a part of English people. I would like him to retain that part. I think it is important.

Bibliography

Ahmad, W.I.U., Kernohan E.E.U. and Baker, M.R. (1989) Health of British Asians: A research review. *Community Medicine* 11 (1), 49–56.

Akhtar, S. (1991) Mothers and daughters. Unpublished MPhil thesis, University of Wales, Cardiff.

—— (1993) *The Muslim Parents' Handbook*. London: Ta-Ha Publishers.

Anwar, M. (1978) *Between Two Cultures*. London: Commission for Racial Equality.

—— (1979) *The Myth of Return: Pakistanis in Britain*. London: Heineman.

—— (1985) *Pakistanis in Britain: A Sociological Study*. London: New Century Publishers.

Anwar, M. and Ali, A. (1987) *Overseas Doctors: Experience and Expectations*. London: Commission for Racial Equality.

Aries, P. (1973) *Centuries of Childhood*. London: Penguin Books.

Aurora, G.S. (1967) *The New Frontiersmen*. Bombay: Popular Parkashan.

Azuma, H., Kashiwagi, K. and Hess, R.D. (1981) *The Effect of Mother's Attitude and Behaviour on the Cognitive Development of the Child: A US-Japan comparison*. Tokyo: University of Tokyo Press.

Bahl, V. (1987) Results of the Asian mother and baby campaign. *Midwife Health Visit Community Nurse*, 23 (2), 60–2.

Baker, C. (1992) *Bilingualism*. Clevedon: Multilingual Matters.

—— (1994) *Foundations of Bilingual Education and Bilingualism*. Clevedon: Multilingual Matters.

Ballard, R. (1994a) Differentiation and disjunction among the Sikhs. In R. Ballard (ed.) *Desh Pardesh*. London: C. Hurst & Co.

—— (ed.) (1994b) *Desh Pardesh: The South Asian Presence in Britain*. London: C. Hurst & Co.

—— and Ballard, C. (1979) The development of South Asian settlements in Britain. In J.L. Watson (ed.) *Between Two Cultures*. Oxford: Basil Blackwell.

—— and Vellins, P. (1985) South Asian entrants to British university: A comparative note. *New Community* 12 (2), 260–5.

Basran, S.G. (1993) Indo-Canadian families: Historical constraints and contemporary contradictions. *Journal of Comparative Family Studies* 24 (3), 339–52.

Bath, K.S. (1972) The distribution and spatial patterns of Punjabi population in Wolverhampton. Unpublished MA thesis, Aberystwyth, University of Wales.

Bellin, W. (1995) Psychology and bilingual education: Intelligence tests and the influence of pedagogy. In B.M. Jones and P.A.S. Ghuman (eds) *Bilingualism Education and Identity* (pp. 189–221). Cardiff: University of Wales Press.

Berry, J.W. (1994) Acculturation and psychological adaptation: An Overview. In A. Bouvy *et al.* (ed.) *Journeys into Cross-Cultural Psychology: Selected Papers*

from the Eleventh International Conference of IACCP, held in Liege, Belgium.
Bhachu, P. (1985a) *Twice Immigrants: East African Settlers in Britain*. London: Tavistock.
—— (1985b) Prenatal education strategies: The case of Punjabi Sikhs in Britain. *Research Papers in Ethnic Relations*. No. 3. Warwick: Centre for Research in Ethnic Relations.
—— (1985c) Multilingual education: Parental views. *New Community* 12 (1), 9–21.
Bhargava, S.K., Ramji, S., Sachdev, H.P. and Iyer, P.U. (1986) Delivery of perinatal care in India: priorities and policies. *Ann Trop Paediatr.* 6 (4), 225–31.
Bhatnagar, J. (ed.) (1981) *Educating Immigrants*. London: Croom Helm.
—— (1981) Multiculturalism and education of immigrants in Canada. In J. Bhatnagar (ed.) *Educating Immigrants*. London: Croom Helm.
Bhopal, R.S. (1986) Bhye bhaddi: a food and health concept of Punjabi Asians. *Sociology of Science Medicine* 23 (7), 687–8.
Birns, B. and Hay, D.F. (eds) (1988) *The Different Faces Of Motherhood*. New York: Plenum Press.
Black, J. (1988) Paediatrics among ethnic minorities. *British Medical Journal* 290, 830–3.
Booth, E. B. and Verma, M. (1992) Decreased access to medical care for girls in Punjab, India: The roles of age, religion, and distance. *Public Health Briefs* 82 (8), 1155–7.
Bornstein, H.M. (ed.) (1991) *Cultural Approaches To Parenting*. Hove and London: Lawrence Erlbaum Associates.
Bouvier, L.F. and Agresta, A.J. (1985) The fastest growing minority. *American Demographics* 7 (46), 31–3.
Brimblecombe, F. (1980) *Child Rearing: Fashion or Science*. Exeter: University of Exeter.
Bronfenbrenner, U. (1986) The ecology of the family as a context for human development: research perspectives. *Developmental Psychology* 22, 723–42.
—— (1994) Foreword. In A. Levine *et al. Child Care and Culture: Lessons from Africa*. Cambridge/University Press.
Brown, C. (1984) *Black and White Britain: The Third PSI Survey*. London: Gower.
Buchignani, N., Indra, M.D. and Srivastiva, R. (1985) *Continuous Journey: A Social History of South Asians in Canada*. Toronto: McMelland Stewart in Association with Multiculturalism Directorate.
Bullivant, M.B. (1978) Towards a neo-ethnographic method for small-group research. *Australia & New Zealand Journal of Sociology* 14 (3), 239–49.
Bullock Report (1974) *A Language for Life*. London: Her Majesty's Stationery Office.
Butler, N. and Golding, J. (1986) *From Birth to Five: A Study of the Health and Behaviour of Britain's Five Year Olds*. Oxford: Pergamon.
Caldwell, J.A.W. and Berthold, M.J. (1995) Aspects of bilingual education in Australia. In B.R. Jones and P.A.S. Ghuman (eds) *Bilingualism Education and Identity*. Cardiff: University of Wales Press.
Cardens, R. (1988) *Parental Behaviour in Diverse Societies*. San Francisco: Jossey-Bass.
Carter, B.D. and Middlemiss W.A. (1992) The socialisation of instrumental competence in families in the United States. In J.L. Roopnarine and D. Carter

(eds) *Parent–Child Socialization in Diverse Cultures.* Norwood: Ablex Publishing Corporation.
Caudhill, W. and Plath, D.W. (1966) Who sleeps by whom? Parent-child involvement in urban Japanese families. *Psychiatry* 344–53.
Chadney, G.J. (1980) Sikh family patterns and ethnic adaptation in Vancouver *AMERASIA* 7 (1), 31–50.
Charlot, M. (1981) The education of immigrant children in France. In J. Bhatnagar (ed.) *Educating Immigrants.* London: Croom Helm.
Cheng, Y. and Heath, A. (1993) Ethnic and class destinations. *Oxford Review of Education* 19 (2), 151–65.
Chetcuti, P., Sinha, H.S. and Levine, I.M. (1985) Birth size in Indian ethnic subgroups born in Britain. *Archives of Diseases in Childhood* 60, 868–73.
Chieu, I. (1987) Child-rearing attitudes of Chinese, Chinese-American and Anglo-American mothers. *International Journal of Psychology* 22 (4), 409–19.
Clark, A.M. and Clark, A.D.B. (1976) *Early Experience: Myth and Evidence.* London: Open Books.
Clarke, M., Clayton, G.D. Mason A. and MacVicar, S.E. (1988) Asian mothers' risk factors for perinatal death – the same or different? A 10 year review of Leicestershire prenatal deaths. *British Medical Journal* 297, 384–7.
Clarke, C., Peach, C. and Vertovec, S. (1990) *South Asians Overseas: Migration and Ethnicity.* Cambridge: Cambridge University Press.
Cohen, R. (1991) East-West and European migration in a global context. *New Community* 18 (1), 9–26.
Commission For Racial Equality (CRE) (1987) *Learning in Terror.* London: CRE.
Dahya, B. (1972) Pakistanis in England. *New Community* 2, 25–33.
Davenport, E. (1983) The play of Sikh children in a nursery class and at home. *Educational Review* 35 (2), 127–39.
Davey, G.A. (1977) Racial awareness and social identity in young children. *Mental Health Society* 4, 255–62.
Daws , D. (1989) *Through the Night: Helping Parents and Sleepless Infants.* London: Free Association Books.
Dekker, J.J. and Groenendijk, L.F. (1991) The republic of God or the republic of children? Childhood and child-rearing after the Reformation: An appraisal. *Oxford Review of Education* 17 (3), 317–35.
de Mause L. (ed.) (1974) *The History of Childhood.* London: Souvenir Press.
Desai, R. (1963) *Indian Immigrants in Britain.* London: Oxford University Press.
Dhaya, B. (1972) Pakistani in England. *New Community,* 2, 25–33.
Dix, T. Ruble, D.N. and Zambarano, R.J. (1989) Mothers' implicit theories of discipline: child effects, parent effects, and the attribution process. *Child Development* 60, 1373–91.
Donoghue, E.C. and Shakespeare, R. (1967) The reliability of paediatric case history milestones. *Development Medicine and Child Neurology* 9, 64–9.
Dosanjh, J.S. (1968) Punjabi immigrant children: Their social and educational problems of adjustment. *Education Papers No. 10.* School of Education, Nottingham University.
—— (1976) Child-rearing practices of Punjabi parents with special reference to lower juniors (7–9). Unpublished Ph.D. thesis. Centre for Child Development, Nottingham University.
Drury, B. (1991) Sikh girls and the maintenance of an ethnic culture. *New Community* 17 (3), 387–400.

Dunn, J. (1988) *The Beginning of Social Understanding.* Oxford: Basil Blackwell.
Dworkin, J.R. (1980) Differential process in acculturation: The case of Asiatic Indians in the United States. *Plural Societies* 11 (21), 43–57.
Eisenman, R. and Sirgo, B.H. (1991) Liberals versus conservatives: Personality, child-rearing attitudes, and birth order/sex differences. *Bulletin of the Psychonomic Society* 29 (3), 240–2.
Eldering, L. (1994) A theoretical model for understanding child rearing in ethnic minority families. Paper presented at the Conference of the IACCP, Pamplona, 24–27 July 1994.
—— (1995) Child rearing in bicultural settings: A culture-ecological approach. *Psychology and Developing Societies.* (In press).
Ellis, J.G. and Petersen, R.L. (1992) Socialization values and parental control techniques: A cross-cultural analysis of child-rearing. *Journal of Comparative Family Studies* 23 (1), 39–54.
Farooqi, S., Perry, I.J., and Beevers, D.G (1993) Ethnic differences in infant-rearing practices and their possible relationship to the incidence of sudden infant death syndrome. *Paediatric and Perinatal Epidemiology* 7, 245–52.
Finkle, D. and McGue, M. (1993) Twenty-five year follow-up of child-rearing practices: Reliability of retrospective data. *Personality and Individual Differences* 15 (2), 147–54.
Firdous, R. and Bhopal, R.S. (1989) Reproductive health of Asian women: A comparative study with hospital and community perspectives. *Public Health* 103 (4), 307–15.
Fontana, D. (1994) *Psychology For Teachers.* London: The British Psychological Society in association with Macmillan.
Forrey, R. and Hegelus, A. (1989) Differences in the upbringing and behaviour of Romany boys and girls. *J. of Multilingual and Multicultural Development,* 10 (6), 89, 515–28.
Garforth, S. and Garcia, J. (1989) Breast feeding policies in practice – 'No wonder they get confused'. *Midwifery* 5, 75–83.
Ghosh, R. (1983) Sarees and the maple leaf: Indian women in Canada. In G. Kurian and R.P. Srivastava (eds) *Overseas Indians: A Study in Adaptation.* New Delhi: A Population Review Book.
Ghuman, P.A.S. (1979) The nature of intellectual development of Punjabi children. *International Journal of Psychology* 13 (4), 1–14.
—— (1980a) Punjabi parents and English education. *Educational Research* 22 (2), 121–30.
—— (1980b) Bhattra Sikhs in Cardiff: Family and kinship organisation. *New Community* 9 (3), 308–16.
—— (1980c) A study of the concept of equivalence and divergent thinking among four sub-groups of Punjabi children. *International Review of Applied Psychology,* 29, 89–99.
—— (1980d) Problems in cross-cultural research – from a Punjabi perspective. *Enface, Special,* No. 4/5, 192–195.
—— (1994a) *Coping With Two Cultures: A Study of British Asians and Indo-Canadian Adolescents.* Clevedon: Multilingual Matters.
—— (1994b) Canadian or Indo-Canadian: A study of South Asian adolescents. *International Journal of Adolescence of Youth* 4, 229–43.
—— (1994c) Indo-Canadian Parents' Perceptions of Canadian Schooling.

Multicultural Education Journal 12 (1), 21–31.
—— (1995) *Asian Teachers in British Schools: A Study of Two Generations.* Clevedon: Multilingual Matters.
—— (1975) *The Cultural Context of Thinking.* Slough: NFER.
—— and Blake, M. (1987) Education of Bangladeshi children in Sylhet and London. *British Journal of Educational Psychology* 57, Abstract, pp. 100.
—— and Gallop, R. (1981) A study of Bengali parents' perceptions of and attitudes to education in Cardiff. *Journal of Multilingual & Multicultural Development* 2 (2), 127–44.
—— and Kamath A. (1993) Bi-cultural identities of primary school children. *The Bilingual Family News Letter* 10 (1), 3–7.
—— and Wong, R. (1989) Chinese parents and English education. *Educational Research* 31 (2), 134–40.
Gibson, A.M. (1988) *Accommodation Without Assimilation.* Ithaca and London: Cornell University Press.
Gill, O. and Jackson, B. (1983) *Adoption and Race: Black, Asian and Mixed Race Children in White Families.* London: Batsford.
Gonzalez-Mena, J. (1993) *Multicultural Issues in Child Care.* Mountain View, California: Mayfield Publishing Company.
Goodnow, J.J. (1988) Parents' ideas, actions, and feelings: Models and methods from developmental and social psychology. *Child Development* 59, 489–505.
Goodwin, R. and Emelyanova, T. (1995) The privatization of the personal? II: Attitudes to the family and child-rearing values in modern-day Russia. *Journal of Social and Personal Relationships* 12 (1), 132–8.
Green, P. (1977) *The Protestant Temperament.* New York: Alfred A. Knopf.
Grindulus, H., Scott, P.H., Belton, N.R. and Wharton, B.A. (1986) Combined deficiency of iron and vitamin D in Asian toddlers. *Archive of Disease in Childhood* 61, 843–8.
Grotberg, E.H. and Bardin, G. (1990) Shifting from traditional to modern child rearing practices in the Sudan. *Early Child Development and Care* 50 (89), 141–150.
Gupta, G.R. (1978) The joint family. In M.S. Das and P.D. Bardis (eds) *The Family in Asia* (pp. 72–88). New Delhi: Vikas.
Guttiereiez, J., Sameroff, A.J. and Karrer, B.M. (1988) Acculturation and SES effects on Mexican-American parents' concepts of development. *Child Development* 59, 250–5.
Hackett, L. and Hackett, R. (1993) Parental ideas of normal and deviant child behaviour: A comparison of two ethnic groups. *British Journal of Psychiatry* 162, 353–7.
—— (1994) Child-rearing practices and psychiatric disorder in Gujarati and British children. *British Journal of Social Work* 24, 191–202.
Hackett, L., Hackett, R. and Taylor, C.D. (1991) Psychological disturbance and its associations in the children of the Gujarati Community. *Journal of Child Psychology and Psychiatry* 32 (5), 851–6.
Hargreaves, D.J. and Colley, A.M. (1980) Parental punishment strategies with eleven-year-old children. In N. Frude (ed.) *Psychological Approaches to Child Abuse.* London: Batsford.
Harkness, S. (1992) Cross-cultural research in child development: A sample of the state of the art. *Development Psychology* 28 (4), 622–5.
Hays, N. (1993) *Foundations of Psychology.* London: Routledge.

Helweg, A.W. (1986) *Sikhs in England.* Delhi: Oxford University Press.

Her Majesty's Stationery Office (1995) *Social Trends.* London: HMSO.

Hilder, A.S. (1994) Ethnic differences in the sudden infant death syndrome: What we can learn from immigrants to the UK. *Early Human Development* 38 (3), 143–9.

Holden, W.G. and Edwards, A.L. (1989) Parental attitudes toward child rearing: Instruments, issues, and implications. *Psychological Bulletin* 106 (1), 29–58.

Holme, J. (1984) Growing up in Hinduism. *British Journal of Religious Education,* Summer, 116–20.

Home Affairs Committee (1986) *Bangladeshis in Britain: Vol. 1.* London: HMSO.

Jackson, R. and Nesbitt, E. (1993) The diversity of experience in the religious upbringing of children from Christian families in Britain. *British Journal of Religious Education* 15 (1), 19–28.

Jones, B.M. and Ghuman, P.A.S. (1995) *Bilingualism, Education and Identity.* Cardiff: University of Wales Press.

Jones, T. (1993) *Britain Ethnic Minorities: An Analysis of the Labour Force Survey.* London: Policy Studies Institute..

Kagan, J. (1984) *The Nature of the Child.* New York: Basic Books, Inc.

Kagitcibasi, C. and Berry, J.W. (1989) Cross-cultural psychology: Current research and trends. *Annual Review of Psychology* 40, 493–531.

Kakar, S. (1979) Childhood in India. *International Social Science Journal* 31, (3), 444–56.

—— (1994) *The Inner World of the Indian Child.* New Delhi: Oxford University Press.

Kapasi, H. and Shier, H. (1994) Asian children's play: Working towards equal opportunities in play for Asian children in the UK. *International Play Journal* 2, 107–17.

Kaye, K. (1982) *The Mental and Social Life of Babies: How Parents Create Persons.* London: Methuen.

Kelly, E. and Cohen, T. (1988) *Racism in Schools: New Research Evidence.* Stoke: Trentham Books.

Kelly, M. and Tseng, Hui-Mei (1992) Cultural differences in child rearing: A comparison of immigrant Chinese and Caucasian American mothers. *Journal of Cross-Cultural Psychology* 23 (4), 444–55.

Kim, Y. and Gudyknust, W.B. (eds) (1988) *Cross-Cultural Adaptation: Current Approaches.* Newbury Park, CA: Sage.

Klucholn, F.R. and Strodbeck, F.L. (1961) *Variations in Value Orientations.* Chicago: Row, Peterson.

Kohli, S.H. (1989) A comparison of smoking and drinking among Asian and white school children in Glasgow. *Public Health* 13, 433–9.

Krause, B-I, Rosser, M.L., Khiani, P. and Lotay, N.S. (1990) Psychiatric morbidity among Punjabi medical patients in England measured by General Health Questionnaire. *Psychological Medicine* 20, 711–19.

Kumar, T.K. (1992) To children with love. *British Medical Journal* 305, 1582–3.

Kurtz, N.S. (1992) *All the Mothers Are One: Hindu India and the Cultural Reshaping of Psychoanalysis.* New York: Columbia University Press.

Kysel, F. (1988) Ethnic background and examination results. *Educational Research* 3(2), 83–9.

La Fontaine, J. (1990) *Child Sexual Abuse.* Cambridge: Polity Press.

Lane, J. (1992) Challenging racism in European child care. *Early Years* 12 (2), 29–30.

La Rossa, R. and La Rossa, M.M. (1981) *Transition to Parenthood: How Infants Change Families*. London: Sage.
Leonard, K. (1992) *Making Ethnic Choices: California's Punjabi Mexican Americans*. Philadelphia: University of Philadelphia Press.
—— (1993) Historical constructions of ethnicity: Research on Punjabi immigrants in California. *Journal of American Ethnic History* 12 (4), 3–25.
Levine, A. (1988) A cross-cultural perspective on parenting. In M.D. Fantini and R. Cardenas (eds) *Parenting in Multicultural Society*. New York: Longman.
Levine, A. *et al.* (1994) *Child Care and Culture: Lessons from Africa*. Cambridge: Cambridge University Press.
Levy-Bruhl, L. (1985) *How Natives Think*. New Jersey: Princeton University.
Li-Repac, D.C. (1982) The impact of acculturation on the child-rearing attitudes and practices of Chinese-American families: Consequences for the attachment process. PhD thesis, University of California, Berkeley.
Lin, C. Chin-Yau and Fu, R.V. (1990) *Child Development* 61(2), 429–33.
Lui, B.J. (1990) Asian-American child-rearing practices and acculturation: a cross-cultural examination. Unpublished Ph.D thesis, University of Washington.
Luschinsky, M.S. (1962) The life of women in a village of north India: A study of role and status. Ph.D. Dissertation, Cornell University.
Maan, B. (1992) *The New Scots*. Edinburgh; John Donald Publishers.
MacArthur, C., Lewis, M. and Knox, G.E. (1993) Comparison of long-term health problems following childbirth among Asian and Caucasian mothers. *British Journal of General Practice* 43, 519–22.
Manderson, L. (1994) Vietnamese attitudes towards maternal and infant health. In P.L. Rice (ed.) *Asian Mothers, Australian Birth: Pregnancy, Childbirth, and Childrearing*. Ausmed Publications.
Mao, J. and Maisnam, P. (1994) Child-rearing practices in Ghari village: A suburban area of Manipur. *Man in India* 74 (1), 87–89.
Mason, E.S. (1990) The Asian mother and baby campaign (The Leicester Experience). *The Journal of the Royal Society of Health* 110 (1), 1–9.
McEnery, G. and Rao, K.P.S. (1986) The effectiveness of antenatal education of Pakistani and Indian women living in this country. *Child: Care, Health and Development* 12, 385–99.
McNally, S., Eisenbeerg, N. and Harris, D.J. (1991) Consistency and change in maternal child-rearing practices and values: A longitudinal study. *Child Development* 62, 190–98.
Michaels, G.Y. and Goldberg, W.A. (eds) *Transition to Parenthood: Theory and Research*. Cambridge, MA: Ballinger.
Miles, R. (1994) A rise of racism and fascism in contemporary Europe?: Some sceptical reflections on its nature and extent. *New Community*, 20 (4), 547–62.
Milner, D. (1983) *Children and Race: Ten Years On*. London: Ward Lock Educational.
Mishra, P.J. and Jain, S. (1994) Child rearing practices and cognitive ability: A study of adolescents. *Psychologia*, 37, 111–15.
Modood, T. (1993) The number of ethnic minority students in British higher education: Some grounds for optimism. *Oxford Review of Education* 19 (2), 167–82.
Moran, S., Smith, P.K., Thompson, D. and Whitney, I. (1993) Ethnic differences

in experiences of bullying: Asian and white children. *British Journal of Educational Psychology* 63, 431–440.
Musgrove, F. (1970) The 'Good Home'. In M. Craft, (ed.) *Family, Class and Education: A Reader.* London: Longman.
Nehru, J. (1946) *The Discovery of India.* London: Deridan Books Ltd.
Neki, J.S. (1976) An examination of cultural relativism of dependence as a dynamic of social and therapeutic relationships. *British Journal of Medical Psychology* 49 (1), 1–10.
Nesbitt, E. (1993) Gender and religious tradition: The role-learning of British Hindu children. *Gender and Education* 5 (1), 81–91.
—— (1994) Valmikis in Coventry: The revival and reconstruction of a community. In R. Ballard (ed.) *Desh Pardesh.* London: C. Hurst & Co.
Newson, J. and Newson, E. (1968) *Four Years Old in an Urban Community.* Harmondsworth: Penguin.
—— (1976) *Seven Years Old in the Home Environment.* Harmondsworth: Penguin.
—— (1986) Family and sex roles in middle childhood. In D.J. Hargreaves and A.M. Colley (eds) *The Psychology of Sex Roles.* London: Harper & Row.
Ogbu, J.U. (1981) Origins of human competence: A cultural-ecological perspective. *Child Development* 52, 413–29.
Ogbu, J.U. (1988) Cultural diversity and human development. In D. Slaughter (ed.) *Black Children and Poverty: A Development Perspective* (pp. 11–28). San Francisco: Jossey-Bass.
Ogbu, J.U. (1994) Understanding cultural diversity and learning. *Journal for Education of the Gifted* 17 (4), 355–83.
Owen, D. (1992) *National Ethnic Minority Data Archive: 1991 Census Statistical Paper No. 1.* Warwick: Centre for Research in Ethnic Relations.
Parekh, B. (1986) The structure of authority within the Indian family. In K.A. Brah (ed.), *Working with Asian Young People.* London: National Association for Asian Youth.
—— (1994) Some reflections on the Hindu dispora. *New Community* 20 (4), 603–20.
Park, K.J. and Honing. S.A. (1991) Infant child care patterns and later teacher ratings of pre-school behaviours. *Early Child Development and Care* 68 (91), 89–96.
Parker-Jenkins, M. (1995) *Children of Islam.* Stoke-on-Trent: Trentham Books.
Parsons, I. and Day, S. (1992) Improving obstetric outcomes in ethnic minorities: An evaluation of health advocacy in Hackney. *Public Health Medicine* 14 (2), 183–91.
Patel, N.V. (1989) Childrearing in Hindu Gujarati Indian families in America: Effects of modernity and acculturation. Unpublished MA thesis, Department of Psychology, University of Houston.
Peel, A. and Clarke, M. (1990) Pregnant women at work: a study of ethnic minority risk in Leicestershire. *British Journal of Industrial Medicine* 47, 649–55.
Penn, R. and Scattergood, H. (1992) Ethnicity and career aspirations in contemporary Britain. *New Community* 19 (1), 75–95.
Phoenix, A., Woollett, A. and Lloyd, E. (eds) (1991) *Young Mothers.* Cambridge: Polity Press.
Power, G.T., Kobayashi-Winata, H. and Kelly, L.M. (1992) Childrearing patterns

in Japan and the United States. *International Journal of Behavioural Development* 15 (2), 185–205.
Press, B.K. (1989) Observations on family life, child rearing and education in the Soviet Union today. *Early Child Development and Care* 50 (89), 11–23.
Pringle, K. (1974) *The Needs of Children*. London: Hutchinson.
Ramanujam, B.K. (1972) *The Indian Family in Transition*. New Delhi: Sterling Publishers.
Raufi, S. (1981) The children of guest-workers in the Federal Republic of Germany: Maladjustment and its effects on academic performance. In J. Bhatnagar (ed.) *Educating Immigrants*. London: Croom Helm.
Rex, J. and Tomlinson, S. (1979) *Colonial Immigrants in a British City: A Class Analysis*. London: Routledge & Kegan Paul.
Rex, J. (1985) The concept of a multicultural society. *Occasional Papers in Ethnic Relations, No. 3*. Warwick: Centre for Research in Ethnic Relations.
Rice, P.L. (ed.) (1994) *Asian Mothers, Australian Birth: Pregnancy, Childbirth and Childrearing: The Asian experience in an English-speaking country*. Melbourne: Ausmed Publications.
Robins, L.C. (1963) The accuracy of parental recall of aspects of child development and of child rearing practices. *Journal of Abnormal and Social Psychology* 66 (3), 261–70.
Roland, A. (1980) Psychoanalytic perspectives of personality development in India. *International Review of Psycho-Analysis* 7, 73–87.
Rona, R.J., Chin, S., Duggal, S. and Driver, A.P. (1987) Vegetarianism and growth in Urdu, Gujarati, and Punjabi Children in Britain. *Journal Epidemiol. Community Health* 41 (3), 233–36.
Roopnariane, L.R. and Carter B.C. (eds) (1992) *Parent-Child Socialization in Diverse Cultures*. New Jersey: Alex Publishing Corporation.
—— and Hossain, Z. (1992) Parent-child interactions in urban Indian families in New Delhi: Are they changing? In L.R. Roopnariane and B.D. Carter (eds), *Parent-Child Socialization in Diverse Cultures*. New Jersey: Alex Publishing Corporation.
Rose, E.J.B. and Associates (1969) *Colour and Citizenship: A Report on British Race Relations*. London: Oxford University Press.
Rowe, C.D. (1990) As the twig is bent? The myth of child-rearing influences on personality development. *Journal of Counselling & Development* 68, 606–11.
Rusk, R.R. (1969) *The Doctrines of the Great Educators*. London: Macmillan.
Rutter, M., Tizard, J. and Witmore, K. (1970) *Education, Health and Behaviour*. London: Longman.
Saran, P. (1985) *The Asian Indian Experience in the United States*. Cambridge, MA: Schenkman.
Saraswathi, T.S. and Dutta, R. (1987) Cross-cultural research in developmental psychology: Retrospect and prospect in India. In Kagitcibasi, C. (ed.) *Growth & Progress in Cross-cultural Psychology*. Berwyn: Swets North America Inc.
—— (1989) Current trends in developmental psychology: A life-span perspective. In J. Pandey (ed.) *ICSSR Third Survey of Researches in Psychology*. New Delhi: Sage.
Sarwar, G. (1983) *Muslim and Education in the UK*. London: The Muslim Education Trust.
Schwartz, T. (1981) The acquisition of culture. *Ethos* 9, 4–17.

Segal, A.U. (1991) Cultural variables in Asian Indian families. *Families in Society: The Journal of Contemporary Human Services* 72 (4), 233–42.
Sethi, R.R. (1990) *Inter-cultural Communication and Adaptation Among First-generation Asian–Indian Immigrants*. Paper presented at the conference on: *Individualism and Collectivism*, held in Seoul, Korea, 9–13 July 1990, organised by the Korean Psychological Association.
Seymore, S. (1976) Caste/class and child rearing in a changing Indian town. *America Ethnologist* 3 (4), 783–96.
Sharma, V.P. (1981) *Indian Urban Families: Child-Rearing Practices and Child Growth*. New Delhi: National Council of Educational Research and Training.
Sharma, N. (1990) Current trends in infant care: An Indian experience. *Early Child Development and Care* 58, 71–9.
Sharp, S. (1976) *Just like a Girl: How Girls Learn to be Women*. Harmondsworth: Penguin.
—— (1984) *Double Identity: The Lives of Working Mothers*. Harmondsworth: Penguin.
Shaw, A. (1988) *A Pakistani Community in Britain*. London: Basil Blackwell.
—— (1994) The Pakistani Community in Oxford. In J. Ballard (ed.) *Desh Pardesh*. London: Hurst & Co.
Sheldon, A.T. and Parker, H. (1992) Race and ethnicity in health research. *Journal of Public Health Medicine* 14 (2), 104–10.
Singh, D.K. (1992) Perceptions of child-rearing practices, adjustment and academic achievement of children of working and non-working mothers. MPhil dissertation, University of Punjab, Chandigarh, India.
Sinha, D. (ed.) (1981) *Socialization of the Indian Child*. New Delhi: Concept.
—— (1982) *Cross-Cultural Psychology: A View From the Third World*. Presidential address to the 6th International Congress of IACCP, Aberdeen, 19–23 July 1982.
—— (1984) *The Family Scenario of a Developing Country and its Implications for Mental Health*. Paper presented at the WHO Workshop on Applications of Cross-Cultural psychology to the promotion of Healthy Development. Mexico City, August, 1984.
Skutnabb-Kangas, T. and Cummins, J. (eds) (1988) *Minority Education: From Shame to Struggle*. Clevedon: Multilingual Matters.
Smith, J.D. (1977) *Racial Disadvantage in Britain: The PEP Report*. Harmondsworth: Penguin Books.
—— and Tomlinson, S. (1989) *The School Effect: A Study of Multi-racial Comprehensives*. London: Policy Studies Institute.
Spock, B. (1958) *Baby and child Care*. New York: Bodley Head.
Steinberg, L., Elmen, J.D. and Mounts, N.S. (1989) Authoritative parenting, psychosocial maturity, and academic success among adolescents. *Child Development* 60, 1424–36.
Stevenson, H., Azuma, H. and Hakuta, K. (1986) *Child Development and Education in Japan*. New York: W.H. Freeman & Company.
Stopes-Roe, M. and Cochrane, R. (1988) Marriage in two cultures. *British Journal of Social Psychology* 27, 159–69.
—— (1989) Traditionalism in the family: A comparison between Asian and British cultures and between generations. *Journal of Comparative Family Studies* XX (2), 142–58.
—— (1990) The child-rearing values of Asian and British parents and young

people: An inter-ethnic and inter-generational comparison in the evaluation of Kohn's qualities. *British Journal of Social Psychology* 29, 149–60.

—— (1991) *Citizens of this Country: The Asian-British.* Cleveland: Multilingual Matters.

Stubbs, M. (ed.) (1985) *The Other Languages of England Linguistic Minority Project.* London: Routledge & Kegan Paul.

Surya, N.C. (1969) Ego-structure in the Hindu joint family: Some considerations. In W. Caudhill and Tsung-Yi Lin (eds) *Mental Health Research in Asia and the Pacific* (pp. 381–92). East-West Centre Press.

Swann Report (1985) *Education for All.* London: HMSO.

Taft, R. (1966) *From Stranger to Citizens.* London: Tavistock Publications.

Taylor, J.H. (1976) *The Half-way Generation.* Windsor: NFER.

Taylor, M.J. and Hegarty, S. (1985) The Best of Both Worlds ...? Windsor: NFER-Nelson.

Thirkell, B. and Worrall, N. (1989) Differential ethnic bias in Bengali and white children. *Educational Research* 31 (3), 181–88.

Tizard, B., Blatchford, P., Burke, J., Farquhar, C. and Pelwis, I. (1988) *Young Children at School in Inner City.* London: Lawrence Erlbaum Associates Publishers.

Tomlinson, J. (1991) Attitude to children: Are children valued? *Early Years,* 11 (2), 39–42.

Tomlinson, S. (1984) *Home and School in Multicultural Britain.* London: Batsford.

Triandis, H.C. (1994) Theoretical and methodological approaches to the study of collectivism and individualism. In K. Uichol *et al.* (eds) *Individualism and Collectivism: Theory, Method and Applications* (p. 41–51). London: Sage Publications.

Troyna, B. and Hatcher, R. (1992) *Racism in Children's Lives.* London: Routledge in Association with the National Children's Bureau.

Trueba, T.H., Lilley, R.L. and Ima, K. (1993) *Myth or Reality: Adaptive Strategies of Asian Americans in California.* London: The Falmer Press.

Turner, P. (1985) Asian infant feeding. *Nursing Mirror* 160 (21), 14–15.

Vaidyanathan, P. and Naidoo, J. (1989) *Asian Indians in Western Countries: Cultural Identity and the Arranged Marriage.* Paper presented at the 2nd Regional Conference of IACCP, Amsterdam.

Vedder, P., Bouwer, E. and Pels, T. (1995) *Multicultural Child Care.* Clevedon: Multilingual Matters.

Verma, G.K. (1986) *Ethnicity and Educational Achievements in British Schools.* London: Macmillan.

——., Zec, P. and Skinner, G. (1994) *The Ethnic Crucible: Harmony and Hostility in Multi-Ethnic Schools.* London: The Falmer Press.

Vernon, P.E. (1969) *Intelligence and Cultural Environment.* London: Methuen.

Visram, R. (1986) *Ayahs, Lascars and Princes.* London: Pluto Press.

Wade, B. and Souter, P. (1991) *Continuing to Think: The British Asian Girl.* Clevedon: Multilingual Matters.

Wadsworth, M.E. (1985) Parenting skills and their transmission through generations. *Adoption and Fostering* 9, 28–32.

Wagner, A.D. and Stevenson, W.H. (eds) (1982) *Cultural Perspectives on Child Development.* San Francisco: W.H. Freeman and Company.

Warrington, S. and Storey, D.M. (1988) Comparative studies on Asian and Caucasian Children. 2: Nutrition, feeding practices and health. *European*

Journal of Clinical Nutrition 42, 69–80.
Webster, R. (1995) *Why Freud Was Wrong: Sin Science and Psychoanalysis*. London: HarperCollins Publishers.
Westwood, S. and Bhachu, P. (1988) *Enterprising Women: Ethnicity, Economy and Gender Relations*. London: Routledge.
Wheldall, K. and Merrett, (1984) *Positive Teaching: The Behavioural Approach*. London: George Allen & Unwin.
Whiting, B.B. and Whiting, J.W.N. (1975) *Children of Six Cultures: A Psycho-Cultural Analysis*. Cambridge, MA, Harvard University Press.
Whiting, B.B. and Edwards, S. (1988) *Children of Different Worlds*. Harvard: Harvard University Press.
Williams, R., Bhopal, R. and Hunt, K. (1993) Health of a Punjabi ethnic minority in Glasgow: A comparison with the general population. *Journal of Epidemiology and Community Health* 47, 96–102.
Williams, R., Bhopal, R., Hunt, K. (1994) Coronary risk in a British Punjabi population: Comparative profile of non-biochemical factors. *International Journal of Epidemiology* 23(1), 28–36.
Williamson, N.E. (1976) *Sons or Daughters: A Cross-Cultural Survey of Parental Preference*. London: Lawrence Erlbaum Associates.
Wilson, A. (1978) *Finding a Voice: Asian Women in Britain*. London: Virago.
Witkin, H. *et al.* (1974) Social conformity and psychological differentiation. *International Journal of Psychology* 9(1), 11–13.
Woollett, A. and Dosanjh-Matwala, N. (1990a) Pregnancy and antenatal care: the attitudes and experiences of Asian women. *Child: Care, Health and Development* 16, 63–78.
—— (1990b) Asian women's experiences of childbirth in the East End: The support of fathers and female relatives. *Journal of Reproductive and Infant Psychology* 8, 11–22.
Woollett, A., Dosanjh-Matwala, N. and Hadlow, J. (1991) Reproductive decision making: Asian women's ideas about family size and the gender and spacing of children. *Journal of Reproductive and Infant Psychology* 9, 237–52.
Woollett, A., *et al.* (1995) The ideas and experiences of pregnancy and childbirth of Asian and non-Asian women in East London. *British Journal of Medical Psychology* 68, 65–84.
Wrench, J. (1992) Employment and Labour Market. *New Community* 18 (4), 603–10.
Wright, C. (1992) Early education: Multiracial primary school classrooms. In D. Gill, B. Mayor and M. Blair (eds) *Racism and Education: Structures and Strategies*. London: Sage Publication in association with the Open University.
Yarrow, M.R., Campbell, J.D. and Burton, R.V. (1968) *Child Rearing: An inquiry into Research and Methods*. San Francisco: Jossey-Bass.
Yee, G. (1991) *The melting pot revisited: A literature review of current literature in multicultural education*. Unpublished manuscript. University of California, Berkeley Department of Anthropology, Special project.
Zaidi, F. (1994) The maternity care of Muslim women. *Modern Midwife*, March 1994, 8–10.

Appendix: Questionnaire

<u>For mothers of ethnic minority children between the ages of seven and nine years.</u>

Interviewer ....
Date..................................

A. 1. BACKGROUND
Child's full name...
Date of birth.............................Sex: Boy/Girl
Address...
....
....

Do you own this property? Yes/No
Sole owner/joint owner/Tenant

2 Family size and position:

For each child in the family, indicate sex and age: include foster children marked F and mark a ring round the child included in the study.

Sex:	
Age:	

HOUSING: Modern detached/Modern semi/ Victorian detached/Victorian semi/ Victorian terraced/ Terrace with bays/Terraced without bays/Self contained flat/rooms/Council house or estate/Council (not estate)/Council flat/Others...

DECORATIONS:
Art reproductions/Punjabi or English calendars/ Paint or paper on walls/Family photographs/Bare walls/Fresh or artificial flowers/Indoor plants/ Others..

OTHER COMMENTS:
Overcrowding/Cleanliness/Others...................................

HEATING: Gas fires/Open fires/Central heating/Others.........................
Television/Hi-fi/Washing machine/Dishwasher/Microwave/Floor coverings/Others........

3. MOTHER: Age.............Not working/Working part-time/Full-time/Occupation if at work..
If working who looks after N/Children?............................

4. FATHER: Age.............Precise occupation..................................

Does he have to be away from home at all except just during the day?...........
Home every night/Up to two nights away per week/Three nights away per week/Normally away/Separation divorce/Dead/Others.............................

Shift work? Yes/No................What shifts.................

5 Country of birth Mother Father
....

If not this country when did you come to this country?.............................
(If applicable) When did your husband come to this country?.....................
(If applicable) When did your father come to this country..........................
(If applicable) When did your grandfather come to this country...................

Where was ..N... born?
Punjab/England/Others......................................

6 Would you mind telling me about your education?
How many years did you spend at school/College/University?
How many years did your husband spend at school/College/University?

FORMAL EDUCATION

	No of years.	Mother	Father
	No education		
Primary:	1 - 2 years		
	Up to four years		
Middle:	5 - 8 years		
Matriculation:	9 - 10 years		
Intermediate:	10 - 12 years		
Degree and Over:	12 - 14 years		
Training			

7 What is your religion?...............Denomination?................................

8 Did you want a baby boy or girl?...

9 BIRTH DATA
Where was ..N... born? Home.Hospital/Others..........................
Apart from the Doctor/ Midwife or Nurse was anybody else present at the time of birth?..
How soon were you out of bed for the whole day?................................
Did you have any special exercises during your pregnancy?........................
If yes, specify for how long and whose advice?....................................

10 Did you have any help after the baby was born?....................................
Husband at home all day/Relative/Neighbour/Friend/Local Authority Home help/Private paid help/Others...
For how long?..
If other than husband, specify whether living in? Yes/No
Do you normally have any help in the house?......................................
Specify how often, whether paid...

11 How was the name of..N...decided? ....
(If applicable) Who decided? ....

12 Did you observe any ritual or custom in connection with ..N?....................
(Prompt after giving time for initial response)
e.g. a Taking ..N...to a temple/mosque within a specified period?....
b Hair cutting ceremomy?..
c Alms giving during special occasions..............................
d can you think of any other of this kind?............................

13 **Feeding :**

History: Age in months

	0	1	2	3	4	5	6	7	8	9
Breast:										
Bottle:										

Breast Feeding

If little or not breast feeding, did you have any special reason for not breast feeding?...

When stopped, how? Sudden/Gradual

Did you have any special reason fro stopping when you did?.......................
....

On the advice of the
Doctor/Others?...

Did the baby mind?...

Sources of advice on feeding schedule.

Doctor/ Midwife/H.V./Hospital/Magazines/Books/Others...........................
....

Solids

How old was ..N.. when you started him giving solid foods?....................
Are there any foods he will not take?...
Full details...

Assessment of mother's attitude: Tick on appropriate line.
Anxious Battles/much coaxing/persuasion for every mouthful)
Mildly concerned/(Much encouragement)
Unconcerned (Takes no notice/lets child leave)

General Personality

14 How would you describe ..N.. to some one who does not know him at all?....

15 Would you say he is a placid child or rather temperamental?......................
Placid/Varies/Temperamental

16 Do you find him easy to manage or is he a bit tricky?
Do you have to feel your way with him?
Easy/Varies/Temperament?

17 Is he the sort of child who usually agrees with what you want him to do Or does he tend to object to things quite a lot?
Agrees/Varies/Objects

Activities

18 We should like to know something now about what sort of things N..likes doing when he is not at school?

19 What about when when he comes out of school in the afternoon? Do you usually fetch him? Yes/No
If no, does he comes straight home, or does he play out or go somewhere else before coming home? Straight home/ plays out/Unspecified/Elsewhere
(Prompt if necessary: Do you have any rule about coming straight home?
Yes/No

20 When he comes home what does he do with his free time until bed time?......
....

21 Some children seem to spend a great deal of time doing one or two special things, like reading, drawing, computing, watching television, playing chess or making models. Has n.. a special hobby of this sort? (Specify)
Does ..N... watch TV Asia? Yes/No

If Yes, which programmes...
Does he watch Indian/Pakistani films?

Does he watch videos? Yes/No what kind of videos?..............

22 Does ..N... has a place of his own where he can keep his own things?
(specify) ....

23 You have mentioned other children a few times:
You have not mentioned other children very much:
Which does ..N... likes best? Playing with other children or playing by himself? Others/ Alone/Equally.

24 With whom does he play as a rule?
Siblings: Often/Sometimes/Never.
Others (Punjabi/West Indians/Others) Often/Sometimes/Never.

25 Do they come and play at your house?
Most weeks/Sometimes/No.

26 Does he go to their houses?
Most weeks/Sometimes/No

27 Are you happy about his friendships?...
this friendship?...

28 Have you ever tried to discourage any friendship between..N... and another child? Yes/No
If Yes, any special reason...
If No, do you think you would ever do this for any reason?.......................
(Specify reason)..

29 In general, would you say ..N...gets on with other children?....................
Does he make friends easily? Yes/Not very/Some difficulty making friends
Do you mean English/Punjabi/West Indian/Others?

30 Does he do a lot of fighting? Do his quarrels come to blows?....................
(Prompt) Siblings: Often/Sometimes/Little fighting
Others: Often/Sometimes/little fighting.

31 Do you (would you ever interfere in ..N's... quarrels and arguments with other children? (English,West Indian,Punjabi) outside the family Yes/No

Fantasy and Tension

32 What sort of games does ..N... mostly play with other children?
Place in order of preference; Prompt if necessary)
.... Rough and tumble/Climbing/Kicking ball around
.... Construction - building, making..................
.... Imaginative games/Roll-playing, "house", "school", etc. (Criterion is plot).

33 Does he ever indulge in play-acting games when he is on his own - either being someone else or making up a story with dolls and toy animals or puppets?
Yes/No (Details)..
....

34 Does he mind listening to these games, or does he stop when you come in?
Likes audience/Does not mind/Prefers privacy/Sometimes each.

35 Does he ever make up stories for you about things that have not actually happened? Yes/No

If Yes, does he tell them as if they were true, or does he explain that this is a story? As true/As story

Fantasy

36 Has ..N... any special fears or worries? Yes/No
(Specify)..
If Yes, has he had that for a long time? Since?..................
Did he come and tell you about it, or could you see that he was afraid?.......
....

37 We are interested in the various odd habits that children seem to have at this age. Does ..N... have any little habits you can think of? ....
Does he bite his nails, for instance......................Yes/No.....................
When he was younger did he suck his thumb?
Does he do that at all now? Yes/No
If No, when did he stop doing that altogether?.....................................

38 Does he ever suck his dummy now? Yes.No
If No, when did he finally give that up that?..
Did you have to do anything about it, or did he just drop it himself?..............

39 Does he ever use his bottle now? Yes/No
If No, when did he finally give up that?..
Did you have to do anything about it or did he give it up himself?................

Transitional objects

(If yes to any of the follow-ups above): Have you tried to stop that, or are you quite happy to let him go on as long as he seems to want it?

40 What about things children do when they are a bit strung-up?
Does he pull his ears or mouth, or pick at his face?
....

41 Does he blink or screw up his eyes? Yes/No

42 Does he ever stammer or stutter when he speaks?..................................
Is there any other habit like these that you have noticed?............Yes/No
Specify...
(If any habit prompt back separately for each)
Have you notice whether he...
....

43 Does he ever have a headache or a temperature because he is anxious or excited?
....
(Prompt): Is he actually sick out of excitement or worry?.....................
If Yes to either; Have you tried to do anything about this?.................

Toilet training

44 How old was ..N...when you started toilet training..............................
How did you go about it?..
How long did it take until he was well trained?.....................................
What did you do about it when he had accidents after he was trained?...........

45 Does he ever wet his bed? Yes/No
If No, how long is it since he last wet his bed?....................................
Did you do anything to keep or make him dry at night?
If Yes, about how often does he have a wet bed?
Most nights/1 - 3 nights per week/less than once a week/less than once a month

Are you doing anything about it, or just waiting for him to grow out if it?.......

46 Does he ever wet his pants in the daytime? Yes/No
If No, when did he become quite dry during the day?..............................

47 Did you ever do anything like telling a story or singing a lullaby to him at bed-time?...
Do you still do that? Yes/No
If Yes, Would he mind if you did not do that one night?
If No, Do you do anything else of that type at bedtime now?.....................
Specify...

48 Does he take anything to bed with him? Yes/No
If Yes, What is it?..
If No, Has he ever done this?...
What was it?..
When did he stop?...

Independence

49 How about following you around and hanging on your clothes?..................
If not much, Did he ever go through a stage of doing this?......................
How do you (did you) feel about it when he hangs on to you and follows you around?...

50 Could you tell me now what sort of things ..N... does on his own?
Does he go on a bus on his own? Not at all/To school only/Otherwise.......
Specify...

51 Does he play or roam around in the street at all? Yes/No

52 Does he go the the shops on his own? Yes/No

53 Do you trust him to cross busy road on his own? Yes/No
54 Have you any rules about how far he can go on his own?
Exact rules/ vague/ ad hoc/ he would ask/No rules/ up to him.

55 Does he ever go to a park or recreation ground by himself?.......................
Swimming bath alone?..............Any where else?................................

56 Does he belong to any clubs/Brownies, or anything like that?
Specify...

57 Does he ever stay the night at someone's house without you? Yes/No
Specify...

58 Does he have any pocket money of his own? Yes/No
Who gives?...........................How much?.................Regular fixed sum?............................(exclude school expenses and school savings)

59 Do you buy him sweets, apart from any he buys with his pocket money? Yes/No

60 If he wants extra money for something, do you give it to him?
What sort of things?..
Freely if can afford/No/Only for...

61 Could he earn extra money from you or his Daddy if he wanted? Yes/No
If Yes, Does he ever?...............Details..

62 We should like to know about the sort of jobs children do around the house at this age. Is there any little jobs you expect..N...to do?............................
(Prompt for each)Is that something he does as a regular thing, or just when he feels like it?...
Suppose he is too busy doing something of his own one day;
What happens?..

63 (If younger siblings): Does ..N... ever help you by looking after his brother/sister/the younger children?...
Do you ever leave him in charge of them for a while?..............................
Does he ever take them out with him?..
Only under supervision/Alone in house for short time/Away from house/In sole charge for periods over an hour.
Ref. siblings aged...

64 Does he ever have time off school either for any of these chores, or for any other purpose?..

65 Has he any animal of his own? Yes/No
If No, has the family any pets Yes/No
Does he look after it/them at all, in the way of feeding and cleaning?.............
Is that his job, or just a thing he does sometimes?
Responsible/Sometimes/No

66 Do you let ..N...choose the toys or do you decide for him?........................
What about clothes, books and other things?..

67 Does ..N... share bedroom with anyone? Yes/No
If Yes, with whom?...
If No, did he share bedroom with anyone before?...................................
Does ..N... share bed with anybody? Yes/No
If Yes, with whom?...
If No, did he share bed with anyone before? Yes/No
When did he have his own bed/bedroom?...

School and Intellectual

68 We should like to know something about how ..N...gets on at school? Does he like school? Very much/well enough/Not much/Strongly dislikes

69 Which school does he attend?...
(If mother demurs ask what type)Private/Local Education Authority/Others.....
Did ..N... go to any school(s) other than the one he attends now? Yes/No
If Yes, where and for how long?...

70 Does he stay for dinners? Yes..........Per week/No
If Yes, does he like that? Yes/No..
If No, is that because he does not want to, or is it because the food at school interferes with your religious beliefs?..

71 Do you know what he enjoys most at school?.....................................
Do you know what he does not like?...

72 Does he naturally come and tell you about school, or do you always have to ask him? Loves telling/Average/Have to ask

73 Does he seem to get on well with his teachers? Yes/No/so-so

74 Has he changed his class teacher in the last twelve months? Yes/No
If Yes, did that upset him at all?...

75 Does he ever complain about anything special at school? Yes/No
(Specify)...
If Yes, What do you say to him about that?..

76 Are you aware of any difficulties ..N... has at school?.............................
What are they?...
Are you satisfied with the way in which the school deals with them?...........

77 Does he ever say that he does not want to go to school to-day?
Often/Sometimes/Never

78 Does he ever pretend he is not well, so as to stay at home from school?..........
Often/Sometimes/Has tried/Not in the last twelve months/Never yet

79 (If any reluctance to go to school): Has he ever refused to go to school?
Often/Occasionally/Not in the last twelve months/Never yet
If Yes, Do you know why?...
What happened?...

80 Does he often take things to school to show his teacher?
Often/Occasionally/No
If Yes, What sort of things?..

81 Does he ever ask you questions about something he has been shown at school?
If Yes, What sort of things?..

82 How good is ..N's...reading?..
Can he read well enough to enjoy a book for its story? Yes/No

83 When he is reading a book to himself, does he say the words aloud or reads silently? Aloud/Mouths/Silently/No mouthing.

84 Is there anybody who has tried to help him with his reading out of school hours at all?..
In what way?..
Who is he/she?...

85 Does he read much/look at books much at home?.................................

86 Does he belong to a library? Yes/No
Does he go there himself? Yes/No
If No, who takes him there?..
Does he choose the books himself?..

87 Has he any books of his own?...
Have the children any books of their own?..
About how many?..
(Real books, not comics. Count total number of probable interest to..N...)

88 Do you get him any comics or magazine regularly?.................................
(Specify)..

89 Do you or anybody else often read to him?..
About how often?........................(Daddy counts, but specify)................

90 What sort of things do you read to him?...
(If long books): Can you tell me some of the books you have read to him which he specially liked?...

91 Do you or his Daddy or anybody else ever help him with other things, like sums or writing, or any other school work?..

92 In general, would you say that you are pleased with the school ..N... goes to? I do not mean is it a good school, but does it suit ..N...?..........................

93 If he showed the ability, how far would you like him to go with his education?
....

94 Have you any idea now about what you would like him to do when he is grown up?..

95 Has ..N... any idea about that?..

96 Do you pay for an extra lesson for ..N...? Music or dancing or anything else at all? Yes/No (Specify)..
Does anybody give him special lessons for which you do not pay?...............

97 Does he do any writing for his own pleasure? Yes/No
If Yes, what does he write?...

98 Does he ever write letters to people? Yes/No
If Yes, what sort of letters does he write?...
What about?..
None/Thank you or Santa Clause only/Occasional others/Many
If any, does he like writing letters, or do you have to go on at him to get them done?..

99 Does anyone play a musical instrument in your family? Yes/No
(Any degree of skill counts - specify who and what) ....
If Yes, Has ..N...learned to play it at all?..

100 Have you ever taken him to pictures/theatre/concert or any place like these?
(Specify)...

101 What about museums and art galleries? Has he been to any with you or his Daddy?....................................(Specify)...................................

102 Is there any other exhibitions or shows or anything like that to which you have taken him?..
(Prompt if necessary) Has he ever been to a zoo or a circus with you?...........

103 Does he ever go to a football match or any other sporting event?..................

104 Does he ever go to a Sikh temple/mosque (service of religious worship) with you or his Daddy?...
Regularly/Sometimes/Used to/Not now/No

105 Does he go to a Sikh temple/mosque on a Sunday/Friday?
Regularly/Sometimes/Used to/Not now/No

106 Do you ever talk to him about religion? Yes/No
If No, what do you tell him about that sort of thing?...............................
(Prompt if necessary) Does he say prayers at home at all? Yes/No

107 What part, if any, did your husband play in looking after ..N... when he was a baby?..
(Pause, the prompt)
a. Changing nappies........................ b. Feeding......................
c. Putting to Sleep........................... d. Carrying about............
e. Playing with...............................

108 Does he give ..N... a lot of attention? Very high/Average/Not much/Ignores

109 Is there any outing that ..N...particularly enjoys?..................................
(Prompt) If you were planning a treat specially for ..N..., what do you think he would choose to do?...
About how often do you do that?..

110 Where did ..N... go on his holidays?...
How long did ..N... stay there?..
Has he been to India/Pakistan? Yes/No If Yes, did he like it?......

Discipline, etc

111 What is it about ..N... that gives you most pleasure?.............................

112 Is he a child who shows a lot of affection? Yes/No
(If not to mother, prompt whether to anyone, including animals if any, specify)
....

113 Do you ever give him a cuddle nowadays, or do you think he is too old for that now? ....
(If too old) Do you kiss or hug him at all?
No kissing/No cuddling/formal kissing /Frequent informal hug or cuddling.

114 What about disagreements? what sort of things make you get on each other's nerves now, you and ..N...? ....

115 (If not smack): What happens if he simply refuses to do something you want him to do?..

116 How do you feel about smacking children at this age?...........................

117 Do you think parents should try to do without smacking children altogether, or do you think smacking is a good way of training children? ....
....

118 In general, do you think smacking has good results with children of this age? (Specify)..
Any bad results?...

119 What effect does smacking has on..N...?...
(Prompt if necessary): Does he behave better?..............................
For how long?................. Dos it upset him?...................................

120 What effect does it have on you?..
Do you feel relieved or upset in any way, or is it just part of the routine?.........
(Omit last part if Mother clearly does not smack routinely)

121 How often does ..N... get smacked?...
Once per day +/Once per week +/Once per month +/Less

122 Do you threaten ..N... to get him smacked by his father?..........................
Does he obey you then?..
Do you, in fact, report the matter to your husband?.................................
Besides you and your husband, is there anybody else in the house who smacks ..N...?.................. If Yes, who is he?..................................
Do you approve of this smacking?..

123 For what sort of things is ..N... most often smacked?..............................

124 Of course, there are lots of other ways of dealing with naughtiness, besides smacking; for instance, do you ever promise ..N... a reward for being good?
Yes/No/Special circumstances

125 Do you ever say that if he is naughty h cannot have something he likes -- ice cream or television or something like that? Yes/No

126 Do you carry out a threat if you have warned him, or do you usually let it go?
Mostly carries out/Sometimes does/Lets it go

127 Do you ever send him out of the room or put him in a room by himself for a bit?
....

128 Do you ever threaten him with someone else - ghosts, the doctor, a policeman- someone like that? Yes/No
If Yes, what do you say?...

129 Do you tell him you will not love him if he is naughty? Yes/No
If yes, when do you say that?...

130 Do you hold up another child as an example? Yes/No
What do you say?..
(prompt either way as necessary): What about the other way round?
Do you ever say,"Look how nicely so-and-so behaves" or "You don't want to be like so-and-so", do you? positive example/negative example/Both/either.

131 Some parents find that rudeness and cheekiness are a problem at this age. Does this happen with ..N...? A lot/Some/Very little

132 What do you do when he is rude to you?..
(Specify rudeness): Smack/Other punishment/Rebukes/Nothing

133 Does he ever seem to get a kick out of smashing up something?
Yes/Destructive/Only expendables/No
How do you feel about children doing that sort of thing?..........................

134 Sometimes it is quite easy for high-spirited children to get themselves into trouble with neighbours or school or with the Police. Has ..N... ever got into that sort of trouble?...
(Specify)..

If yes, What did you say to ..N... about it?..

135 Does ..N... ever get into a real rage - shouting and stamping and banging doors?.......................
About how often does that happen?...
What usually starts of off?...
Do you do anything about it?..

136 Do you find how strict you are depends a great deal on your mood at the time?
....

137 I think everyone agrees that temperamentally some children are much easier than others. Compared with other children, would you say that ..N... is very easy, or fairly easy, or fairly difficult?
Very easy/Fairly easy/Fairly difficult/very difficult

138 Can you think of any other problems which have not been asked/ Yes/No
If yes, what are they?...
Explain what you would do about them?...
If no, did you any problems before?...
At what age and how were they solved?..

139 Does ..N... ever talk back to you? Yes/No
If yes, what do you do?..
When you want to stop ..N... from doing something what do you say or do?
....
Do you ever say to him, "What will other people say if they see you?" Yes/No
If Yes, Do you mean Punjabis/English/Both?

140 Have you any English/West Indians/Punjabis/Others friends?....................
Do you take ..N... with you when you visit them?.................................
How often? Frequently/sometimes/Rarely/Never
Do they return the visit?..

Bilingualism

141 Which language does ..N... use whilst talking to
a. you?................................b. his Daddy?..........................
c. siblings..............................d. his grandparents.?.................
e. Relatives............................f Other Punjabi children?...........

142 Which language does he use most at home?..

143 Does anyone talk to him in his mother tongue? Yes/No
If Yes, who? .... How often?..........................
Often/Sometimes/Rarely
If No, did anybody ever talk to him in his mother tongue? Yes/No
(Specify when it stopped)...

144 Was there any provision for the use of mother tongue in the:
a. play group (if he attended) Yes/No
b. nursery school (If he attended) Yes/No
c. Infant school Yes/No

145 Is there any provision for the use of mother tongue in the school he attends now? Yes/No

146 Do you want him to learn to read and write his mother tongue? Yes/No
If Yes, what practical steps have you taken for this?...............................
(Prompt if necessary) Does he go to any community/religious school on weekends? Yes/No
If No, do you intend sending him to one?
(specify)...

Identity

147 What do you consider yourself to be?...
(Prompt, if necessary) Indian/Pakistani/British/others
Do you ever tell ..N... to do certain things as English children do? Yes/No
if Yes, what sort of things?...
Do you ever tell ..N... not to do certain things what English children do? Yes/No
What sort of things?..

148 What other aspects of the British culture you would not mind ..N... taking up?
(Specify):...
Prompt if necessary) food........music.......customs......others.................
What aspects of ` culture you would definitely like ..N... to retain?
....

149 Suppose you think ahead a bit, how would you react if ..N... wants to marry someone of a different race?
Strongly disapprove/Object but accept/Approve/will not mind

150 Do you think ..N... will be accepted by the whites? Yes/No
in school?...............In his place of work?...............Socially?.............

151 Are you going to tell him about racism? Yes/No
If Yes, when?.................. how?..

152 How important is ..N's religious education?
Very important/important/Does not matter

153 Is religious instruction being given to ..N...? Yes/No
If Yes, who is providing this?
You/Daddy/School/Sikh temple/Hindu temple/Mosque/Others...........

154 What, in your view, will his national identity be when he grows up?
British/Indian/Pakistani/Others

155 If facilities are available would you send ..N... to a school run along the lines of your religion? Yes/No

Gender Equality

156 In your view, should girls be treated the same as boys? Yes/ No
If Yes, do you (would you) treat your daughter(s) the same as your son(s) ? a. in education?..
b. choice of clothes?............at school?............at home..................
c. opportunity to work in another city?.......................................
d. going out?...
e. household chores?..
f. others?..

If No, what kind of restrictions would you place on your daughter?.............
(Specify)..

Prospect and retrospect

157 Now, looking to your childhood, how would you compare the way your mother raised you with the way you are raising your children?..................
....

158 Would you say that you have altered your ideas about bringing up children since you had your first baby? Yes/No
If Yes, in what respects?..
....

159 Suppose you think ahead a bit , to when ..N... is about sixteen. Do you look forward to that age or you think that children are nicest when they are at this age?..
....

160 In what ways is your lifestyle different from that of your parents?................
....

Index